D0198107

Codependency
FOR
DUMMIES®

by Darlene Lancer

WILEY

John Wiley & Sons, Inc.

Codependency For Dummies®

Published by
John Wiley & Sons, Inc.
111 River St.
Hoboken, NJ 07030-5774
www.wiley.com

Copyright © 2012 by John Wiley & Sons, Inc., Hoboken, New Jersey

Published by John Wiley & Sons, Inc., Hoboken, New Jersey

Published simultaneously in Canada

WILEY

About the Author

Darlene Lancer, JD, MFT is a marriage and family therapist, specializing in addiction and codependency. In her private clinical practice, she has treated individuals and couples for over 24 years. As program director she managed Brookside Institute's Los Angeles office for addiction rehabilitation. For two decades, she's been a consultant and workshop presenter at many rehabilitation facilities, including St. John's, St. Joseph's, and Brotman Hospitals, West Area Opportunity Center, Malibu Horizon, The Canyon, Milestones Ranch Malibu, and Promises Treatment Centers.

In addition to hosting two weekly Internet radio programs, Relationship S.O.S. and Decode Your Dreams, she's a frequent guest speaker on radio and has taught at universities, colleges, and various organizations, including the California State Bar Association. Ms. Lancer has also conducted meditation groups and trainings.

She was a senior mediator for the Los Angeles County Conciliation Court, where she helped families resolve custody and visitation disputes and domestic violence problems.

Ms. Lancer is the author of "10 Steps to Self-Esteem – The Ultimate Guide to Stop Self-Criticism" and has been published widely in professional and popular periodicals, including *The California Therapist, Somatics, Family Law News and Review, Shared Transformation,* and *Whole Life Times.* Her blogs appear on numerous websites, including www.Mentalhelp.net, www.Selfgrowth.org, www.WhatisCodependency.com, www.facebook.com/codependencyrecovery, and www.DarleneLancer.com.

Prior to becoming a psychotherapist, she had a successful law career, during which time she co-chaired the Beverly Hills Bar Entertainment Law Committee, edited two volumes for the Los Angeles Superior Court, and authored professional articles. She received a Masters in Psychology from Antioch University and a Juris Doctorate and American Jurisprudence Award from the School of Law at U.C.L.A.

Darlene Lancer is available for speaking engagements, expert interviews, and workshops. More information about her seminars and coaching packages are available on her website, www.whatis codependency.com.

Dedication

I dedicate this book to my children who grew up in a family rife with dysfunction and suffered from my ignorance and codependency before I embarked on recovery. I'm so grateful that today they're wonderful parents and have much healthier families of their own.

Author's Acknowledgments

There are many people I want to thank who have contributed to my own growth and knowledge about codependency over decades of experience. This book wouldn't have been possible without the love and support I found in Al-Anon when I timidly crossed the threshold of my first meeting 33 years ago. There were sponsors, therapists, and many individuals along the way who guided my recovery.

I'm fortunate to have been trained by outstanding professors and supervisors who inspired me, in particular Drs. Hal Stone and George Oliver, as well as pioneers in the recovery field who helped and influenced me: Robin Norwood, Melody Beattie, Pia Melody, and Earnie Larson.

Additionally, I'm grateful to the women I sponsored and the many individuals and couples who entrusted me with their pain and healing and allowed me the privilege of participating in their transformation to wholeness.

I'm indebted to the encouragement and tolerance of my girlfriends who tirelessly listened and forgave me when I jabbered about codependency or was too busy to talk at all because of writing deadlines. I especially appreciate the theoretical conversations with colleagues Flora Golden and Dr. Shari Butler.

I'd like to acknowledge the excellent staff of John Wiley & Sons, Inc., the steadfast vision of my acquisitions editor Erin Mooney Calligan, and the help of my project/copy editor Susan Hobbs.

Publisher's Acknowledgments

We're proud of this book; please send us your comments at http://dummies.custhelp.com. For other comments, please contact our Customer Care Department within the U.S. at 877-762-2974, outside the U.S. at 317-572-3993, or fax 317-572-4002.

Some of the people who helped bring this book to market include the following:

Acquisitions, Editorial, and Media Development

Project Editor: Susan Hobbs

Acquisitions Editor: Erin Calligan-Mooney

Copy Editor: Susan Hobbs

Assistant Editor: David Lutton

Editorial Program Coordinator: Joe Niesen

Technical Editor: Leslie Ferris

Editorial Manager: Carmen Krikorian

Editorial Assistant: Rachelle Amick

Art Coordinator: Alicia B. South

Cover Photos: © Jupiter Images / Steve West

Cartoons: Rich Tennant (www.the5thwave.com)

Composition Services

Project Coordinator: Sheree Montgomery

Layout and Graphics: Carrie A. Cesavice, Timothy C. Detrick, Corrie Niehaus, Joyce Haughey, Cheryl Grubbs, Lavonne Roberts

Proofreaders: Melissa Cossell, Bryan Coyle, Toni Settle

Indexer: Christine Karpeles

Publishing and Editorial for Consumer Dummies

    Kathleen Nebenhaus, Vice President and Executive Publisher

    Kristin Ferguson-Wagstaffe, Product Development Director

    Ensley Eikenburg, Associate Publisher, Travel

    Kelly Regan, Editorial Director, Travel

Publishing for Technology Dummies

    Andy Cummings, Vice President and Publisher

Composition Services

    Debbie Stailey, Director of Composition Services

Contents at a Glance

Table of Contents

Part III: The Skills: Taking Action *169*

Chapter 11: Finding Your Voice. 171

Chapter 12: Recovery and Your Family,
Friends, and Lovers. 191

Introduction

*1*f you're reading this book because you wonder whether you are or may be codependent, you're not alone. Some think the majority of Americans are codependent. If you decide to recover from codependency, you join the fortunate minority.

The term *codependency* has been used for more than three decades. Today, and the perspective taken by this book, is that codependency applies to many more people than originally thought. Different types of people and personalities may be codependent or behave in a codependent manner. Codependence manifests in varying degrees of severity. Not all codependents are unhappy, while others live in pain or quiet desperation. Here are some people who may be codependent:

> An older couple, Manny and Faye are happily married for many years. Faye calls Manny "Daddy," and Manny calls Faye "Mother." Faye defers to her husband, who frequently corrects her. They agree about most everything and that Manny comes first. If you ask Faye her opinion, she quotes her husband.

> Sid and Ina have lived together for several years, but their relationship lacks passion and intimacy. Sid is having an affair with Myra and is unsure about marrying Ina, whom he claims lacks Myra's wildness. He feels trapped. He can't commit to either woman. He fears both leaving and getting closer to Ina.

> Angie's a top film director. Men find her attractive, and she's had several intense, brief relationships that end when the passion does.

Codependents are attracted to codependents, so there's little chance of having a healthy relationship. The good news is the symptoms of codependency are reversible. It requires commitment, work, and support. Even so, sometimes they can sneak up on you and affect your thinking and behavior when you least notice it. Codependency is not something you heal from and are forever done with, but you can one day enjoy yourself, your life, and your relationships. Should you choose to embark on recovery, you're beginning an exciting and empowering journey. A new way of living and seeing the world opens up. I hope you decide to do so, and wish you well.

About This Book

I faced a problem organizing this book, because a self-help book is linear and compartmentalized — you read a sentence or paragraph that discusses one thing at a time. However, people exist through four dimensions of space/time. Moreover, codependency is holographic. It affects everything in the way you live your life. It's neither linear, nor two-dimensional. Every trait affects every other. This book breaks down codependency into parts in order to discuss its various aspects, but that's not how you experience codependency. For instance, just answering "Yes," or "No" to a question is impacted by your self-esteem, values, boundaries, feelings, and reactivity — all at once. On top of that, there are things from your past or the present, about which you may be unconscious and in denial. They, too, affect everything you say and do. Even when you understand all the moving variables, the process is impossible to understandably explain in a few sentences.

I decided to organize the book the way you'd experience embarking on recovery — first understanding the definition, symptoms, and causes, and then the evolving process of changing and healing. However, feel free to jump around and read it in any order that you choose. There are cross references to other chapters that are relevant to the topic being discussed.

This book is very comprehensive and details everything you need to know about codependency in one place. It provides tools you can implement to take an active role in your recovery. There are exercises, which are an important part of the book. If you're a professional, feel free to copy and use these exercises with your clients. If you're tempted to skip the exercises, you miss out on a major feature, which is included for your benefit to help you change. One strategy is to read through the book, and then go back and do the exercises at your leisure. After you do them, you can also repeat an exercise you find helpful months or years from now and will most likely acquire new knowledge about yourself. Some of the exercises are meant to be repeated, and like any exercise, every time you do it, you benefit.

Those new to codependency probably won't be able to implement advice found in later chapters. If that happens, don't be dismayed. If you begin recovery and pick up this book down the road, you may read it with different eyes and glean new insights and understanding.

An Important Message for You

Not all codependents are in a relationship with someone who suffers from an addiction. Whether or not you are, this book is for you as you relate to your loved one. If you're recovering from an addiction to a substance or process, such as alcohol, eating, hoarding, shopping, working, sex, gambling — the list goes on — and are ready to work on your issues revolving around codependency, then this book is an ideal place to start. However, the focus of this book is not about overcoming those addictions, but on your relationships.

Conventions Used in This Book

This book contains a number of examples to illustrate a point that may be more abstract. For instance, because denial operates at an unconscious level, you may not relate to it unless you read how other people experience it. The examples are composites of clients and people I've known, including myself, and resemblance to a real person is coincidental, as specific details and facts have been changed. The names are made up and appear in **boldface.** Other conventions used in this book include the following:

- As mentioned earlier, there are people with all different kinds of addictions. Throughout this book, when I refer to "addict," I'm not referring only to a drug addict, but also a person with any type of addiction. In some cases, I specifically refer to alcoholics.

- **Boldface** is also used to highlight key words in some lists.

- *Italicized terms* when used for the first time are followed by a definition.

- In a few cases I use acronyms, like CoDA for Co-Dependents Anonymous, but first explain what it means.

- Some words are *italicized* for emphasis.

- Web addresses show up in `monofont` type.

What You're Not to Read

I believe that every chapter in this book provides valuable information, and I hope that you agree. On the other hand, you needn't read it all to benefit. If you don't want to read it cover-to-cover, use the Table of Contents to select what's important to you. Two things you may want to skip and come back to later are paragraphs indicated by the Technical Stuff icon and sidebars, containing interesting nonessential information.

Foolish Assumptions

Not knowing your familiarity with codependency, in writing this book, I assumed you may be totally new to the concept, someone already in recovery, or a mental health professional who is seeking more information. I've tried to write so that nonprofessionals are able to understand all the concepts; however, some ideas are profound and written for the person who wants to comprehend the deeper psychology underlying codependency. *It's certainly not written for dummies.*

How This Book Is Organized

This book contains five parts, divided into 20 chapters. It's modular, so that you can pick and choose what you want to read first and move around. However, it is laid out so that the chapters build upon one another, from the point of view of how recovery proceeds. If you're new to codependency, it makes more sense to read the book in order.

Part 1: What is Codependency and Who is Codependent?

If codependency is new to you, probably the first thing you're asking is what is it and whether you or someone close to you is codependent. The answer isn't clearcut; this part explains how the definition has evolved over the last few decades. From my clinical practice and codependency literature, I present a definition in Chapter 2. Chapters 3 and 4 discuss typical symptoms of codependency. Not all are necessary to be codependent, but you may relate to some.

Part 11: Breaking the Cycle of Codependency: Beginning Recovery

This important part discusses denial, which can keep you from changing and getting help. Even if you know you're codependent, this part contains information that's significant in recovery. Chapter 7 describes how you may have become codependent. Chapter 8 is essential. It's about getting to know yourself, which is the cornerstone of self-esteem and setting boundaries. Letting go, covered in Chapter 9, is the first step to help you focus on yourself. Chapter 9 provides important insight into nonattachment and tools for achieving it. Codependents in recovery may appreciate the value of Chapter 10, which can help you build your self-esteem.

Part III: The Skills: Taking Action

In Part III, you're ready to take action. It shows you how to communicate assertively and set boundaries and provides information on resolving conflict and dealing with your family, partner, and dating. It touches on what codependency looks when it comes to sex. Chapter 14 emphasizes the necessity of bringing positive experiences into your life. Chapter 15 deals with how to cope with relapse, which is an integral part of change. For those familiar with codependency and serious about recovering, Chapter 13 introduces you to deeper healing work that's necessary for lasting change, particularly for people who have experienced abuse or trauma in their past.

Part IV: Standing on Your Own: Leaving Codependency Behind

In this part, you're guided to take charge of your life and put your newfound self-esteem into action by setting goals and pursuing your passions. Many codependents have never witnessed what a healthy relationship is like. Chapter 16 details what to look for and explains that creating a healthy relationship is an evolving process, which grows out of working on yourself and building your self-esteem. Finally, Chapter 18 provides resources that you can check out, including psychotherapy, self-help groups, and further reading.

Part V: The Part of Tens

There's a lot of information in this book, and it may even be overwhelming if you're looking at codependency for the first time. In order to change and heal, you have to work at it regularly. Chapter 19 provides you with practical ideas you can start using to build your self-esteem and self-love, the core of recovery. Chapter 20 provides daily reminders to help you do that.

Icons Used in This Book

What's cool about *For Dummies* books is that there are icons throughout letting you know what's really important and what you can skip. Here are the icons used in this book

This icon marks paragraphs that are important. In some places, it was difficult to decide where to place the icon because all the information in the chapter is important, but the paragraphs with the icon stand out as information you should continue to think about.

The Tip icon indicates that there's a valuable suggestion to put into practice in overcoming codependency.

This icon signifies that the information is technical psychological stuff, which you may not be interested in. Reading it depends how much in-depth understanding about codependency you'd like to have.

Look out for this icon, which alerts you to a warning about avoiding some pitfalls of codependency or beginning treatment.

The Self-Discovery icon indicates that this paragraph begins some exercises or suggestions for healing work that you can do on your own at home.

Where to Go from Here

Where you start reading depends on how much you know about codependency. If you're ready to begin recovery, I recommend that you get a journal to take notes, write about yourself, and do the many exercises that are designed to enlighten you and further your recovery.

I've reiterated throughout this book that reading is only a beginning. It opens your mind to the problem. It takes time, work, and support to overcome codependency. There's specific information on getting outside support and where to find it in Chapters 6 and 18. Read all you can, talk to other recovering codependents, and find a sponsor in a Twelve Step program or a professional coach or mental heal professional to help guide you on your journey.

Part I

What is Codependency and Who is Codependent?

The 5th Wave   By Rich Tennant

...and finally, do you feel well connected to the other members of your department?

In this part...

This part introduces you to codependency by defining what it is and determining if you are codependent. It offers several pages of questions that help you assess your codependency level, and looks at self-esteem and denial. Boundaries are also explored, as is recognizing codependent communication patterns. This is the place to start your recovery.

Chapter 1

When Relationships Hurt

All relationships have their troubles. There are times when people you love the most hurt and disappoint you, and you worry when they're suffering. Addicts obsess about their "drug" of choice, whether it's alcohol, food, or sex. They plan and look forward to it. Codependents do that in relationships. Their lives revolve around someone else — especially those they love. Their loved ones preoccupy their thoughts, feelings, and conversations. Like jumpy rabbits, they react to everything, put aside what they need and feel, and try to control what they can't. The stress of it feels normal, but it's not. This chapter introduces you to codependency and what it means to be codependent. It explores the goals and the process healing process, called recovery.

What Is Codependence?

The term *codependence* is controversial. What it is and who has it has been debated for decades. There's also disagreement about whether or not it's a disease. (See Chapter 2.) Experts agree that codependent patterns are passed on from one generation to another and that they can be unlearned — with help. In 1989, 22 leaders in the field convened at a national conference and came up with a tentative definition of codependency:

"Codependency is a pattern of painful dependence upon compulsive behaviors and approval of others to find safety, self-worth, and identity. Recovery is possible."

That didn't end attempts to define codependency. My definition in Chapter 2 cuts to the core cause.

The controversy

 The controversy around codependency is divided into two camps — for and against. At one end are mental health professionals who advocate that codependency is a widespread and treatable disease. On the other is an array of critics of codependency, who argue that it's merely a social or cultural phenomenon, is over-diagnosed, or is an aspect of relationships that doesn't need to change. They state that it's natural to need and depend upon others. They claim that you only really thrive in an intimate relationship and believe that the codependency movement has hurt people and relationships by encouraging too much independence, and a false-sense of self-sufficiency, which can pose health risks associated with isolation.

 Other naysayers disparage the construct of codependency as being merely an outgrowth of Western ideals of individualism and independence, which have harmed people by diminishing their need for connection to others. Feminists also criticized the concept of codependency as sexist and pejorative against women, stating that women are traditionally nurturers and historically have been in a nondominant role due to economic, political, and cultural reasons. Investment in their relationships and partner isn't a disorder, but has been necessary for self-preservation. Still others quarrel with Twelve Step programs in general, saying that they promote dependency on a group and a victim mentality.

 I have lobbied for it to be recognized as a mental disorder by the American Psychiatric Association, which would allow insurance coverage for treatment. A major obstacle is the lack of consensus about the definition of codependency and diagnostic criteria. For insurance purposes, clinicians usually diagnose patients with anxiety or depression, which are symptoms of codependency.

Codependency's detractors are correct to claim that people are meant to love, care for, and depend upon others, and need and thrive in relationships; however, it's not the concept of codependency that's to blame for the increase in divorce, loneliness, and unhappiness. Part of the problem of codependency is an inability to have satisfactory intimate relationships. When you look at codependent relationships up close, you discover that many of the benefits of healthy, intimate relationships elude codependents due to their dysfunctional patterns of interacting. Instead of feeling supported and enhanced by relationships, the symptoms and consequences of codependency provoke anxiety in relationships and cause pain. Codependents complain of feeling lonely and unhappy *in* their relationships. Often when they're not in relationships, their untreated codependency causes them to isolate, rather than reach out to connect with others.

Recovery from codependency doesn't necessitate ending a relationship to become independent. The goal is to be able to function better and more independently *in* the relationship. I've worked with many codependent individuals and couples whose relationships benefited when they became more autonomous and assertive. Having a false sense of self-sufficiency is part of codependency. Ignoring their needs is typical of people who are invested in caring for others. Calling it what it is doesn't create the problem. People feel rewarded and contented doing that, but where codependency is involved, it usually leads to self-sacrifice, control, resentment, and conflict.

Some recovering codependents choose to leave an abusive or painful relationship as an act of self-preservation. Remaining in such a relationship may also pose health risks from the chronic stress. Separation doesn't have to lead to isolation. There're healthy ways to cope with loneliness. Recovery helps individuals receive support in healthy, nurturing, interdependent relationships.

Finally, I agree that the term *codependency* shouldn't be used to judge people. It arose out of Western socio political thought and should be considered in a cultural and ethnic context. There may be instances where codependency is adaptive, and change would be disruptive. This poses a problem as American and European ideas spread to Asia, the Middle East, and Africa. I've received correspondence from men and women who feel conflicted between their eager desire for independence and the oppressive restraints of their religion and culture. Many don't have the institutional or cultural support necessary for change that exists in the West.

A brief history

The first proponents of codependency were clinicians in the trenches. They witnessed the self-destructive patterns of family members of alcoholics who tried to get the drinker sober and maintain order amidst chaos. (See Chapter 2.) They saw husbands and wives who'd lost themselves and become empty shells trying to control an uncontrollable situation. Surprisingly, they noticed that codependent patterns predated the alcoholic marriage and continued even after the alcoholic sobered up. Still later, it was observed that those patterns appeared in others who weren't involved with an addict but had grown up in dysfunctional families. (See Chapter 7.)

Karen Horney's "neurotic trends"

Horney described three personality styles that people develop in order to cope with self-alienation and the fear, helplessness, and isolation of childhood. Underneath brews feelings of anxiety, hostility, and unworthiness that are repressed to varying degrees. The first group is made up of individuals who believe they can only feel loved and secure if they're passive and comply. The second includes those who view life as a struggle and conclude they must be aggressive and in control, while the third group ensures their safety by withdrawing emotionally from interactions.

Horney identified ten neurotic trends or needs that underlie these three styles. Although the needs may overlap and remind you of normal needs, they're *neurotic* because they're compulsive, driven by anxiety, and out of proportion to reality. They're inappropriate and indiscriminate in application. It's normal to want to please your boss, but wanting to please everyone is neurotic. Several of these trends describe codependents:

The first style — Neurotic compliance

1. The need for affection and approval

2. The need for a partner, believing that love will make you happy and that your partner will fulfill your expectations and responsibilities

3. The need to restrict your behavior and expectations within narrow borders, underestimating your potential and living an inconspicuous life

The second style — Neurotic aggression

4. The need for power and domination of others with contempt for weakness

5. The need to exploit and manipulate others, viewing them as objects to be used

6. The need for social recognition or prestige

7. The need for admiration of your ideal self

8. The need for personal achievement combined with resentment when others don't recognize you

The third style — Neurotic withdrawal

9. The need for self-sufficiency and independence to the extent that you avoid close relationships

10. The need for perfection, worrying about possible errors and defects, and feeling superior to others

3. (repeated) The need to restrict your behavior and expectations within narrow borders, underestimating your potential and living an inconspicuous life

Eventually in 1986, the self-help program Co-Dependents Anonymous (referred to CoDA) was founded by two therapists, Ken and Mary, who both grew up in dysfunctional, abusive families and had histories of addiction. CoDA is modeled on the Twelve Step program, Alcoholics Anonymous (AA).

Around the time AA was getting started in the late 1930s and early 1940s, leading neo-Freudians and humanists began focusing on the development of personality. They believed that individuals were fundamentally good, but due to poor parenting and cultural influences, they were thwarted in their natural striving to actualize their true nature. One of the leading proponents for self-actualization was psychoanalyst Karen Horney. She conceptualized a compliant personality alienated from the real self that today resembles the traits of a codependent. Some of her other personality categories apply to codependents, too.

Codependency is real and painful

Codependency is insidious and powerful. It robs you of joy, peace of mind, and the ability to have sustained, loving relationships. It affects your relationship with yourself and with others, in some cases all your relationships and sometimes only one person — a spouse or romantic partner, a parent, sibling, or child, or someone at work. Ask yourself if your relationships feed you or drain you.

Codependents live with a high degree of shame, stress, and reactivity. They suppress their feelings or explode, and have behaviors that stem from fear, guilt, and the need to control others. This limits flexibility in the relationship and the flow of communication. Often codependent relationships involve emotional or physical abuse and addiction. Even when that's not the case, codependents feel trapped and unhappy because they give up themselves by denying or suppressing their needs and feelings and fear being alone or rejected. To cope, they sometimes disregard what's actually happening in the present. Problems with intimacy and communication arise due to confusion about personal boundaries and responsibilities to themselves and others. Instead of bringing couples closer, frequently communication is avoided or used to manipulate and leads to conflict. (Chapter 3 takes a closer look at the characteristics of codependency.)

Codependents feel uncomfortable being themselves. They develop a persona in the world that reacts to others, to their own self-criticism, and to their imagined ideal of who they *should* be. To be acceptable to others and to themselves, they hide who they are and become who they aren't. Shame due to earlier trauma conceals their real, core self, which they can't access. Many codependents aren't even aware of how self-critical they are, yet they suffer "tyranny of the shoulds," a phrase coined by Horney. Even though you may not relate to this, it still may be operating beneath your conscious awareness. You may only be aware of your persona illustrated in Figure 1-1 and nothing on the inner circles.

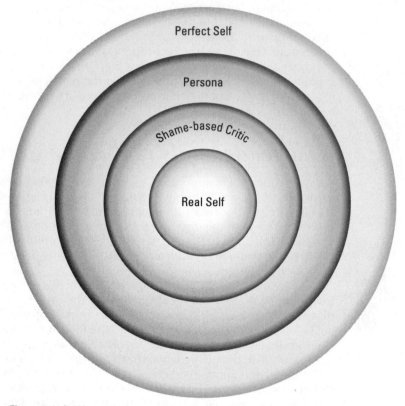

Figure 1-1: Self in confusion.

Dysfunctional parenting in childhood (such as, critical, indifferent, rigid, invasive, inconsistent, or rejecting parents) causes codependents to repress their authentic feelings and develop deep, shame-based beliefs about who they are and their rights, needs, and lovability. Sometimes their beliefs are due to abuse, and sometimes they're inferred from the behavior of indifferent or emotionally unavailable parents. Shame is also the result of the anger they turned against themselves, instead of directing it toward the parents they looked up to and relied upon for survival. (See Chapter 7.)

To get by, many codependents learned to comply and measure up to an imagined ideal. Others withdrew or rebelled. As adults, some codependents constantly feel inadequate, whereas others identify with their ideal self and think they have high self-esteem. Many become perfectionists to balance the self-hatred they feel inside. They may strive to be loving, good, beautiful, accomplished, or successful in an effort to prove their worth and/or to be independent and never again need anyone. Yet, the more they try, the more depressed they become, because they're abandoning the real self that wasn't nurtured by their original caretakers. Some enter therapy because of an addiction or relationship problem, while others come because they don't understand why they're depressed despite the fact that everything in their life is working.

Facing the Problem

Maybe you're wondering if you're codependent. (See Chapter 4.) It may be hard to tell at first, because, unless you're already in recovery, denial is a symptom of codependency. (See Chapter 5.) Whether or not you identify as codependent, you can still benefit from alleviating any symptoms you recognize, enabling you to function better both in and out of relationships. Recovery helps you to be authentic, feel good about yourself, and have more honest, open, and intimate relationships.

The spectrum of codependency varies from individuals who show only slight symptoms to others who have all the typical characteristics. (See Chapter 3.) The horizontal vector in Figure 1-2 illustrates how opposite codependent personality traits can manifest in a relationship. Individuals may reverse roles. For example, you may be the pursuer in one relationship and a distancer in another, or flip back and forth in the same relationship. In an alcoholic marriage, the sober spouse may scold and blame the irresponsible, needy alcoholic, who behaves like a victim. Then their roles switch, and the alcoholic dominates and controls his or her partner. Sometimes the spouse who acts needy or "crazy" gets well, and the self-sufficient, invulnerable partner breaks down.

The disease and recovery exist on a scale represented by the vertical vector in Figure 1-2. Codependent behavior and symptoms improve with recovery, described at the top, or if you don't take steps to change, become worse in the late stage indicated at the bottom.

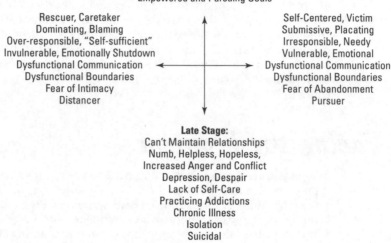

Recovery:
Self-Esteem
Aware of Feelings and Needs
Creative and Spontaneous
Practices Self-Care
Interdependent Relationships
Assertive Communication
Intact, Flexible Boundaries
Empowered and Pursuing Goals

Rescuer, Caretaker
Dominating, Blaming
Over-responsible, "Self-sufficient"
Invulnerable, Emotionally Shutdown
Dysfunctional Communication
Dysfunctional Boundaries
Fear of Intimacy
Distancer

Self-Centered, Victim
Submissive, Placating
Irresponsible, Needy
Vulnerable, Emotional
Dysfunctional Communication
Dysfunctional Boundaries
Fear of Abandonment
Pursuer

Late Stage:
Can't Maintain Relationships
Numb, Helpless, Hopeless,
Increased Anger and Conflict
Depression, Despair
Lack of Self-Care
Practicing Addictions
Chronic Illness
Isolation
Suicidal

Figure 1-2: The continuum of codependency.

As you get better acquainted with the symptoms and characteristics of codependents, you may see yourself. If you feel overwhelmed by the thought of having codependency, instead, focus on the patterns and behaviors you want to change. If you're committed to change, it really doesn't matter whether or not you consider yourself a codependent. However, it's important to realize that codependency won't get better or go away by itself. Support is essential, because you won't be able to make permanent changes on your own.

The Stages of Codependency and Recovery

Counselors treating alcoholic families considered codependency to be a chronic disease like other addictions (see Chapter 2), because they observed that codependency was progressive. Addiction counselors noticed that the addicts' spouses showed progressively worsening symptoms that paralleled those of alcoholics. In the later stages, both had serious mental and/or physical problems. Left untreated, codependency spiraled downward, just like alcoholism did. However, both markedly improved when treatment began and shared a similar trajectory of recovery. You can commence recovery at any time to reverse codependency's adverse progression — the sooner, the easier. This section generally summarizes significant characteristics of the early, middle, and late stages of codependency and recovery as they apply to relationships. Notice that over time the symptoms on the left side of the following Tables 1-1, 1-2, and 1-3 get progressively worse, while the symptoms on the right side improve. Reference to addict and other addictions only apply if you're involved with an addict, in which case, symptoms and progression are more pronounced. There's more dysfunction, feelings of helplessness, and conflict. However, you may relate solely to symptoms in the early stage, or only a few of the symptoms. If you start making changes now, you can turn things around more quickly.

Early stage of codependency and recovery

The early stage of codependency begins by becoming attached to someone and ends with unhealthy dependency on him or her. In recovery, the early stage ends with starting to reclaim yourself

The disease process

You may be attracted to a needy person or be overly involved with a family member and naturally want to help or please him or her. Gradually, you become increasingly emotionally dependent upon and obsessed with that person to the extent that you lose focus on yourself and start to give up personal friends and activities.

The recovery process

You begin coming out of denial (see Chapter 5), which means you squarely confront the problem and acknowledge reality — a prerequisite to changing it. This shift may be inspired by someone else's recovery, by reading this book, or, more likely, it's triggered an event — a wakeup call, referred to as *hitting bottom* — that makes change imperative. Instead of ignoring or minimizing the facts, you recognize them as difficult and painful, but true. You don't have to like them, but you see them as they are.

Beginning recovery starts with getting information and reaching out for help. By reading this book, you've already begun searching for new answers and options. Many people start psychotherapy or join a Twelve Step program, which gives them hope and starts the process of rebuilding their identity. Table 1-1 shows the progressive stages of early codependency and recovery.

Table 1-1   Early Stage of Codependency and Recovery

Progression of Codependency	Recovery from Codependency
Attracted to needy person; offers help, gifts, meals	Hits bottom and reaches out for help for self
Attempts to please the person	Learns about codependency and addiction
Obsessed with the person and his or her behavior	Joins Twelve Step program and/or therapy
Rationalizes and doubts own perceptions	Begins to have hope
Denial about addiction, but concern grows	Comes out of denial
Gives up own activities to be with the person	Learns recovery is for self
Family and social life affected	Refocuses on self
Increasingly emotionally dependent on the person	Begins to build own identity

Middle stage of codependency and recovery

The important middle stage of codependency is where denial, painful emotions, and obsessive-compulsive behavioral patterns are prevalent. You increase attempts to control, while feeling more out of control. When in recovery, you reclaim independence, balance, and greater peace of mind.

The disease process

Without support, denial and isolation continue, and problems get worse. You may minimize and hide from yourself and others painful aspects of your relationship and withdraw from outside activities and friends. Meanwhile, your obsession with the relationship or addiction and accompanying anxiety, resentment, and guilt increase. You do more to help, enable, and control the other person or the addiction, and may even take over his or her responsibilities. (See Chapter 3.) As mood swings and conflict increase, some codependents turn to drugs, food, spending, or other addictive behavior to cope.

The recovery process

The middle stage is where most of the work of recovery takes place. You begin to practice nonattachment and grasp your powerlessness over others and your addiction. (See Chapter 9.) As the focus on yourself grows, so do self-responsibility, self-awareness, and self-examination, which are part of psychotherapy as well as Twelve Step programs. AA emphasizes that an alcoholic's success is based upon rigorous self-honesty as the key to recovery. This is also true for codependents and one of the 12 steps of CoDA, which are derived from AA. Blaming others and external circumstances denies your power to effect change and achieve happiness. Even if you're a victim of abuse, you find the power to change your circumstances when the center of control shifts from the perpetrator to yourself. Self-examination also includes working through childhood issues that may have led to your codependency. (See Chapters 7 and 13.)

Although insight about your behavior is necessary, it's insufficient for change. Decisions, actions, and risk-taking are required during the middle stage. (See Chapter 17.) They happen when you're ready and can't be forced. It's hard to change even when you know things would improve — like taking a better job or moving to a desirable area — but taking risks where the outcome is uncertain requires courage — courage to venture from discomfort that's familiar into new territory. This is one reason why support is essential. (See Chapters 6 and 18.)

During the middle stage, you make new friends, participate in outside activities, and develop the ability to be assertive and set boundaries. (See Chapters 11 and 14.) As you become more emotionally independent, you take better care of yourself, and reactivity, enabling, and controlling behavior diminish.

Table 1-2 shows the progression of codependency and recovery in the middle stage.

Table 1-2   Middle Stage of Codependency and Recovery

Progression of Codependency	*Recovery from Codependency*
Denies/Minimizes painful aspects of relationship	Understands powerlessness
Hides from others painful aspects of relationship	Begins reliance on a spiritual source
Anxiety, guilt, and self-blame increase	Begins to detach

(continued)

Table 1-2 *(continued)*

Progression of Codependency	*Recovery from Codependency*
Self-esteem lessens	Self-awareness grows
Withdraws from outside family and friends	Makes new friends
Obsessively watches the person and addiction	Develops outside activities
Tries to control by nagging, blaming, manipulation	Stops enabling and controlling
Anger and disappointment due to broken promises	Learns assertiveness
Resentment at inability to control the person	Takes responsibility for own self
Mood swings and increased conflict and violence	Increases self-care and self-esteem
Enables and manages the person's responsibilities	Sets boundaries and less reactive
Hides family secret (addiction)	More emotional independence
Uses food, alcohol, drugs, shopping, work to cope	Heals childhood wounds

Late stage of codependency and recovery

In the late stage of codependency and recovery, the contrast between disease and health are most pronounced. The untreated codependent's world has significantly narrowed, and his or her levels of health and functioning have severely declined, while the recovered codependent's world has expanded to include greater risk-taking, relationships, and new goals.

The disease process

As the disease progresses, anger and conflicts are more common, and self-esteem and self-care further decline. Hopelessness, emptiness, and depression prevail. The chronic stress of codependency manifests in new symptoms, such as stress-related health problems (see Chapter 3) and new or more advanced obsessive-compulsive behaviors and addictions. These behaviors and addictions may include regularly monitoring the addict, enabling, cleaning house, dieting, overeating, having affairs, exercising, spending, or using legal or illegal drugs.

The recovery process

In the late stage of recovery, your self-esteem and confidence return. You're empowered to pursue your own goals and are more expansive, creative, and spontaneous. (See Chapter 17.) You desire to fully express yourself for the sheer joy and freedom of it. As your focus shifts away from someone outside yourself, you fully understand that your happiness doesn't depend upon others, and you no longer have a desperate need to be in a relationship. At the same time, you're more desirous and capable of authentic intimacy. (See Chapter 16.)

Table 1-3 shows the progression of codependency in the late stage if you do nothing, and the rewards you reap if you stick with recovery.

Table 1-3   Late Stage of Codependency and Recovery

Progression of Codependency	*Recovery from Codependency*
Develops physical symptoms	Happiness doesn't depend on others
Feels angry, hopeless, and depressed	Self-esteem and confidence return
Obsessive-compulsive behavior, addictions	Has own power and pursues goals
Further decline in self-esteem	Is expansive, creative, spontaneous
Despair and lack of self-care	Experiences self-love
Increased conflicts	Capacity for interdependency and intimacy

Recovery from codependency requires ongoing maintenance in or out of a relationship. This is why people continue in Twelve Step programs after they've left an addict or addiction behind. Only after a number of years do the changes and tools of recovery and health become part of you.

Goals of Recovery

The overall goal of recovery is to become a full-functioning individual. That entails knowing, valuing, trusting, and freely expressing yourself congruently with your feelings and values. To that aim, this book addresses objectives with respect to your thoughts, feelings, actions, and self-esteem, as listed in this section. Consider tracking your progress as you work through the coming chapters and continue to grow in recovery. Add your own goals as you go along.

How you think

The first priority is to heighten your awareness and open up your thinking and understanding about codependency and addiction and how each has and continues to affect your family and your life. Specific cognitive goals include understanding your separateness from others, letting go and giving others the dignity to be responsible for themselves while taking responsibility for yourself. Ongoing goals are developing awareness of your thoughts, rationalizations, values, beliefs, needs, and behavior and getting a handle on your obsessive, repetitive worries and negative self-talk. Your list may include:

Understanding codependency (see especially Chapters 1, 2, 3, and 4)

Understanding addiction and your family dynamics (see Chapters 5, 7, and 12)

Understanding how addiction may have affected you (see Chapter 7)

Coming out of denial (see Chapter 5)

Accepting your powerlessness over addiction (see Chapter 9)

Understanding and practicing the concept of nonattachment (see Chapter 9)

Becoming aware of separateness between yourself and others (see Chapter 3, 12, and 16)

Gaining awareness of thoughts

Judgments of self and others (see Chapter 10)

Worries and fears (see Chapter 9)

Rationalizations (see Chapter 5)

Fantasies and obsessions (see Chapters 5 and 9)

Gaining awareness of your needs and how to meet them (see Chapters 3, 10, and 13)

Gaining awareness of beliefs and values (see Chapter 8)

Testing your thoughts and beliefs against reality (see Chapters 5, 7, and 8)

Developing decision-making skills (see Chapter 17)

Gaining awareness of codependent behavior (see Chapter 3)

Pleasing

Manipulating

Controlling (see also Chapter 9)

Enabling

What you feel

Because either you weren't taught to name your feelings or your childhood environment prevented their free expression, it's likely that you're not often aware of your feelings. Having emotion is different. Codependents can cry and rage, but aren't able to name a feeling or know why they're upset. Typically codependents feel guilty for other people's negative feelings and think other people make them feel guilty or angry. Taking responsibility for your feelings and not those of others is a gradual, but essential, learning process. Important goals are to be able to identify, name, and express your feelings openly. This latter step may be disturbing if you're not used to crying or feeling vulnerable, but this is a healthy part of healing. People who are overwhelmed with feelings need to contain and understand them. Down the line, you want to be able to appropriately express your feelings to others. Your goals may include:

Replacing despair with hope (see Chapters 6, 14, and 18)

Gaining awareness and acceptance of feelings about you, your work, and people in your life (see Chapter 8)

Being able to name and accept your feelings (see Chapter 8)

Journaling feelings (see Chapter 8)

Connecting thoughts, needs, feelings and actions (see Chapter 8)

Distinguishing your feelings from others' (see Chapters 3 and 9)

Taking responsibility for your feelings (see Chapters 3, 8, 9, and 10)

Not taking responsibility for other people's feelings (see Chapters 3 and 9)

Sharing feelings in a group or with a therapist (see Chapters 6 and 18)

Taking charge of your anger (see Chapter 3, 13, and 14)

Grieving your losses (see Chapter 13)

Sharing my feelings in safe, personal relationships (see Chapters 12 and 16)

Being able to soothe yourself when you have negative feelings (see Chapters 10, 13, and 14)

Your self-esteem

Your self-esteem reflects how you feel about yourself. It enhances or impairs your relationships, professional success, your moods, and sense of well-being. Replacing shame and low self-esteem with self-respect and self-worth is the cornerstone of recovery. (See Chapter 10.) Pursuing all of the goals outlined in this chapter improves your self-esteem, but you can benefit by giving specific attention to:

Confronting negative self-talk (see Chapter 11)

Healing shame (see Chapters 3, 7, 11, and 13)

Being kind to yourself (see Chapters 10 and 13)

Taking responsibility for your actions (see Chapters 8, 9, 10, and 15)

Affirming yourself (see Chapters 10 and 17)

Accepting yourself (see Chapter 10)

Reducing guilt and forgiving yourself (see Chapters 10 and 15)

Meeting your needs (see Chapters 5, 8, 9, and 13)

Sharing in Twelve Step meetings and in therapy (see Chapters 6 and 18)

Trusting and loving yourself (see Chapter 10)

Nurturing and giving yourself pleasure (see Chapters 13 and 14)

What you say

Practicing assertive communication improves your relationships and also builds self-esteem. Your communication goals may include:

Being honest and direct (see Chapter 11)

Making "I" statements (see Chapter 11)

Taking positions (see Chapter 11)

Becoming aware of abusive communication (see Chapters 3 and 11)

Setting boundaries and saying "No" (see Chapter 11)

Being able to problem-solve in your relationships (see Chapter 11)

Handling conflict (see Chapter 11)

What you do

There's a maxim in AA: "Take action, and the feelings will follow." Your thoughts and feelings determine how you behave, but actions also change your mood and feelings. Reading about and under-standing codependency and how you came to be codependent are important, but taking risks and behaving differently actualizes your understanding and changes you. Taking action doesn't mean jump-ing in to "fix" everyone's problem. That complicates matters and prevents things from working themselves out naturally. There's another — almost opposite saying in Al-Anon, the Twelve Step pro-gram for families of alcoholics: "Don't just do something, sit there." It requires courage and strength to do the opposite of what you ordinarily do and to refrain from habitual behavior. Action goals include communicating differently and setting boundaries. They also include:

Journaling

Attending Twelve Step meetings and/or counseling (see Chapters 6 and 18)

Not enabling (see Chapters 3 and 9)

Practicing nonattachment (see Chapter 9)

Minding your own business (see Chapter 9)

Creating a spiritual practice (see Chapter 14)

Developing interdependent behavior (see Chapters 12 and 16)

Developing hobbies and interests (see Chapter 14 and 17)

Taking action to meet your needs (see Chapters 5, 8, 9, and 13)

Setting and pursuing goals (see Chapter 17)

Trying and discovering new activities (see Chapters 14 and 17)

Building supportive relationships (see Chapters 6, 14, and 18)

Reaching out when you're in pain (see Chapters 6 and 18)

Don't be discouraged if you're unable to achieve some of these goals. Many manifest in the middle and later stages of recovery. You're on a journey — a wonderful, sometimes painful, but joyous adventure of self-discovery.

Chapter 2

A New Definition of Codependency

Clinicians like labels in order to talk about and study an illness. It helps them identify symptoms, utilize tested treatments, and understand the origin of a disorder. It also spawns research.

I don't like labels because they ignore each person's uniqueness and make people feel badly about themselves! Codependents especially already feel badly about themselves! They already feel ashamed or deficient. On the other hand, the benefit of a definition is that when you clarify and can name a problem, you know where to go for help and how to approach treatment. Your situation has a name . . . and hopefully a solution. A diagnosis enables you to take responsibility for your problems. Once identified, you're able to find others who share your experience and provide information, tools, and support. Instead of wandering around a store, looking at things to buy, you can head directly to the department that has the answers you need.

If you don't like the term *codependency,* disregard it; but if you resonate with some aspects discussed, focus on those and then utilize the suggested action steps that you find helpful.

Defining Codependency

The term *codependency* evolved out of clinical work with alcoholics, following the founding of Alcoholics Anonymous in 1935 by Bill Wilson to help alcoholics find sobriety.

Soon after, the founder's wife, Lois Wilson, saw that the spouses, mostly wives at that time, needed support. She started holding meetings in members' homes. It expanded to include all relatives and friends of alcoholics, and Al-Anon was born. In the 1950s, a main office was established in New York City to coordinate groups that had spread nationwide, and today worldwide. They discovered that many of the problems in the family persisted even after the alcoholics found sobriety, and that their spouses' patterns continued when they entered into new sober relationships. They realized that they had to recover independently of the person and relationship that brought them to Al-Anon.

This evolution concurred with advent of family therapy in the mental health field. Theorists and therapists were increasingly viewing mental illness in a family context. In clinics, counselors noticed that some patients improved, but when they returned to their families, their symptomatic behavior returned. They deduced that the family dynamics were maintaining or even causing the illness, and began focusing on family interactions. Family system theories emerged from the study of cybernetics, systems theory, and systems psychology.

Therapists who worked with alcoholics observed repetitive patterns among the spouses and families of the alcoholics that reinforced drinking behavior. These family members were initially referred to as *co-alcoholics.* They uniformly displayed dysfunctional characteristics. They reproached and tried to manage the alcoholic, unaware that they were trying to control an uncontrollable illness. From years of disappointments, their self-esteem and despair were as low as that of the alcoholics.

The term *codependency* was born in the late 1970s, and by the 1980s was being applied to addicts and their relatives, families of someone with chronic mental or physical illness, and caregiving professionals.

The codependency movement

In the United States, other *Twelve Step* anonymous programs began to form based on the model of Alcoholics Anonymous, which had proven so effective. Soon they proliferated.

Addiction and Twelve-Step Programs

After Al-Anon founded its headquarters, Narcotics Anonymous began in 1953, followed by Overeaters Anonymous in 1960 and Gamblers Anonymous in 1961. The 1970s saw the arrival of Emotional Health Anonymous, Sex Addicts Anonymous, Sex and Love Addicts Anonymous, Debtors Anonymous, and Adult Children of Alcoholics. The list grew in the 1980s to include, among others, Workaholics Anonymous, Nicotine Anonymous, Clutterers Anonymous, Cocaine Anonymous, Marijuana Anonymous, Sexual Compulsions Anonymous, and Co-Dependents Anonymous. The meeting of the First National Conference on Co-dependency was held in 1989.

A codependent society

As the awareness of addiction grew, more habits and compulsions began being characterized as addictions, and increasingly people seemed to have codependent traits that compromised their relationships, both among the addicts and those close to them. Family systems author and theorist Virginia Satir commented that of the 10,000 families she'd studied, 96 percent exhibited codependent thoughts and behaviors. By the end of the 1980s, America was referred to as an addictive society by author and former psychotherapist Anne Wilson Schaef in her 1988 book, *When Society Becomes an Addict.*

It may be that all the focus on relationships is the sign of the times, reflected in the growth of family therapy and the women's, sexual liberation, and human potential movements. Intimacy is considered a need today, but in prior generations it was left to romance novels, poetry, and fantasy because the focus was on survival and productivity. It's no coincidence that the codependency movement arose in America, the champion of romantic love with the highest divorce rate. Americans want romance to work! Whatever the reason, just about everyone wants a fulfilling intimate relationship — something that seems to elude codependents.

Definition of codependency

Today, no consensus exists on a definition of codependency. It hasn't been recognized by the American Psychiatric Association for inclusion in the *Diagnostic Statistical Manual of Mental Disorders,* which is published periodically to describe agreed-upon criteria for mental diagnoses. Nonetheless, therapists familiar with codependency can name it when they see it.

Various attempts were made to define codependency during the expansion of the movement. Depending upon the orientation of the expert, definitions focused on causes, behaviors and symptoms, family dynamics, or a person's ability to form loving relationships. Some of these definitions are too general and others too narrow. Critics argued that the definitions included "normal" people, and, therefore, weren't useful. I disagree for the following reasons:

- ✔ These so-called "normal" people are suffering. It's normal to worry about and help someone who's in trouble or is ruining his or her health and relationships because of an addiction, but those helpers become dysfunctional when the problem takes over their mind, spirit, and health.

- ✔ Codependency has become "normal." That doesn't make it healthy.

- ✔ Most codependents "look good." The critics may personally know or work with codependents who seem agreeable, reliable, and do more than their share or work, but aren't aware that they're anxious and guilt-ridden inside.

- ✔ Most schools, bureaucracies, and corporations rarely encourage independent thinking, and reward compliance.

- ✔ More and more people are using prescription and street drugs and addictive behavior to cope with underlying codependency.

 Codependency causes pain in relationships whether or not there's an identifiable addict and whether or not the person lives alone or tries to control someone else's behavior. My definition cuts to the core of codependency: A lost Self, which includes addicts as well as many of those who love them.

 A *codependent* is a person who can't function from his or her innate self, and instead, organizes thinking and behavior around a substance, process, or other person(s).

A *process* is an activity. For example, it may be gambling, sex, shopping, or working. Although this definition includes people addicted to substances and processes, sobriety or abstinence from the process must be obtained before tackling the underlying codependence. (In some cases, such as working and eating, abstinence may mean moderation within certain guidelines.)

The Core of Codependency – A Lost Self

You were born unique with an innate capacity to feel and respond to both your internal awareness and external environment. That's how you learn, plan, create, and relate to others from your authentic experience. Development of this natural process was interrupted or denied to codependents.

The term *Self* is vague and difficult to identify and define. It's your unique, essential being. Perhaps it's encoded in your DNA, waiting to be embodied, developed, and expressed. I capitalize it to remind you that it's this larger Self you don't usually think about. Famous psychoanalyst Carl Jung thought it's a coherent, unifying principle that integrates the totality of all that you are — both the center and whole of your psyche. It comprises your:

- ✔ Personality

- ✔ Unconscious

- ✔ Consciousness

- ✔ Ego, which helps you deal with reality, makes up only a small part

For a codependent, it's as if the Self adapted and reacted to others' behavior in order to cope, instead of referring back to its own internal impulses. Over time, these impulses became obscured and veiled by a proxy personality and the ability to access them weakened. Chapters 7 and 13 discuss how that happened.

Codependents complain that they feel like "a fraud," or that they experience a gap between their public and inner selves. When you can't connect to your Self, you find it hard to identify feelings, make decisions, and set boundaries. Sometimes, you may feel resentful, lost, and confused, which leads to depression. You react to people and situations and look to others for answers, validation, and approval. Hence, the motto of Co-Dependents Anonymous' is, "To thine own self be true," which is a real challenge. Codependents remain in unhappy relationships because of the pain of rejection and loneliness. Some, forego commitment and stay on their own due to avoid losing themselves again.

The continuum of codependency

Like most things, codependency varies on a scale from minimal to severe. When you're under stress, symptoms flare. As you read this book, some characteristics and examples may sound foreign, while you can relate to others. The severity of codependency varies depending on a number of things, such as:

- ✔ Genetics

- ✔ Culture, including religious beliefs

- ✔ Your family's dynamics

- ✔ Your experience of trauma

- ✔ Your role models

- ✔ Your addictions or use of drugs

- ✔ Intimate relationships with addicts

If you're codependent, generally symptoms show up to some extent in all your relationships, and in intimate ones to a greater degree. Codependency may not affect you as much at work if you've had effective role models or learned interpersonal skills that have helped you manage. Maybe you weren't having a problem until a particular relationship, boss, or work environment triggered you. Perhaps you only have problems in one relationship — for instance, with a parent or child, but not with your spouse. One explanation may be that the parent has a difficult personality or the child has special needs, and the couple has adjusted to their roles and to one another, but avoids intimacy.

Is it a disease?

That codependency is a disease was first suggested in 1988 by psychiatrist Timmen Cermak. *Disease* may sound morbid, but it's only a condition with discernible, progressive symptoms that impair normal functioning.

Alcoholism was termed an illness by the American Medical Association (AMA) in 1956. In 1991 the AMA categorized it as a disease along with drug dependencies. AA and clinicians had adopted the disease medical model long before, following the 1960 publication of *The Disease Concept of Alcoholism* by E. Morton Jellinick. This was considered a victory because it removed much of the shame around alcoholism for the individual and in society at large.

Since then, addiction experts have applied the medical model of disease to sex, food, and gambling addictions. So, too, with codependency. Some people object to the disease label because they claim it stigmatizes, discourages, and disempowers the person who is trying to recover. They claim that it makes people believe they have no power to stop their addictive behavior and that they can never get well. Others disagree, saying that it removes shame and the punitive treatment of addiction, which should be treated with the same empathy and vigilance as a physical disease, such as diabetes or hypertension.

For years, people argued about whether a biological component of addiction was required to qualify addiction as a disease, and whether one could be identified. Today, brain scans of addicts reveal defects in the brain's pleasure center that processes dopamine, which creates feelings of pleasure or satisfaction. The same was found true for a behavioral addiction, like gambling. Whether the dysfunction in the pleasure center predates the addiction is an open question. Investigation continues to examine how genes play a part in addictions. Research has shown that environmental factors, including parenting and trauma, affect gene expression and the development of an addiction. Trauma and depression affect brain chemistry, but so do psychotherapy and behavioral changes, including positive thoughts and feelings.

Whether or not you believe codependency is an addiction or a disease, the choice to recover is yours. If you don't like the labels, don't use them.

Codependency and addicts

Addicts by definition are dependent. They become dependent and reliant upon the object of their addiction in order to function, and more time is spent in connection with the addiction. When addicts abstain, many develop cross-addictions. To witness cross-addiction first hand, you only have to attend an Alcoholics Anonymous (AA) meeting to see how many people are smoking. Sober alcoholics start chain smoking, overeating, developing sex addictions, and so on. Some food addicts who've had bariatric surgery to lose weight eat less, but become alcoholics or shopaholics.

There are many causes for addiction, but neuroscience research has demonstrated that when addicts stop practicing their primary addiction and adopt another addiction, *it is at just the same level of addiction.* For example, when a compulsive gambler abstains from gambling, he or she's at risk to start drinking as if he or she were an alcoholic all those years. Aside from physical reasons, on the emotional level, he or she hasn't done the emotional recovery work to heal his or her lost Self. This is where codependency comes in.

When addicts give up their addiction, they then have to deal with their emotions. Instead, many who are single want to rush into romance (jokingly called "13th stepping" in AA). They're squarely confronted with all the relationship and intimacy problems that they've avoided. There are those who sponsor newcomers and try to manage the newcomer's life, and even obsess about him or her. Again, the underlying problem of codependency is surfacing. Sometimes, it's years before they're willing to face their codependency issues, if ever, which can contribute to relapse.

Switching addictions and obsessing can also happen to those in Al-Anon or Co-Dependents Anonymous. When I stopped my codependent behavior, I started dieting compulsively. I went to Overeaters Anonymous to let go of my diet obsession, which had replaced my obsession with my husband. The mental obsessions were my means of coping with repressed feelings I wasn't able to access. (See Chapter 5 for more information on denial.)

This book focuses on the codependent's relationship with the lost Self and interactions with others. It doesn't deal specifically with overcoming addiction to drugs or other processes, although healing the Self is part of that. To learn more, check out *Addiction & Recovery For Dummies* by Brian F. Shaw, Paul Ritvo, and Jane Irvine (John Wiley & Sons Publishing).

Women and codependency

I see many codependent men in my clinical practice; however, women comprise the majority of codependents. There are many reasons:

- ✔ **Biological:** Women are biologically wired for relationships. Their deep limbic systems increase their ability to bond and their sensitivity to feelings. Under stress, men prepare men for action, while women's hormones prepare them to tend to children and befriend others.

- ✔ **Developmental (gender identity):** Generally, girls are more dependent upon and emotionally involved with their parents. For them, loss of a relationship is their biggest stressor. They're more accepting of parental values, and a separation that threatens the emotional attachment with their parents creates anxiety. Autonomy is their biggest challenge. Unlike girls, boys must separate from their mothers and identify with their fathers in order to establish their male identities. For males, intimacy is a challenge.

- ✔ **Political:** Universally, women have been subordinated to men and marginalized from access to equal money, rights, and power. Oppression for generations has made women more compliant. This continues today. They're traumatized by physical and sexual abuse far more than men, which lowers their self-esteem.

- ✔ **Cultural:** In most cultures, girls are more restricted and have less opportunity for autonomy. Both hormones and societal norms encourage adolescent boys to be more rebellious and autonomous. They're given more freedom and are willing to struggle for it.

- ✔ **Societal:** Women suffer from low self-esteem and depression far more than men. It's not clear whether this is a cause, by-product, or concurrent with codependency; however, societal attitudes are a contributing cause. A Dove study found that over 40 percent of women are unhappy with their looks, and over two-thirds suffer low confidence about their bodies. Many blamed the airbrushed, ideal models for setting unrealistic, unattainable standards. Unfortunately, it starts in childhood. Seven in ten girls are dissatisfied with their looks. A large number practice self-destructive behavior.

What Codependency Is Not

It's important to note that any definition of codependency may include people who have one or more other mental disorders; for example, obsessive-compulsive disorder, attention deficit disorder, bi-polar disorder, and/or personality disorders, such as narcissistic, dependent, or borderline. They require diagnosis to determine the most appropriate care. Specific treatment is beyond the scope of this book. Diagnosis should be left to a professional, and mind-bending time spent diagnosing someone close to you — a common codependent activity — would be better spent working on yourself.

Codependency is also not caregiving, kindness, or interdependency. I've heard people complain that they were labeled "codependent" because they were taking care of a sick relative or helping someone. Codependent behavior in a specific situation doesn't make a person codependent. An evaluation of codependency is based upon a larger pattern of behavior and accompanied by other characteristics described in Chapter 3. This section takes a look at the difference between what's codependent and what's not.

Caretaking vs. caregiving

Many people, particularly women, enjoy nurturing and caring for others. Some make it a profession, me included. Mothers are wired to care for their children. Codependent caretaking is different from giving care to someone. In fact, with codependency, there may be more "taking" than giving, when the needs of the giver take precedence. This is because caregiving comes from abundance, and caretaking emanates from need and deprivation. When does caregiving become codependent caretaking? Read the following cases, and decide for yourself.

Jill and **Jane** quit their jobs, each to care for her dying mother; one woman is codependent, and the other isn't. Take a look at the following cases, and think about what makes one codependent. (For more on caretaking, see Chapter 3.)

Jill enjoys her job. She is the only relative who can care for her mother. Reluctantly, she realizes spending the last months of her mother's life with her is a priority, so she leaves her job. She arranges for part-time help a few days a week to in order to make time for herself. Jill exercises, talks to friends for support, and does her best under the circumstances to maintain balance and harmony in her life, which nurtures both her and her mother.

Jane feels obligated to leave her job to help her. She blames and resents her siblings for not sharing her burden, yet doesn't ask that they pitch in. She feels responsible for and worries about her mother's medical treatment. She spends all day with her mother and tries unsuccessfully to convince her to see a faith healer. Her mother encourages her to get some rest, but Jane feels too guilty and preoccupied to take time for herself and is tired all the time.

Jane's codependent caretaking has inappropriate responsibility and control written all over it. She feels guilty and resentful because she feels responsible for her mother, yet she neglects her responsibilities to herself. Jane takes over her mother's treatment, gives unwanted advice, and doesn't ask others for help so she can maintain control. Finally, she's too worried and guilty to take care of herself, even though her mother seems to need her less than the daughter acknowledges. Jill, however, gives care to her mother, but doesn't neglect her needs, so she doesn't become resentful. Codependents give until it hurts.

Pleasing vs. kindness

It's certainly natural and satisfying to be helpful and kind to others. However, codependent pleasing emanates from low self-esteem — more to get than give. Many codependents don't have a choice! They can't say no. As with care-giving, it's not so much the actions that determine codependency, but the pleaser's state of mind. The essential question is whether you are giving from a place of self-esteem or from guilt, fear, or insecurity.

Assume **Bill, Brad,** and **Bob** love and enjoy giving to their girlfriends and always let them choose where they dine.

> **Bill** lets his girlfriend choose to avoid disappointing her and a potential conflict, because he's afraid of losing her.
>
> **Brad's** self-esteem is boosted by letting his girlfriend pick pricey restaurants, even though he'd rather order takeout.
>
> **Bob** doesn't care where he eats, but asserts himself on other matters.

Bill fears abandonment, so letting his girlfriend choose the restaurant is sort of bribery. Most people enjoy pleasing and showing kindness to others and feel good when it's appreciated, but they don't fear that the relationship is at risk. Brad is mainly concerned with his self-image. He can't let her know who he really is — also because he fears abandonment. Only Bob is acting out of free choice, rather than fear and low self-esteem.

Codependency vs. interdependency

When it comes to relationships, whether the dynamics are codependent or healthy, interdependency may not be apparent at first. The following are the extremes, so you get the idea. Most relationships fall somewhere in between.

Relationship hell

Although from the outside a codependent couple may look physically, intellectually, and financially independent, in reality, there are two emotionally dependent and insecure adults. Rather than equality and respect, there's a power imbalance and/or power struggles. One person may anticipate the other's needs and then feel guilty, anxious, or resentful about it. They're not just affected by each other; they react to and feel responsible for each other's feelings and moods. They directly or indirectly try to control the other in order to get their needs met. They feel less free in the relationship and fear both intimacy and separateness, which threaten their insecure selves.

Relationship heaven

Attachment normally develops in intimate relationships. When two people love each other, it's natural for them to want to be together and to miss and be concerned about one another. Over time, their lives and routines become intertwined. They enjoy helping and encouraging each other. They need, depend upon, and are affected by one another, but are equals and take responsibility for their own lives as well as their contribution to the relationship. Their lives are interdependent. They don't fear intimacy, and independence is not seen as a threat to the relationship. In fact, the relationship gives them each more freedom. They respect and support each other's personal goals, but are committed to the relationship. (See Chapter 16 for a deeper look.)

Two couples, the **Jones** and **Browns,** always spend their weekends playing doubles tennis in a tournament circuit, one couple is codependent.

The **Jones** consider each other best friends. They enjoy the tennis tournaments and socialize with other couples they meet. They leave uplifted and relaxed, and are able to talk about the challenges of their game, their mistakes, and strategy with an attitude of helping one another and their game.

The **Browns** bicker after each game. The wife has tried to quit, but the husband threatens to tour the tennis circuit alone. She's usually late getting ready. He's angry, she feels guilty, and they don't talk on the way to the game. Afterwards, he critiques her playing. They rarely socialize, except when they win, but even then, the husband tries to improve her game.

It's not the time spent together, but the relationship dynamics that are determinative. The Jones cooperate and treat each other with respect. They are fed by each others' company. The Browns are emotionally reactive to one another because of the incompleteness of their individual selves. The power is imbalanced, and the husband is emotionally abusive. The wife tries to express her power and anger by being chronically late, but she cannot quit the game because she's afraid of abandonment. So is he, which is why he threatens to leave by playing without her, but doesn't. They're in bondage to one another and unable to talk about their problems.

Chapter 3

Characteristics of Codependents

. . . .

In This Chapter

▶ Defining self-esteem and internalized shame

▶ Explaining boundaries

▶ Understanding dependency

▶ Recognizing codependent communication patterns

▶ Identifying caretaking and control

▶ Taking a look at denial

▶ Finding out about painful emotions

. . . .

*E*veryone has wounds; some people have a lot more than others. As a codependent, you have your share of wounds. You may be afraid to get close, afraid to be alone, afraid of being hurt, afraid of being controlled, afraid of being judged. These are your wounded places. You don't realize this or that deep down, you don't believe you matter. Sadly, your wounds make you ashamed of who you are — of being human — so you hide them from others, even from yourself. This is your denial.

In this chapter, I describe the major traits and symptoms of codependency. You may have some, but not all, or not all the time or with everyone. Symptoms and severity vary among codependents.

Low Self-Esteem

Self-esteem reflects your real opinion of yourself — deep down. It's a self-appraisal. Your self-esteem may be high or low, but isn't based on what others think. Instead of Self-esteem (a capital "S" to emphasize *self*-evaluation), codependents look to others for their value and validation. Other people and things make them feel good or bad. You can say that codependents are "other defined."

You know how it feels to complete a difficult project, win a competition, or just have a great day with your friends. People with high self-esteem feel that way most of the time. Usually, people feel down when they're reprimanded by their boss, have a financial setback, or become ill, but these feelings are transient and don't reflect true Self-esteem, positive or negative. Good self-esteem doesn't vary significantly with external events. You won't feel bad about yourself when bad things happen because they're external and not a reflection of your essential Self. You know that you have the resources to recover. But when people with low self-esteem suffer loss or disappointment, they feel defeated. Table 3-1 compares the signs of high and low self-esteem.

Table 3-1	Signs of High and Low Self-Esteem
High Self-Esteem	*Low Self-Esteem*
Know you're okay	Feel not enough; compare and improve self
Know you have value and matter	Lack self-worth and value
Feel competent	Need others' approval; ask others' opinion
Exhibit honesty and integrity	Feel indecisive; defer to, agree with, and please others
Trust yourself	Doubt self; feel disconnected from needs and wants
Display self-acceptance	Are critical of self and others; are sensitive to criticism
Show responsibility to self and others	Discount own feelings, wants and needs
Are hopeful	Lack confidence and self-efficacy
Respect and compassion for self and others	Lack self-respect and self-compassion

As a codependent, you probably have low self-esteem. You may believe you're never enough, that you're not doing enough, attractive enough, smart enough, or good enough. You may base your self-worth on money, beauty, prestige, or by excelling at something — even being a great parent — yet none of this is self-esteem. How will you feel about yourself if you lose your money, looks, prestige, or if your child becomes a drug addict? There are successful, beautiful celebrities who dislike themselves, and average, ordinary people with high self-esteem. Nor is true self-esteem based upon performing well if your actions are motivated by a desire to win others' approval or recognition — thus the expression, "You're only as good as your last performance." You'd be seeking "other" esteem. There's a catch here, because you may think highly of yourself, not realizing it's all based on these externals.

Because codependents are typically disconnected from themselves, you may not trust yourself and may lack the ability to know or follow inner guidance. You may be confused or unable to make up your mind, always asking someone else's opinion. You may not know what you really want and defer to others in order to be liked and loved. When you know your needs and desires, you may dismiss or talk yourself out of them, or go along with someone to avoid conflict — especially in intimate relationships.

Low self-esteem can make you super-critical, so that you find fault with just about anything concerning yourself — how you feel, act, look, and what you need, think, say, or create. You may even hate and loathe yourself. Like most people, you probably don't realize the extent of your self-judgment. It makes you sensitive to criticism and even feel criticized when you're not. When you receive praise, attention, compliments, or gifts, you're embarrassed and make excuses, because you don't feel deserving. Being self-critical also makes you critical of others.

Don't be discouraged. There's hope. Your self-esteem is learned, and poor self-esteem can be transformed into self-worth. This book and its exercises are designed to start you on that path.

Internalized shame

Whereas self-esteem comes from your thoughts, shame is a painful feeling of humiliation and self-disgust. When others are around, you may feel exposed and alienated, like they can see your flaws. It makes you want to hide and become invisible. Everyone has shame, including people with high self-esteem who generally feel good about themselves. Shame is healthy when it prevents you from doing something you consider unethical. Physical signs of shame are:

- Avoiding eye contact
- Withdrawing
- Freezing

- Perspiring

- Slumping your shoulders

- Hanging your head

- Dizziness

- Nausea

Normally, shame passes after an embarrassing incident, but for codependents shame is internalized. It sits there waiting to be activated and persists long after the event, like an open wound that has never healed. You're ashamed of who you are. It's all pervasive, paralyzes spontaneity, and defines you. You don't believe that you matter or are worthy of love, respect, success, or happiness. You think that you're bad, defective, inadequate, a phony, a failure, or worse. Chronic internalized shame leads to hopelessness and despair. Extreme, prolonged shaming and humiliation can cause psychic numbing, like becoming a living zombie. Some codependent symptoms and feelings that stem from low self-esteem and internalized shame are listed in Table 3-2. Others include pleasing, control, caretaking, depression, and perfectionism.

Table 3-2	Core Codependent Feelings		
Low Self-Esteem	*Shame*	*Fear*	*Guilt and Blame*
You Lack:	*You Feel:*	*You Fear:*	*You Feel Guilt About:*
Self-confidence	Unworthiness	Abandonment	Your feelings
Self-trust	Unlovable	Rejection	Your acts and needs
Self-responsibility	Unimportant	Criticism	Others' feelings
Self-efficacy (agency)	Undeserving	Failure and success	Others' acts
Self-respect	Self-loathing	Intimacy	Others' needs
Self-value/worth	Judgmental	Own power	Others' problems

Feeling a lot of shame creates a chronic sense of inferiority. You may envy and compare yourself negatively to people you admire. Because shame is painful, you may be unconscious of your shame and think you have good self-esteem. You may boast or feel self-important and superior to those you teach or supervise, people of a different class or culture, or anyone you judge. By devaluing others, you boost yourself higher to hide your shame from yourself. Most codependents fluctuate between feeling inferior and superior.

Pleasing — the pretzel dilemma

There are codependents who turn themselves inside out to accommodate others. They're not centered in themselves and desperately want others to validate them, like them, love them, or at least need them. If that's you, you want other esteem so much that you try to turn yourself into a human pretzel in order to please, accommodate, and win someone else's approval. You feel anxious if others are unhappy with you, and you give their needs, feelings, and opinions precedence over your own. In fact, you silence, sometimes even to yourself, your own needs, feelings, thoughts, opinions, and values to become what you believe is expected or desired by someone else, especially in romantic relationships — where the rubber meets the road. You try to fit in, be perfect, be nice, look good, be responsible, do well, and take care of others, further hiding your wounds, your shame, and your pain. When you feel extremely insecure, you may mimic other's actions and feelings or pretend to feel and behave the way you assume another person wants.

The more you look outward in order to measure how you should feel, think, and behave, the greater is the estrangement from your inner Self, and the stronger is the need and addiction to something or someone, just as an addict takes a drug to fill the emptiness created by the separation from the Self. Pleasing gives only temporary relief and builds a need for more, until the attraction to that "other" becomes an addiction.

Guilt

Guilt is different from shame. Whereas shame is a bad feeling you have about yourself as a person, guilt is a feeling about what you've said or done that violates your personal standards, a law, or ethical principle, such as hurting someone. For codependents, guilt is hard to let go of and gets compounded when it taps in to underlying feelings of shame. You may feel guilty, "I shouldn't have done that," followed by shame, "I'm so selfish (or a loser, etc.)."

David is an accountant. On Saturday, he realized that he'd made a mistake on a client's tax return. He hadn't submitted it to the client or the IRS, but David was so guilt-ridden and angry at himself that he couldn't wait until Monday to correct the error. He interrupted a family outing to go to his office. His unhealthy guilt robbed him of peace of mind because it triggered internalized shame.

Feelings are part of our humanity, but codependents feel guilty and ashamed about them. You judge your feelings and tell yourself you shouldn't feel the way you do — feeling guilty when you're angry or thinking there's something wrong with you when you're sad or depressed. You wonder what's normal. You review prior events and conversations and blame yourself for perceived "mistakes." Figure 3-1 shows the Self shrouded by the negative thoughts and emotions of codependency. Notice the broken boundary.

Susan was dating someone new. Each week in therapy, she'd detail what happened and what was said during their previous date. She'd conclude with, "So, what do you think?" She wanted to know if she'd said or done anything "wrong," and what the man may be thinking about the relationship. Her focus was on adapting herself to win him in order to complete her deficient Self.

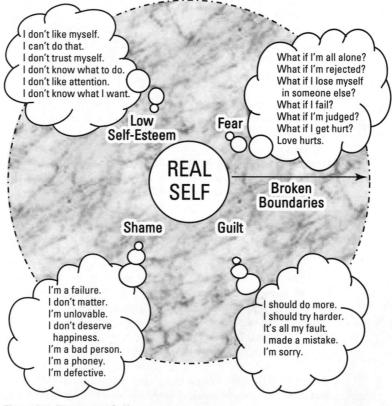

Figure 3-1: The buried Self.

Codependents also feel guilt and shame about their needs, making it difficult to ask for help or what they want. They judge themselves as weak, indulgent, needy, or selfish.

Shirley had learned to be self-sufficient at a young age, so when she was undergoing radiation treatment for breast cancer, she drove herself there. When I suggested she ask a friend or relative to accompany her, she protested, "I just couldn't." She assumed her needs were as burdensome to others as they'd been to her parents.

Stanley had years of executive experience setting limits with employees and enforcing the needs of his employer's company, but when it came to his needs, he was the opposite. Even though he resented his demanding wife, he couldn't say "No" to her or ask for what he wanted without feeling guilty. He kept putting off buddies who invited him on a fishing weekend, convincing himself that his desire to go was selfish. He didn't realize that devaluing his needs reflected his low self-worth, but blamed his wife instead.

Codependents feel guilty not only for their own feelings, but also about other people's feelings. They mistakenly feel responsible for them. You may feel guilty if your spouse didn't like the movie you chose, even though he or she agreed to see it. In relationships, you can't disagree without feeling guilty. You're always saying, "I'm sorry," for your "mistakes," and try harder, often instead of confronting your partner's behavior. If he or she has a painful emotion, like anger or sadness, even when you're not being blamed, you first think, "What did I do wrong?" You get defensive. Guilt gets in the way of hearing the other person, perpetuating conflict.

Feeling unworthy and undeserving can make you a sucker for punishment. You're susceptible to accepting others' abusive anger and blame as further proof that you're the one in the wrong — even when you're accused of causing the other person's addictive or abusive behavior. Because of low self-esteem, rather than set boundaries, you try even harder to please the blamer and win approval. However, blamers are codependents, too. They don't take responsibility for their actions because of their low self-esteem, and defend against shame by blaming others for their own behavior. Neither the blamer nor the pleaser are centered within their own Self.

Perfectionism — when nothing's good enough

"Perfection" doesn't exist in the world, but only in the mind of a perfectionist. It's an illusory standard that's always out of reach. As a perfectionist, you never know what's good enough. You're always failing in your mind. Ongoing self-comparison to ideal standards create continual self-judgment and self-shaming — not only for a specific behavior, but of yourself as a person. As with David, the accountant in the above example, compulsive actions in pursuit of perfection defend against these feelings.

The combination of shame, guilt, and perfectionism is especially self-defeating when you seek love from someone who's unable to love or can give it only sporadically. You try harder to be perfect to earn love and prove that you're good or lovable in order to validate your self-esteem and quell your inner feelings of shame.

Some codependent high achievers try to prove their worth through accomplishments. Their compulsion is driven by internalized shame that they're flawed. An A student who obsesses over an A- on a test or that he missed a question is a perfectionist driven by shame. Others don't try to achieve because they think they're hopeless failures. Students who believe shaming messages that they're lazy, failures, or stupid are unable to excel in school.

Another example is a woman whose appearance must always be "perfect." Even her home must be spotless. Her personal shame is projected onto her environment, which she sees as a reflection of her intolerable flawed Self. Something chipped, dusty, or out of place can create painful anxiety, which she can stem only by fixing it rather than fixing her feelings about herself.

Dysfunctional Boundaries

Boundaries are part of an expression of self-esteem. They define where you end and others begin and set limits between you and others, allowing you to embody your individual Self. Awareness of boundaries both protects you from others and prevents you from violating others' boundaries. They are learned growing up when parents protect and respect your boundaries, and teach you not to invade others'. If you weren't taught, you won't recognize when you're being inappropriate, and if your parents invaded your boundaries, it feels natural when others do. Having healthy boundaries begins with getting to know yourself and your feelings and limits. Figure 3-2 shows three dysfunctional boundaries.

Types of boundaries

Boundaries affect every aspect of your life and affect how you interact with the world. For the purpose of discussion, I divided them into different types. Four major boundaries are:

✔ Material

✔ Physical, including sexual

✔ Mental

✔ Emotional

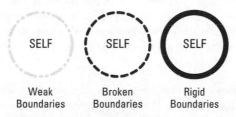

SELF	SELF	SELF
Weak Boundaries	Broken Boundaries	Rigid Boundaries

Figure 3-2: Degrees of boundaries.

Material boundaries

Material boundaries refer to sharing your possessions and money. People without boundaries give and loan without discretion. Taking or borrowing money or belongings without permission or without returning them also shows a lack of respect for others' boundaries.

Physical and sexual boundaries

Physical and sexual boundaries refer to your privacy and how, whom, and when you allow someone to enter your space or touch you. When children are denied a right of privacy or control over their bodies, their physical boundaries are violated. You can get a sense of people's boundaries by how close they stand to you, whether they offer a handshake, hug, or kiss. If you pull away and they persist, then you know that they're not respecting your boundaries and that theirs are different than yours. Another example is someone who telephones at inappropriate hours or launches into a one-sided monologue without sensitivity to the listener. Yet, the listener, in by not setting limits, also lacks boundaries. Boundaries can change in different relationships, as shown in the following example.

Jill's mother gave her mixed messages. She forbade Jill to go into her purse or belongings, but invaded Jill's boundaries by reading her mail and rummaging through her drawers. When Jill married, she didn't want to be like her mother and respected her children's boundaries, but didn't feel she had a right to privacy with her husband and felt guilty taking time for herself or locking the door.

If you've been physically or sexually abused as a child you may have trouble stopping physical abuse or unwanted sexual advances due to weak or non-existent physical or sexual boundaries. Sexual boundaries can also be violated with inappropriate nudity, flirtation, or provocative language.

Francis was molested as a child by her babysitter. She wasn't protected, and the words "Stop it" weren't in her vocabulary. As an adult, she was unable to stop her husband's violence. When it came to sex, she thought it was a marital duty even when she didn't want it, because she hadn't healed her molestation trauma and believed she didn't have a right to say "No" to her husband's advances.

Physical boundaries can differ between spouses because of the way they were raised, and can lead to conflicts that range from sharing money, bathrooms, information, and personal belongings to locking doors, nudity, lending, and spending.

Mental boundaries

Mental boundaries apply to opinions and beliefs, and whether you can formulate and hold on to your own when challenged, without becoming rigid or dogmatic, which would indicate inflexible boundaries. If, as a child, you were denied the right to think for yourself, make your own decisions, or have your ideas and opinions respected, then you may not know what you think or believe. If you express an opinion and become confused, lose hold of it in an argument, or become very angry, you may be reacting from your past when parents dismissed, criticized, or silenced your views.

Emotional boundaries

Emotional boundaries are subtle and difficult to understand. They define your emotional rights and responsibilities and separate your feelings from others. People with healthy emotional boundaries don't lose themselves in intimate relationships. As shown in Figure 3-3, each person's emotional identity is clear. Because the integrity of each Self is maintained, they can each be close and remain whole.

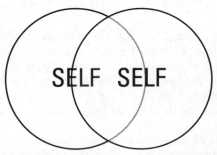

Figure 3-3: Healthy Selves.

Codependents don't have healthy emotional boundaries. If your feelings weren't respected as you were growing up, you may be unable to sense differences between your feelings and someone else's or know when your boundaries are disrespected. You may not know why you're upset or what you're feeling and be unable to name your hurt, humiliation, or anger. You may not get angry for days, if at all. You can't tell someone to stop hurting you until you know it. Even then, you may not feel entitled to assert your rights.

Poor emotional boundaries can make you feel responsible for, and at times, even guilty when you hear someone else's problem or negative feelings. You have the impulse to do something when someone else is upset. Their problems and responsibilities become yours. You take on more than 50 percent of the responsibility in a relationship, and if it's not working, blame yourself. You try to meet your partners' needs, but don't consider your own. You may even blame yourself for your partner's sexual dysfunction, addiction, or depression. But it doesn't help, so both of you end up unhappy.

Your boundaries are weak if you allow someone to blame, control, abuse, or take advantage of you. You feel at fault when blamed and react, instead of saying, "I don't take responsibility for that," or "I disagree." You lack limits as to how much you allow or give. On the other hand, if you blame or tell others what they should do, you're ignoring their separateness and crossing their boundaries. When you expect, blame, or control someone in order to make *you* feel better, you're not taking responsibility for your own feelings. You imply that someone else is responsible for how you feel, denying the separateness between you. (See later discussion on responsibility.)

We're one — no boundaries — egad!

Maybe being one with someone you love sounds wonderful, but in reality no two people are alike. They may be very similar, but each person's unique, and that includes you and your history, genetics, preferences, thoughts, interests, desires, and emotional responses. Even identical twins develop and respond to things differently. Your boundaries are crossed when others assume what you're thinking, feeling, or what's right for you. Respecting others' boundaries honors their separateness.

People with weak or no boundaries feel vulnerable being alone and also being in close relationships where they lose themselves. They get into them quickly, have sex with strangers, and say "Yes" when they want to say "No." They trust anyone and reveal privacies to acquaintances. When the boundary between you and someone else doesn't exist or is very blurry, it's called *enmeshment*, shown in Figure 3-4. It can make relationships scary and painful.

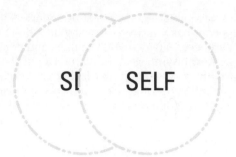

Figure 3-4: Enmeshed Selves.

When you're enmeshed, you feel responsible for and react to your partner's feelings, moods, and problems, but don't think clearly about your own needs and feelings, nor take responsibility for them. It's "I'm glad when you're glad, and "I'm sad when you're sad." This leads to conflict and sometimes abuse. Couples very enmeshed may appear as if there's only one controlling person in the relationship. This is because the two are fused. There's no room for discussion, disagreement, or separateness. One person is a doormat or caretaker without a sense of separate rights, values, and feelings.

Rigid boundaries

If your boundaries are rigid or thick for self-protection, you end up lonely out of fear because you haven't learned to protect yourself. You're distant and seem invulnerable, and your relationships lack sharing and are full of inflexible rules. You may isolate socially, or use work, addiction, or activities to avoid intimacy — sometimes only being intimate during sex. You may erect self-protective walls of silence, anger, distrust, and cynicism about people and life. Rigid boundaries create problems for others who aren't allowed get close. Your body language tells people to stay away, like a wounded animal that withdraws in self-protection because it feels vulnerable. If your family lacked closeness or touching or had negative rules about self-expression, then you may have learned to have rigid boundaries. Rigid boundaries can also be a reaction to trauma.

Broken and mixed boundaries

If you have broken boundaries, you have limits some of the time, in certain situations, or with certain people. You may have good boundaries, but lose them under stress, or be able to set limits with friends, but not with authority figures. You may have good boundaries or even distant, rigid boundaries with your mate, but are enmeshed with a child to whom you give too much or try to control.

When your boundaries are mixed, you flip from weak to rigid boundaries after feeling hurt. If you get close too quickly, you may lose interest or feel uncomfortable, because you're afraid of intimacy, and then boomerang to being alone. If you're in recovery and begin to have healthier boundaries, when you're with your family, you can start to feel crazy and confused. You can be having a hard time holding on to your fragile, new sense of Self.

Needing Someone Too Much

Codependents joke that at the moment of death, someone else's life flashes before them. The reality is that so much of yourself is invested in others that you lose who you are — your feelings, needs, hobbies, and goals. Your thinking and actions revolve around getting, changing, worrying about, and reacting to someone else. In advanced stages of the disease, codependents have become shells — their entire life having been squandered on someone else in the way that a compulsive gambler or debtor squanders their life savings.

Codependents are by definition "dependent" — dependent on something or someone outside of themselves. Dependency comes from low self-esteem and fear of abandonment. Signs include:

✔ Excessive thinking, worrying, or talking about someone

✔ Valuing others' opinions over your own

✔ Difficulty making decisions on your own

✔ Often giving up plans, hobbies, or interests to be with someone

✔ Fear of being left or rejected

✔ Feeling unhappy, empty, or discontent being with yourself

✔ Fear of being alone

✔ Inability to go places or start projects on your own

✔ Adapting to others' tastes or point of view

✔ Following, researching, or snooping on someone

✔ Feeling unhappy or trapped in a relationship you can't leave

✔ Seeking relationships for happiness, power, meaning, security, or excitement

✔ Focusing your energy on someone else's problem or life

✔ Feeling loyal to someone who's hurting you

✔ Unable to let go or get over losses and break-ups

You may not have spent time alone to get to know and develop yourself and formulate your own opinions and goals. You're usually looking for someone to make you happy if you're single, and when you're in a relationship, you focus on making that someone happy, in neither case taking the time to make yourself happy. You're rarely content with yourself, and become overly invested in pleasing or helping someone else, whom you begin to depend upon to fill in gaps in your Self. Soon you're reacting to and controlled by that person's feelings, needs, and moods, so you try to control the other person, rather than honor your needs and feelings.

Please don't leave

Fears of being left, rejected, or being alone play a big role in dependent relationships. Some codependents can't sleep alone. If you're disconnected from yourself, you won't feel complete. You won't have an inner life to sustain and nurture you, and being alone can feel empty — like no one's home. If you're unable to meet your needs, you hope that someone else will. Relationships add to your life but can't fix what's missing inside. You can feel just as lonely in a relationship, and once attachment bonds take hold, dependency on the relationship turns into addiction.

Abandonment in early childhood can produce shame, low self-esteem, and insecurity about whether you're loved and cared for, and whether you can count on it in the future. (For more on early abandonment, see Chapter 7.) Abandonment needn't be an actual leaving due to death or divorce, but may be emotional, as when someone isn't present emotionally or withholds love or attention. Emotional abandonment also leads to feelings, fears, and perception of rejection and contributes to codependency in adult relationships.

When fear of abandonment is pervasive, you feel that you're never enough and unworthy of love. You hide your flaws, try to please and accommodate your partner, walk on egg shells, tolerate abuse, make yourself needed, and become a human pretzel — all to avoid being alone or rejected. Losing a relationship is agony because it can trigger an earlier abandonment and because you're losing parts of yourself — the parts that were already missing. You may attract unavailable partners or your persistent accusations or pleas for attention or reassurance may produce your worst fear and push them away. The cycle of abandonment is shown in Figure 3-5.

Figure 3-5: Cycle of abandonment.

"Can't get you out of my mind"

When I was 15, my teacher asked me to participate in a research project, but didn't describe it. I entered a small interview room. A woman introduced herself and explained that she would tape record our interview. She gave no instructions and waited for me to talk. I had no idea what to say without being asked. As we sat in silence, I became increasingly uncomfortable and annoyed for what seemed like an eternity. I began talking about my parents and siblings until I ran out of things to say. Later, I thought the entire meeting was strange and also strange that I'd spoken about every-one but myself.

This is what codependents do. You're invested in other people, and think and talk about them. You try to figure out their motives, what they need, what they could or should be doing, and solve their problems. Sometimes, you can talk casually about the person who's captured your thoughts. Other times, your attention is laser focused on that person to the exclusion of all other sensory input. When someone asks you how you're feeling, you report on the other person. You're not even aware that you haven't answered the question, even when repeated. This is obsession. Your thoughts race out of control, repeat themselves in circles, search for answers, worrying and going over conversations. They grip your mind in an inescapable preoccupation that takes possession of you. Obsessions are driven by fear and pain. It can be fear of being abandoned or rejected, fear of being unlovable, or fear that your loved one will either destroy you or him or herself. Bottled up emotion steals you away from the present — minutes and hours add up to days. Your life disappears. The consequences can be devastating.

When a relationship is new, it's normal to want to be with and spend time thinking of the man or woman you love. He or she is the center of your world *for a while,* but for codependents, it never stops, and it doesn't have to be about a love relationship, you can obsess about anyone close to you. Moreover, you give up what's important to you to be with or go along with that person.

Obsessions are a way to avoid deeper emotional pain, but are not necessarily painful. In fact, they may be pleasurable fantasies of what you'd like to experience in your relationship, how you'd like someone to act, or memories of better times. Whether visions or endless chatter fill your mind, it keeps you out of touch with reality — including longings for connection, unmet needs, or fears of what may happen. The distance between your fantasy and reality reveals the depth of what you're missing.

You're my mojo

People who are happiest, healthiest, and the most successful have an *internal locus of control,* meaning they feel they control outcomes in their lives. They take responsibility for themselves and effect changes to create their happiness, whereas dependent men and women find self-responsibility and self-efficacy difficult. Rather than act, you react; rather than change, you adjust to your circumstances. You need another person or structure, such as an assignment, in order to take action, risk, create, or produce. You find it hard to motivate and sustain your efforts on your own. This is more pronounced with women, whose autonomy isn't usually encouraged (see Chapter 2). For a man, the necessity of supporting a family motivates him. Some women don't have that imperative. Other reasons for this lack of agency are:

- Fear of success, failure, disappointment, or change
- Low self-esteem — talking yourself down
- Passivity and indecision
- Attention and energy wasted on someone else
- Needing another's support and validation
- Lack of self-trust
- Blaming others, God, circumstances, and feeling like a victim
- Underlying depression from abuse in childhood
- Having felt like your words or feelings didn't matter growing up
- Having had an authoritarian or narcissistic parent
- Having been told you won't succeed
- Having been told your dreams were unattainable

How You Communicate

Communication is the most important factor in determining the kinds of relationships you have, and it reveals a lot about your self-esteem to the listener. Healthy communication that is clear, concise, honest, and assertive reflects good self-esteem. The purpose of communication is to impart feelings and information, but an important part of communication is listening. Codependents have poor communication skills. You're so preoccupied that often you don't really listen. The other person's words get filtered through layers of fear and low self-esteem.

Interpersonal oral communication falls into the following categories — listed from what's generally easiest to the most difficult:

✔ Sharing or requesting information and experiences

✔ Expressing thoughts and opinions

✔ Active listening

✔ Expressing feelings

✔ Requesting satisfaction of wants and needs

✔ Stating boundaries

You start learning communication before you're able to speak. Even in utero, you're learning the rhythm and sound of your mother's voice. Your parents were your role models, but better communication skills can be learned. (See Chapter 11.)

Saying what you think and feel

Do you say what you think and feel? Because of fear and low self-esteem, codependents typically have some of the following poor communication habits:

✔ Make threats you don't keep

✔ Say "yes" when you mean "no"

✔ Agree to things you swore you wouldn't just to keep peace

✔ Hide what you think and feel or the fact that you don't know

✔ Edit what you say in order to avoid controversy or criticism

✔ Expect others to read your mind, understand you, and meet your needs without having to be asked or told

✔ Speak indirectly — hint at what you want

- ✔ Ask questions instead of making statements
- ✔ Talk about someone other than yourself or give advice
- ✔ Blame someone else for causing your feelings

Fear, often driven by shame, is the biggest obstacle to being direct in your communication. Awareness of your fears can help you risk being honest. Common fears that derail communication are fear of:

- ✔ Being disliked or criticized
- ✔ Rupturing the relationship
- ✔ Being an imposition or burden
- ✔ Making a mistake
- ✔ Hurting someone's feelings
- ✔ Experiencing retaliation

Fear, guilt, and lack of boundaries can result in avoidance of serious conversations about problems in your relationships because you worry about what the other person will think, instead of considering the actual facts and your thoughts and feelings. Talking about problems can feel as if you're in a life-threatening situation — that your only option is to blame, hide or shade the truth, or apologize and agree in order to please, appease, or control someone else's feelings. This is *defensive manipulation* because it's motivated by fear to avoid conflict. Sometimes by lying or through covert behavior, codependents manipulate to protect themselves or to get what they want. They're easily manipulated with criticism and guilt trips. Manipulating focuses on someone else whose reaction becomes the measure of your self-esteem. Ask yourself:

- ✔ Do your insides match your words, or do you edit the truth?
- ✔ How often do you ask questions rather than make a statement?
- ✔ Do you use "I" statements?
- ✔ Do you express your feelings without saying "you"?
- ✔ Do you listen?
- ✔ Are you clear and concise?
- ✔ Are you able to say "No?"
- ✔ Do you make direct, polite requests to satisfy your wants and needs?

Being a human reactor

Codependents *react*. This means you act in response to outside influences. A few words in a text message can hit you like a cyclone and blow you off course from what you're doing, feeling, or thinking. It destroys your mood and what you think of yourself, and can ruin your day or even your week. You take personally what others say as a reflection upon you. This instantly surrenders your self-esteem and emotions to whatever or whoever has triggered them. You lose your center because your Self is other-defined, and your locus of control is others. This makes you easy to manipulate.

Reacting doesn't necessarily mean flying into a rage, although it may. For example, you can also react with silence when being interrupted, rather than respond by setting boundaries. Both rebellion and compliance are reactions, just opposite sides of the coin. (Read more in Chapter 9.) Sometimes, major life choices are reactions to a parent, spouse, or other influential person.

Having a fragile Self and poor boundaries contribute to reacting, but living under constant stress, whether as a child or as an adult, can make you hyper-vigilant and reactive — like a traumatized animal quick to flinch — every little thing becomes a crisis You make mountains out of molehills and scream at your kids or computer for something others would take in stride. Rather than thinking about options and taking constructive action, you react in fruitless attempts to control in ways that worsen the problem. Other times, a minor event may set you off because it's the last straw in a series of problems or insults that you may have overlooked or complained about in the past. Your reaction is a signal that you must seriously find new constructive solutions and perhaps seek professional help.

To *respond* to influences is much different. It's a proactive reply or answer. It's *responsible* behavior that requires you to think, problem-solve, or act in ways appropriate and in your best interest. It implies choice and puts you in charge of both your outward expression and internal feelings. You can also choose to respond with silence or ignore a stimulus. Responding diffuses emotions instead of escalating them. When you're tempted to react, try this:

    🖊 Take long slow breaths, emphasizing the exhale.

    🖊 Change your activity — play and have some fun.

    🖊 Talk over the situation to get objective feedback.

    🖊 Consider whether the facts and your life actually changed.

    🖊 Choose not to give the other person or event control over you.

    🖊 Think about whether you agree and your values.

> ✓ Say "Stop" to negative replays in your head.
>
> ✓ Be loving and empathic with yourself with positive statements.
>
> ✓ Consider whether past reactions have brought you peace of mind or resolved a problem.

Abusive communication

Verbal abuse is the most common form of emotional abuse, but it's often unrecognized. It always violates the other person's emotional boundaries. Abusive communication is speech or behavior that is punishing, derogatory, controlling, or manipulative. You may be a victim of abuse, particularly if you're in a relationship with a drug addict, or you may be communicating abusively to control someone else. Abuse may be said in a loving, quiet voice, or may be concealed — as in a joke. Subtle verbal abuse can be just as damaging as overt forms, particularly because it's harder to detect. Over time, verbal abuse has an insidious, deleterious effect causing you to doubt and distrust yourself. Here are examples:

Blaming

This is the most frequent abuse tactic intended to control, put down, and make someone else responsible for events or your feelings or actions. When you blame, you disempower yourself and others. It communicates that you feel like a helpless victim and is very different from assertive expression, such as, "I'm angry at you."

Name-calling

Name-calling is a kind of bullying that's intimidating and insulting. It's intended to humiliate and put someone down.

Raging

Raging or screaming violates other's boundaries designed to intimidate and control.

Covert aggressive manipulation

This is distinguished from defensive manipulation. Here the motive is aggression, albeit hidden. It's an indirect power play to get someone to act or feel the way the manipulator wants using charm, implied rewards, compliments, veiled suggestions of punishment, helplessness, guilt, shaming, self-deprecation, or playing a victim role. On the outside, a manipulator doesn't appear aggressive and may *act* like the aggrieved party, so the person being manipulated feels guilty, defensive, or confused.

Ordering

Instead of requests, ordering someone to do something is an expression of control that's demeaning and treats another person like a slave.

Judging and criticizing

Judging and criticizing include evaluating, giving unwanted advice, and telling someone what he or she "should" do.

Play, jokes, sarcasm, and teasing

Sarcasm is a witty or ironic remark, sometimes overt praise, that's intended to inflict a wound. It can be painful to the recipient. Judgment cloaked as playful teasing or joking is no less hurtful.

Opposing

The abuser treats you as an adversary and argues against anything, challenging perceptions, opinions, and thoughts, without listening or volunteering thoughts or feelings, in effect saying "No" to everything, so a constructive conversation is impossible.

Blocking

This tactic is used to abort conversation, by switching topics, making accusations, or using words that in effect say, "Shut up."

Discounting and belittling

Discounting and belittling are forms of abuse that minimize or trivialize feelings, thoughts, or experiences. It's a way of saying that another's feelings don't matter or are wrong.

Undermining and interrupting

Undermining with statements, such as "You don't know what you're talking about," finishing sentences, or speaking on another's behalf without permission are meant to damage self-esteem and confidence.

Lying and denying

Whatever the motive, conscious lying is manipulative. Some addicts and abusers deny that agreements or promises were made or that a conversation or event took place, including prior abuse, and instead declare love and caring. This is crazy-making and makes the victim gradually doubt his or her memory and perceptions. A persistent pattern is called gas-lighting, named after the movie, *Gaslight,* where Charles Boyer used denial to make his wife, played by Ingrid Bergman, believe she was losing her grip on reality.

Control and Caretaking

Normally, people think of control as ordering or other overt abuse, but control can include indirect, nonverbal behavior. You may use these "soft" methods of control, if you're afraid of being direct:

- ✔ Helplessness or passivity
- ✔ Withholding
- ✔ Isolating
- ✔ Talking
- ✔ Silence
- ✔ Gifts and favors
- ✔ Seduction
- ✔ Pleasing and caretaking

Caretaking is associated with giving physical aid to someone, but being a "good fella" or "nice girl" is also caretaking. I use caretaking to refer to emotional, financial, spiritual, or intellectual help given to control when you silence your feelings and needs in order to accommodate and *take care of* someone.

There's chaos all around

It's normal to need control and predictability, but the family of an addict or abuser is in perpetual crisis. You try to control someone out of control and contain disruption in the family. If you grew up in that environment or in a high-conflict family, fear of upsetting a parent meant staying in control. You learned to control your feelings and behavior to feel safe. You'd never again want to be at someone's mercy. As an adult, you don't feel safe, may be anxious, dread disaster, and try to control people and events because of your *past* fear even when there's no evidence for it in the present.

A warped sense of responsibility

Healthy relationships consist of two people, each taking responsibility for their half of the relationship and their individual Selves as pictured in Figure 3-6. This works well when you know what you think, feel, and need, and how to fill those needs.

Figure 3-6: An equal relationship.

Codependents don't know how to meet their needs and believe that others can't take care of themselves. They attract needy people and invade their boundaries by trying to control them, while not taking responsibility for their own side of the fence. Many addict codependents are irresponsible when it comes to work, money, childcare, or personal safety, health, and hygiene.

Codependents especially don't take responsibility for their feelings and emotional needs in relationships. It's a haywire system in which you may be unaware of your feelings and needs, but instead try to control and blame someone else in order to get your needs met. The unspoken contract is, "I'm responsible for you, and you for me. I meet your needs, and you meet mine." You may say, "You made me do that," or "You're making me feel guilty." This externalizes control of your actions and feelings and puts your partner, who you expect should make you happy, in charge of your self-esteem. It relinquishes responsibility for your own life and relieves you of responsibility for your self-care, choices, and actions to create your happiness, because you believe it depends on what others think and do. You may try endlessly to control, advise, and manipulate someone whose feelings and opinion are critical to your sense of well-being. The result that is you focus on, feel responsible for, and react to the feelings and needs of others. You may go to extremes not to disappoint anyone and feel very guilty if you do.

Control through kindness

Caretakers genuinely want to help. It makes them feel good to be helpful. However, caregiving and codependent caretaking are different (see Chapter 2). The former has no strings attached, whereas the latter is an unconscious form of manipulation.

Healthy caregiving

True caring entails listening to others' thoughts and feelings with understanding and allowing them to brainstorm solutions. You respect others' separateness and boundaries, and offer support without guilt or an urge to fix their problems, trusting that others will find appropriate solutions to their problems and pain, and it's not your job to change or direct their lives. When you do give, it's without expectations or control. You don't give up yourself.

Motives behind caretaking

Caretakers give love to get love. They give more in relationships, and on the job, they work harder and longer than others. They don't feel worthy of love unless they're giving because they don't believe that they're lovable and enough as they are. Caretaking allows you to both hide the needs, feelings, and flaws you're ashamed of, and also compensate for them by giving, being needed, and becoming indispensable. It's insurance against being abandoned. Because caretaking emanates from guilt, shame, and fear more than love, you give with expectations to fulfill your own unmet needs — usually unconscious needs for love, acceptance, or validation that you're a good person. There are strings attached — especially when gifts, financial aid, or sex is offered.

When you can't stop yourself

Codependents can't stop trying to help. It's a personality style that's been learned and become habitual. You believe you know what's best for others and how to run their lives, even in situations in which you have no experience. Because of an exaggerated sense of responsibility for others — their happiness, feelings, thoughts, behavior, needs, expectations, and desires — you can easily become invested in their problems, try to rescue them and control the outcome. You anticipate others' feelings and needs and offer unsolicited aid and suggestions without being asked. When your advice isn't taken or your help isn't appreciated, you get frustrated, annoyed, and resentful, but continue to help whether or not you're able to change the other person. You may not even be deterred if the person you want to help doesn't believe he or she has a problem. When your offer is refused, you feel rebuffed and hurt. Some people take advantage of caretakers who can't say "no." Even though they volunteer help, they don't take responsibility for their behavior. In the end, they feel used or resentful and insufficiently appreciated, loved, or rewarded for their efforts (see Chapter 9).

Top Dog, Underdog

If you're living in a family where someone behaves irresponsibly or self-destructively, it's normal to take up the slack and assume increased responsibilities and control in order to protect the safety and stability of the family. It seems obvious that you're doing the "right" thing and the other person isn't. But soon, you end up in a parental role and start minding other people's business. Perhaps you were attracted to an irresponsible or dependent person in the first place, allowing you to be a caretaker and in control. You wouldn't feel close in a relationship with someone who has no problem to solve — who wouldn't need you. You're used to being Top Dog looking down on Underdog, as seen in Figure 3-7, unaware that your wish — that Underdog shape up and be responsible — is also your greatest fear. For without having someone to fix, you wouldn't be needed. You'd have no one to blame for your unhappiness.

Top Dog can remain long-suffering and self-righteous while in control and the spotlight is not on him or her. "Who else would want me?" Top Dog thinks. Underdog needs a caretaker — someone dependable, to lean on and to provide the structure that he or she is lacking. Underdog is also codependent and feels "Who else would want me?" In many cases, when Underdog starts to improve, Top Dog unwittingly sabotages Underdog's recovery to avoid becoming the Underdog. That would threaten his or her entire personality structure of being self-sufficient, invulnerable, strong, and flawless. A crisis, illness, or financial reversal, could cause their roles to flip.

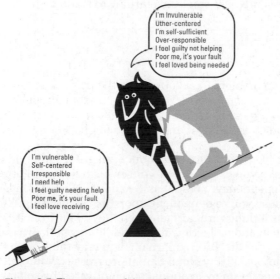

Figure 3-7: The seesaw of dependency.

Enabling

Enabling refers to caretaking that removes the natural consequences of someone's irresponsible behavior. It also includes handling responsibilities for someone that they can *and should* be handling. Often Underdog will badger, blame, and manipulate Top Dog into enabling. Originally, *enablers* were co-alcoholics who suffered the consequences of the alcoholic's drinking and did their best to literally clean up after the alcoholic, made excuses to the boss and friends, got the alcoholic into bed, and bailed him or her out of jail and other messes. The conclusion was that alcoholics would remain in denial and never get sober until *they* suffered the consequences of their disease, and that the pressure to change would come not from others' persuasion, but from the alcoholics' own experience of the serious damage alcoholism was causing in their lives. Today enabling is more widely applied to behavior that enables anyone to continue acting in a self-destructive manner. Enablers have a warped sense of responsibility and feel extremely guilty not enabling, even though they're not responsible for the problems created by others.

Mary indulged her unemployed adult son, who spent his time on the Internet. Although resentful, Mary believed that providing room and board, cooking, and doing his laundry was necessary and loving, justifying it on the fact that her son was depressed. She thought he needed more love and was unable to support himself. Her enabling reinforced his lack of confidence in meeting his adult responsibilities and removed the consequences of passivity. Her real motives were her unconscious needs for companionship and to be needed, which prevented her son from learning to stand on his own.

Denial

Denial is an inability to acknowledge the truth of something. It's considered the *hallmark of addiction,* and that applies to codependents, too. Denial can prolong codependency for years or decades. Denial and overcoming it are covered in Chapter 5.

You're as likely to be in denial concerning the addiction of someone close to you as you are of your own addiction to others — your codependency. You put aside and deny what you know to be true because you're dependent upon the relationship. You pretend and act as if things are normal when they're far from it, worsening the problem and deflecting accountability from the irresponsible person in your life. By comparison, you may think you're acting sanely and unselfishly, yet if denial progresses, your behavior becomes increasingly irrational and motivated by self-interest.

Children of addicts often deny that their parents' problems affected them, believing that leaving home or the addict-parent's recovery put an end to their problems. They don't realize that they're still affected, nor want to think about their painful childhood. Even if they only had an alcoholic grandparent, this made their parent codependent, and as a result they've been affected, as well.

Codependents also are unaware of their needs, wants, and feelings. Even if you're conscious of your feelings, you may feel too vulnerable to express them, fear rejection, or think that you're selfish, needy, or self-indulgent, like Stanley in the previous example. Instead, you wait, depend on, and expect others to fill your needs without being asked, or become self-reliant and not depend on anyone. When ignoring your needs and feelings, you assess what others need and feel to gauge your response. Many of the characteristics of codependency are both symptoms of this denial and further reinforce it, because when you're focused on someone else, you don't feel yourself.

Painful Emotions

Despite being in denial, codependents still experience churning emotions. Predominant are anger and resentment and mood swings from fear and anxiety to hopelessness and despair. All of this stress over time leads to depression, which is a lack of feeling.

Fear and anxiety

Fear can breed anxiety, and anxiety can create fear. Earlier I listed some common fears that stem from low self-esteem, including fears of abandonment, rejection, intimacy, criticism, power, success, and failure. On a daily basis, codependents live with yet more fears — the fear of being themselves, of being alone, of showing their feelings, of others' reactions, especially anger, and of taking risks. Some people also have specific physical fears and phobias.

If you live with a drug addict or abuser, it's natural to fear for your safety and the safety of your children and the addict. You're living in a war zone, never knowing when or where a bomb will drop. You're afraid your wife can't care for the children, or your husband won't go to work or will be fired. Will he return home safe and sober? You may dread the sound of opening cans or his car arriving home, and answering questions from debt collectors, concerned friends and relatives, or police at your door. You don't have a chance to recover from one disaster before another one hits. You learn to fear family holidays that end up a battleground or another disappointment. Somehow you learn to live with constant fights, insecurity, even suicide attempts, and still try to go to work, raise children, and maintain an appearance of normalcy. This has become y*our normal;* a life lived in terror is *NOT* normal.

When codependents aren't afraid, they're anxious. Unpredictability and powerlessness add to anxiety. Our bodies are designed to respond to fear by fighting or fleeing, but when you can neither escape nor control a situation, anxiety results. Interspersed with rationalizations and fantasies about how they'd like things to be, you project your fears into the future — even when there's no evidence that they will occur. Worry and obsession grow. You rehearse the negative and live on the edge of "What if . . ." another fight, binge, or financial crisis. You become guarded and constantly walk on eggshells. Gradually, you become more isolated from friends and family, which escalates your feelings.

Anger and resentment

Codependents have anger for good reason. It's a healthy reaction to someone who constantly breaks promises and commitments, violates your boundaries, disappointments you, and/or betrays your trust. Many codependents feel trapped, burdened with troubles, responsible for children, and saddled with financial problems. They don't see a way out and yet still love the one they blame for their woes or feel too guilty to leave. Some are angry at God, yet it's codependency that is the root of their anger.

Anger is a powerful energy that seeks expression. Sometimes, action is required to correct a wrong. It needn't be loud or hurtful. (See Chapter 11 on handling conflict.) Codependents don't know how to cope with their anger. Everyone handles it differently. Some scold, explode, or blame. Others repress it or try to understand an abuser rather than express anger, or they take it out on those less powerful. If you can't be direct, it can come out sideways in the form of:

- ✔ Sarcasm
- ✔ Tone of voice
- ✔ Cold looks
- ✔ Slamming doors
- ✔ Withholding love
- ✔ Withholding sex
- ✔ Silence
- ✔ Forgetting
- ✔ Being late

Many codependents don't feel or even acknowledge their anger. You realize it days, weeks, or years after an event. Buried and unexpressed, it hardens into resentment. Others feel guilty expressing this normal, human emotion. You're afraid your anger will hurt, alienate, or even destroy someone you love. You hold it in and please or withdraw to avoid conflict, while mentally rehearsing grievances and feeling victimized. You can become bitter and desire revenge. Anger can get redirected toward yourself. You criticize, blame, and push yourself and never confront the offender. Nothing changes, and you continue to accept unacceptable behavior. This can lead to depression and physical symptoms.

Difficulty with anger is due to poor role models in childhood, where one or both parents were aggressive or passive. Growing up, you learn to do one or the other. As an adult, you may fear turning into your aggressive parent. If you were taught not to raise your voice or were punished for expressing anger, you learned to stifle it. Some believe it's unchristian or not spiritual or nice to express anger. It's a misconception that you have to vent or rage at someone. The most effective path is to be assertive. Rather than scold someone or stuff your anger, journal, discuss it, and then express it. Channel rage into physical or creative activity. You can also observe anger in meditation or analyze the contributing factors, including your part.

Despair and depression

Without recovery, despair and hopelessness are the natural outcomes of the late stages of codependency. Some reasons are:

- ✔ A chronic sense of inferiority and shame
- ✔ Unending crises that you can't escape
- ✔ Having a series of unsuccessful relationships
- ✔ Being trapped in an unhappy relationship
- ✔ Feeling defeated by daily stress and lack of safety and peace
- ✔ Loneliness
- ✔ Never getting your needs met
- ✔ Loss of faith in the possibility of change for a better future
- ✔ Feeling abandoned by God

Despair can lead to depression — feeling numbness and a lack of feeling, as if life had been drained from you. You lose interest in things. You may feel sad or cry, but without relief. Depression can result from "de-pressing" or holding down feelings, especially anger. Negative self-talk also causes depression (see Chapter 10).

Many codependents have a chronic low-grade depression of which they're unaware. The excitement of romance, sex, an unavailable partner, melodramatic relationships, a busy schedule, and the tasks of being a caretaker provide sufficient stimulation and distraction from the depression that's just beneath the surface. A peaceful relationship or calm environment would soon be "boring," without the adrenalin that drama and stress to mask underlying depression.

Physical Symptoms

It's a fact that stress is a major contributor to ill health and chronic illness. Years of stressful relationships and emotions wear down the body's immune and nervous systems and its ability to repair and replenish itself. The chronic stress of codependency can result in health problems, including heart disease, digestive and sleep disorders, headaches, muscle tension and pain, obesity, ulcers, temporomandibular joint disorder (TMJD), and chronic fatigue syndrome. These and other physical symptoms, such as sexual disorders, cystitis, allergies, sciatica, tinnitus, and eating disorders, may also be manifestations of repressed emotions.

Chapter 4

So, Are You Codependent?

· ·

In This Chapter

▶ Assessing your codependency with questionnaires

▶ Identifying codependent patterns from Co-Dependents Anonymous

· ·

*T*his chapter contains three codependency assessments. The first two were developed for research and clinicians to use in assessing clients. The third is patterns identified by Co-Dependents Anonymous (CoDA) that are common among codependents. Because there isn't one definition of codependency, there isn't one test you can take. Symptoms and their severity vary among different people, depending on many factors, but the questionnaires and patterns identified by CoDA give you more information with which to understand yourself, which is the main objective.

Codependency Assessment

The following are two assessments used to identify codependents. The questions require a yes or no answer. The first was developed by Ron and Pat Potter-Efron. They considered a codependent to be someone who has or had an involvement with an alcoholic, chemically dependent, or other long-term, highly stressful family environment, including long-term illness that can be physical or mental health-related. To meet their criteria, you must have answered positive at least two of the questions in five of the following eight categories in Table 4-1.

Table 4-1	Codependency Assessment		
1. Fear:		Yes	No
a. Do you become preoccupied with the problems of others, especially those of the user?		____	____
b. Do you try to "keep things under control" or "keep a handle" on situations?		____	____
c. Do you take more than your fair share of responsibility for tasks that have to be done?		____	____
d. Are you afraid to approach others directly, in particularly the user?		____	____
e. Do you often have anxious feelings or worry about what will happen next?		____	____
f. Do you avoid taking risks with others because it is hard for you to trust?	____		____
2. Shame/Guilt:			
a. Do you often feel ashamed not only about your behavior, but also about the behavior of others, especially the user?		____	____
b. Do you feel guilty about the problems of others in your family?		____	____
c. Do you withdraw from social contact when you're feeling upset?		____	____
d. Do you sometimes hate yourself?		____	____
e. Do you ever cover up bad feelings about yourself by acting too confidently?		____	____
3. Prolonged Despair:			
a. Do you often feel hopeless about changing the current situation?		____	____
b. Do you tend to be pessimistic about the world in general?	____		____
c. Do you have a sense of low self-worth or failure that does not reflect your skills and accomplishments?		____	____
4. Rage:			
a. Do you feel persistently angry with the user, other family members, or yourself?		____	____
b. Are you afraid of losing control if you let yourself get really mad?		____	____

c. Are you angry at God? ___ | ___

d. Do you ever get back at others in sneaky ways, perhaps without being fully aware of this behavior at the time? ___ | ___

5. Denial:

a. Do you feel yourself denying the basic problems in your family? ___ | ___

b. Do you tell yourself that these problems are not *that* bad? ___ | ___

c. Do you find reasons to justify the irresponsible behavior of others in your family? ___ | ___

6. Rigidity:

a. Do you tend to think in either/or terms when there are problems, instead of looking at many alternatives? ___ | ___

b. Do you feel troubled if anyone upsets your usual routines? ___

c. Do you tend to see moral issues in black-and-white terms? ___

d. Do you "get stuck" in certain feelings such as guilt, love or anger? ___ | ___

7. Impaired Identity Development:

a. Do you have trouble asking for what you want and need? ___ | ___

b. Do you feel pain right along with another person who is in pain? ___ | ___

c. Do you need to have another person around in order for you to feel worthwhile? ___ | ___

d. Do you worry a great amount about how others perceive you? ___ | ___

8. Confusion:

a. Do you wonder what it means to be "normal"? ___ | ___

b. Do you sometimes think that you must be "crazy"? ___ | ___

c. Do you find it difficult at times to identify what you are feeling? ___ | ___

d. Do you have a tendency to be taken in by others — to be gullible? ___ | ___

e. Do you have a hard time making up your mind — are you indecisive? ___ | ___

The second assessment is drawn from a new questionnaire, the Composite Codependency Scale, published in 2011. Research confirmed that it's a valid measurement of core codependency symptoms of emotional suppression, interpersonal control, and self-sacrifice.

1. I try to control events and people through helplessness, guilt, coercion, threats, advice-giving, manipulation, or domination

2. I become afraid to let other people be who they are and allow events to happen naturally

3. I try to control events and how other people should behave

4. I feel compelled or forced to help people solve their problems (for example, offering advice)

5. I feel that without my effort and attention, everything would fall apart

6. I live too much by other people's standards

7. I put on a show to impress people; I am not the person I pretend to be

8. In order to get along and be liked, I need to be what people want me to be

9. I need to make excuses or apologize for myself most of the time

10. I always put the needs of my family before my own needs

11. It is my responsibility to devote my energies to helping loved ones solve their problems

12. No matter what happens the family always comes first

13. I often put the needs of others ahead of my own

14. What I feel isn't important as long as those I love are okay

15. Because it is selfish, I cannot put my own needs before the needs of others

16. If I work hard enough, I should be able to solve almost any problem or make things better for people

17. Feelings often build up inside me that I do not express

18. I keep my emotions under tight control

19. I keep my feelings to myself and put up a good front

20. It makes me uncomfortable to share my feelings with others

21. I don't usually let others see the "real me"

22. I hide myself so that no-one really knows me

23. I push painful thoughts and feelings out of my awareness

24. Very often I don't try to become friends with people because I think that they won't like me

25. I put on a happy face when I am really sad or angry

Your Codependent Patterns

CoDA has put together this list of patterns to help you evaluate your thinking, feelings, and behavior to see if the CoDA Twelve Step program may be helpful to you.

Denial patterns

I have difficulty identifying what I am feeling.

I minimize, alter, or deny how I truly feel.

I perceive myself as completely unselfish and dedicated to the well-being of others.

I lack empathy for the feelings and needs of others.

I label others with my negative traits.

I can take care of myself without any help from others.

I mask my pain in various ways such as anger, humor, or isolation.

I express negativity or aggression in indirect and passive ways.

I do not recognize the unavailability of those people to whom I am attracted.

Low self-esteem patterns

I have difficulty making decisions.

I judge what I think, say, or do harshly, as never good enough.

I am embarrassed to receive recognition, praise, or gifts.

I value others' approval of my thinking, feelings, and behavior over my own.

I do not perceive myself as a lovable or worthwhile person.

I constantly seek recognition that I think I deserve.

I have difficulty admitting that I made a mistake.

I need to appear to be right in the eyes of others and will even lie to look good.

I am unable to ask others to meet my needs or desires.

I perceive myself as superior to others.

I look to others to provide my sense of safety.

I have difficulty getting started, meeting deadlines, and completing projects.

I have trouble setting healthy priorities.

Compliance patterns

I am extremely loyal, remaining in harmful situations too long.

I compromise my own values and integrity to avoid rejection or anger.

I put aside my own interests in order to do what others want.

I am hypervigilant regarding the feelings of others and take on those feelings.

I am afraid to express my beliefs, opinions, and feelings when they differ from those of others.

I accept sexual attention when I want love.

I make decisions without regard to the consequences.

I give up my truth to gain the approval of others or to avoid change.

Control patterns

I believe most people are incapable of taking care of themselves.

I attempt to convince others what to think, do, or feel.

I freely offer advice and direction to others without being asked.

I become resentful when others decline my help or reject my advice.

I lavish gifts and favors on those I want to influence.

I use sexual attention to gain approval and acceptance.

I have to be needed in order to have a relationship with others.

I demand that my needs be met by others.

I use charm and charisma to convince others of my capacity to be caring and compassionate.

I use blame and shame to emotionally exploit others.

I refuse to cooperate, compromise, or negotiate.

I adopt an attitude of indifference, helplessness, authority, or rage to manipulate outcomes.

I use terms of recovery in an attempt to control the behavior of others.

I pretend to agree with others to get what I want.

Avoidance patterns

I act in ways that invite others to reject, shame, or express anger toward me.

I judge harshly what others think, say, or do.

I avoid emotional, physical, or sexual intimacy as a means of maintaining distance.

I allow my addictions to people, places, and things to distract me from achieving intimacy in relationships.

I use indirect and evasive communication to avoid conflict or confrontation.

I diminish my capacity to have healthy relationships by declining to use all the tools of recovery.

I suppress my feelings or needs to avoid feeling vulnerable.

I pull people toward me, but when they get close, I push them away.

I refuse to give up my self-will to avoid surrendering to a power that is greater than myself.

I believe displays of emotion are a sign of weakness.

I withhold expressions of appreciation.

Part II

Breaking the Cycle of Codependency: Beginning Recovery

In this part...

Part II looks at the problem of denial that gets in the way of overcoming codependency. It examines the causes of codependency, makes suggestions for getting started, and answers some common questions. This part helps you get better acquainted with yourself, learn about nonattachment and acceptance, and begin building your self-esteem. In this part, you learn how to value yourself.

Chapter 5

Crossing De-Nile to Recovery

*T*his chapter offers a detailed description of denial, which was first mentioned in Chapter 3 as a characteristic of codependency. It's impossible to change until you face that you have a problem and that what you've been doing to manage it isn't working. This is why coming out of denial is the crucial, first step in the healing process. In this chapter, you learn the function of denial, the different types, how to recognize it, and some tips in working with it.

Why You Experience Denial

Plain and simple, denial is a defense mechanism. Everyone does it. It's the first defense that our brain is capable of using. It operates automatically and unconsciously. The brain can actually distort sensory information and interpret it in such a way that makes facts nonthreatening, using some of the following strategies to block what's going on. Because it's unconscious, it's difficult to spot in yourself. Here are the usual suspects:

▶ **Forgetting:** Overlooking something that you don't want to do

▶ **Self-deception:** Believing the opposite or variation of the truth

▶ **Lying:** Asserting the opposite of the truth (different from a lie)

▶ **Minimizing:** Making less of something than is the reality

▶ **Rationalizing:** Justifying with excuses or arguments

▶ **Repressing:** Removing awareness of feelings, thoughts, needs, desires, traumatic events, or memories

Although you don't choose to be in denial, you alter your perception of reality to protect yourself from being overwhelmed with emotion or facing something you fear. This means that if you don't perceive something is wrong or threatening, then you don't have to experience painful or conflicting feelings about it. If it doesn't exist — there's no problem. Some reasons codependents deny are:

✔ To avoid painful thoughts or feelings if you were to face the facts about someone you love, yourself, or your relationships

✔ To avoid emotional conflict with someone else or conflict within yourself about making difficult choices or taking action that may bring about pain or loss

✔ To avoid a perceived threat, usually of loss, abandonment, physical or emotional harm, serious illness, or death

✔ To cope with a shock or trauma often caused by physical, sexual, or emotional abuse that may have happened long ago

Levels of Denial

When it comes to addiction and codependency, denial isn't healthy; in fact, it can be dangerous. By not facing the problem, you deprive yourself of learning constructive measures that can improve and potentially save your life and those of others. Codependents have multiple levels of denial. Four are explored here.

In level 1, there may be denial about someone's behavior or addiction. This usually works only in the early stages of codependency and addiction. In level 2, there also may be denial about how your codependency is contributing to the problem. The more you learn about codependency and yourself, the more you overcome denial. Level 3 is denial of your feelings, and deeper is level 4 when you deny your needs. (See Chapter 3.)

And then there's denial of the original issues and pain that led to your codependency. These are discussed in Chapters 7 and 13.

Level 1: Denial about someone's behavior or addiction

The first level of denial is denying that someone in your life has an addiction or that his or her behavior is causing a problem or is negatively affecting you. It's common with codependents because:

✔ You may have grown up with addiction or the problem behavior in your family, so it feels familiar and normal.

✔ Addicts and abusers don't like to take responsibility for their behavior. They deny it and blame other codependents who are willing to accept this as the truth.

✔ Growing up in dysfunctional families, you learn to not trust your perceptions and what you know.

✔ Acknowledging the truth would cause feelings of shame because of the stigma attached to addiction and abuse.

✔ Low self-esteem lowers your expectations of being treated well.

✔ You lack information about the signs of addiction and abuse.

Because denial keeps you from acknowledging the truth, you won't have to confront someone's upsetting behavior or addiction, experience the pain, or take action. If you love an addict and can pretend that the dangers facing him or her don't exist, even for a little while, you can function better. You don't have to think about the repercussions of his or her addiction and behavior, such as a fatal drug overdose or auto accident, bankruptcy due to gambling losses, cirrhosis of the liver, or the myriad of other problems.

Denial doesn't mean that you're not bothered by their behavior. It means you don't recognize it for what it is, such as abuse, infidelity, an addiction, or other issue. The fleeting possibility may cross your mind, but you don't think about it. You may dismiss it as unimportant, or minimize, justify, or excuse it with explanations and rationalizations. You tell yourself that things aren't so bad, that they'll get better, and meanwhile have fantasies about how you'd like them to be. You may even doubt your own perceptions and believe lies or excuses you know are false. This is normal when you don't want to admit that someone you love has a serious problem, but the troubles mount up, and one day you find you're making excuses for behavior you never thought you'd tolerate. That's what happens with denial. Things get worse.

Examples may be parents of a teen using drugs or alcohol who ignore the problem and blame falling grades on the bad influence of friends or time he spent playing video games. Others may admit that their child drinks too much, but minimize this as youthful indulgences. Denial of a child's addiction is common when a parent is in denial of his or her own addiction.

Recognizing drug abuse

Most people aren't fully aware of the symptoms of substance abuse. A complete discussion is beyond the scope of this book.

(See *Addiction and Recovery For Dummies* by Brian F. Shaw, Paul Ritvo, Jane Irvine, and M. David Lewis; John Wiley & Sons Publishing.) Each drug affects sleep, mood, and thinking differently. Alcohol first acts as a depressant and then has a delayed stimulus effect, which disrupts sleep, so alcoholics can both pass out and later get the jitters. Not all alcoholics slur their words; in fact, some can sound logical and alert. Addicts often deny promises and conversations. Sometimes, they don't remember due to alcoholic blackouts.

Mood altering effects vary depending upon the drug and the individual. A drug may cause depression or anxiety, or both. Some people withdraw, whereas others get angry, more jovial, or talkative. Alcohol exaggerates the drinker's mood, impairs judgment and thinking, and relaxes inhibitions. Alcohol and drugs still affect users sometimes days after use. What addicts have in common is that they're less present in personal interactions, and with greater dependency, drug use interferes with work and relationships.

A frequent pattern of denial is to focus on a symptom, such as depression, anger, or lying, but to deny the bigger problem of addiction. I've heard many codependents deny that their partner was addicted, and instead attribute their relationship problems to a side effect. One woman was concerned about her husband's anger, but overlooked that he stopped at bars after work and arrived home "plastered." When I commented that it sounded like he had a drinking problem, she denied that alcohol was an issue. In another case, a husband concerned about his wife's depression was in denial about her addiction to pain medication. When she'd pass out, he thought she was napping.

You may want to get more information if you're worrying about someone who:

- ✔ Exhibits behavior that embarrasses, hurts, or angers you and negatively impacts your relationship, his or her job, health, social life, or finances

- ✔ Hides drugs (or bottles) or is lying to you

- ✔ Violates the law

- ✔ Blames you for his or her behavior

- ✔ Forgets where they've been or behaves in unreliable ways

How do you know if you're in denial?

If you're in denial about someone's behavior, you won't know it. In fact, most people will deny they're in denial! Try to be honest, and write a paragraph about each of the following questions:

✔ Do you spend time thinking about how you'd like things to be?

✔ Do you say to yourself, "If only, he (or she) would . . .?"

✔ Do you make excuses for someone to others? To yourself?

✔ Do you minimize or rationalize bad behavior or your hurt feelings?

✔ Do you believe promises or assurances that have been broken?

✔ Do you think the relationship or behavior will improve when some future event occurs (like a vacation, job offer, engagement, or having a baby)?

✔ Do you continue to make concessions or change yourself, hoping that the relationship or the person's behavior will · improve?

✔ Do you cover up or not reveal to family or friends aspects of your relationship that embarrass you?

Level 2: Denial that my codependency is part of the problem

Generally, if confronted, codependents deny their codependency. This is level 2. Codependents believe that they have no choices about their situation and/or blame others. They deny their own disease to avoid deeper pain. You may not think you're codependent, but when the characteristics outlined in Chapters 3 and 4 seem to line up one by one, it may be worth considering.

Another reason that it may be difficult for you to admit you have a problem and seek help is because you're not used to looking at yourself. Focusing on others protects you from facing your pain and taking responsibility for your own happiness. It keeps you stuck pursuing the fruitless goal of trying to change others or looking for the right person to make you happy, based on the erroneous premise that your happiness lies in others. Blaming others or feeling superior to them is a way to avoid looking at yourself, as shown in the following examples.

Jim had been attending Alcoholics Anonymous meetings for a few weeks when another member, **Beverly**, suggested that it would be helpful if his wife **Connie** attended Al-Anon. Beverly called Connie and wisely suggested that she go to Al-Anon "to help Jim's sobriety." Connie was all for that, and so she went. Had Beverly initially told Connie that *she* needed help, Connie wouldn't have listened because she was convinced that she was blameless and that Jim, being the addict, was the one in trouble — not hard because he regularly screwed things up.

Trish focused all her attention on dating, believing "the right man" held the key her to happiness. She blamed her discontent and unsuccessful relationships on the lack of "good" men and was unwilling to look at her codependent behavior.

Some people, including healthcare professionals, know a lot about codependency, but only see it as applying to others. Denial keeps them from looking at themselves. There are also those who admit their codependency, yet think they don't need help. They've figured out their problems in their mind and believe they can manage on their own or by reading and talking to friends. They underestimate the impact of codependency on their lives and don't get help, like Sandra in the following example. In fact, this denial is a symptom of codependency — often because of their internalized shame — in the same way that shame keeps drug addicts from getting treatment.

Sandra was a nurse who experienced burn-out due to working long shifts and over-involvement with her patients. She'd taken continuing education classes in codependency that addressed these problems and knew her health was suffering as a result, but she didn't believe that she needed professional help.

Level 3: I'm fine, thank you — denial of feelings

Codependents are usually good at knowing what other people feel and spend a lot of time worrying about them, often with resentment, but aren't much aware of other feelings, and may not even be aware of their resentment. This denial of feelings is level 3. When people are obsessing about their addiction — whether it's to a person, food, sex, work, or a drug — it's usually a distraction from what they're really feeling. If you ask them how they're feeling, they say "I'm fine," or ask what they're feeling, they say "Nothing." They understand physical pain but not emotional pain, because they're in denial of their true feelings, which would be upsetting to experience. Growing up, they never learned to identify their feelings, nor felt safe expressing them, especially if they had no one to comfort them. Instead, they buried and repressed their feelings. (See Chapter 8 for help on identifying your feelings.)

Feelings, including painful ones, serve a purpose. They help you recognize your needs and adapt to the environment. Awareness of feelings is vital to healthy interactions with others.

- ✔ Fear tells you to avoid danger, including people who may harm you emotionally.

- ✔ Anger tells you that action is required to right a wrong or to make changes.

- ✔ Healthy guilt helps you act congruently with your values.

- ✔ Sadness helps you let go and encourages empathy and human connection.

- ✔ Shame helps you fit in to society and keeps you from harming others.

- ✔ Loneliness motivates you to reach out to others.

When you deny or repress feelings, you can get stuck. The feeling never gets released and stays in your unconscious — sometimes for years. Pain accumulates, and more pain requires more denial. An unintended consequence of denying painful feelings is that you become depressed or numb to joy, gratitude, and love, too. Energy that can be used creatively and constructively gets channeled into holding down feelings, like trying to keep the lid on a pressure cooker. Some people *act out* their repressed feelings with behavior that releases emotional tension without experiencing the feeling. Often codependents who deny their feelings marry someone who has volatile emotions, allowing them to experience feelings vicariously.

Alexis had been cutting herself, but didn't know why. She gave monosyllable answers and was shut down and depressed. Her husband was her opposite — a controlling, passionate, and angry man. She had to ask him for household spending money and justify each expense. She denied her rage at him. Yet, he expressed the anger that she wouldn't allow herself to feel. Alexandra's expression of her fury would have prevented her self-mutilation.

When you deny your feelings, it keeps you from responding appropriately and creates more problems. In some cases, you can identify the feeling, but have denied its buried, repressed meaning. When this happens, you can still remain fixed in a cycle of re-experiencing the feeling and repeating the associated behavior, because the deeper pain isn't resolved. This was the case with Mona and Ira who saw me for conjoint therapy. As often happens, they were locked into a pattern of reacting to one another that was based upon feelings they'd denied from interactions with their parents.

Mona had a cheerful personality and a lively sense of humor. She and **Ira** got along "great," except she complained that Ira wouldn't share his feelings. She asked him frequently, but he always said he was "fine." Sometimes, she gave him multiple choices, which didn't elicit much feedback and escalated her frustration and anger. When I turned to Ira, I was surprised that with a little help he could identify feelings of being judged and smothered by Mona's interrogations. He recalled how he'd recoiled when his mother nagged him and his father. After exploring with Mona what led up to her badgering, she admitted feeling all alone as she had with her arrogant father. Soon she was sobbing. After speaking at length about him, she said, "I always feel good until I'm here and realize how much pain I've been hiding from myself." I encouraged her to sense and express her vulnerable feelings of loneliness whenever they arose instead of focusing on Ira and delving into his feelings. Ira needed help in setting boundaries in order to reflect on and express his feelings. Both Mona and Ira could acknowledge some present feelings, but the meanings behind them were buried in their childhoods.

Level 4: You don't know what you're missing — denial of needs

Codependents are very good at anticipating and filling the needs of others, yet they deny or minimize their own needs. This is level 4. (See Chapter 8 on identifying your needs.) On the other extreme are those who demand and expect everyone else to meet their needs. Some codependents were neglected, and basic physical needs weren't met. If they were abused, they may never have experienced safety in a relationship and don't expect it — something normally consider a prerequisite. Others had their material needs met and assume that's all they require. But humans have many needs. Recognizing a need that was never filled is like asking a blind person to describe color. Here's a partial list of needs.

Autonomy	Mental stimulation	Meaning
Nurturance	Beauty	Play
Integrity	Peace	Humor
Respect	Inspiration	Passi won
Love	Appreciation	Trust
Friendship	Security and safety	Community
	Creativity	Pleasure

Good parents make it safe for children to ask for what they want. Then as adults, they're able to identify their needs, function on their own, and express their needs. If key needs were shamed or ignored in your childhood, you grow up doing the same to yourself and shut down feelings associated with those needs. Why feel a need if you don't expect it to be filled? It's less painful to deny it entirely.

Expressing needs in the context of a relationship requires trust, so you'd feel particularly vulnerable around needs that require the participation of another person and deny and/or feel ashamed of your needs for support, nurturance, and the most human of all — the need for love. Even if you know that you were loved, if you never received nurturing or had your feelings respected, you may attempt to fill this void with an addiction. Addictive relationships serve as a substitute for real connection. Some people are caretakers who hope to receive love in return, but are unable to experience real intimacy or maintain an intimate relationship. (See Chapter 16 on intimacy.)

Many who don't recognize their needs for support and comfort isolate — especially when they're hurting. Even with awareness of their needs, asking someone to meet them can feel humiliating.

Anna came to see me about stress at work and her lack of a social life. She was used to being self-sufficient. Then she was unexpectedly diagnosed with colon cancer. She was preparing for surgery and said that a friend was dropping her at the hospital. Concerned, I inquired who would be with her. She replied: "I'm okay. I'll be unconscious during the operation anyway." I asked Anna if she'd feel more at ease having someone at her side while waiting to be anesthetized. "I hadn't thought about someone being there," she answered, adding, "but I'll be fine."

After the surgery, Anna reported that her friend stayed with her prior to the surgery, and that it had been an enormous comfort — more than she could have imagined. She'd both minimized her fear of the surgery and denied her need for emotional support.

Marlene said she was very happy in her marriage and work, but was extremely depressed for no apparent reason. I later learned that her husband had been impotent during their 20-year marriage, but it didn't seem to bother her. She said, "It's not that important to me. I've gotten used to going without." She was in denial of her sexual needs and didn't connect her deprivation to her depression.

Peeling the Onion's Layers

As you progress in recovery, you uncover more levels of denial because you don't know what you don't know. The expression "peeling an onion" is apt because gaining awareness of unconscious material is an ongoing process, like peeling back layers of an onion. People can go to Twelve Step meetings for years, but deny the extent of their codependency. Like Ciena, in the following example, they make some changes, but deny the depth of the problem.

Ciena made progress in recovery, but continued to struggle in her marriage. Her self-esteem and communication with her workaholic husband greatly improved, and she no longer nagged, pleaded, or tried to control him. There was less conflict, but she'd been changing herself in order to change him — classic codependency. Her denial kept her from facing the emptiness in her marriage, her own intimacy issues, and her fears of being alone if the marriage ended.

In many cases, the addict enters recovery, or the codependent gains enough independence and self-esteem to leave the problematic relationship. Life improves, and he or she thinks that codependency is cured, but the causes haven't been addressed, so problems recur.

Cynthia ended her relationship with a drug user. She was happy, focusing on her career, and thought codependency was a thing of the past, only to be dismayed to see her behavior return all over again in a new relationship with a clean and sober man. He was responsible, kind, and fun to be with. Cynthia was convinced he was her soul mate, but his schedule never allowed him enough time with her. She started obsessing about him and dropped plans with friends and activities in order to be available when he called. After turning into a pretzel to win his love, she became as unhappy as she'd been with her ex, whom she began to miss because at least he needed her.

Chapter 6

The Process of Recovery

*B*ecause you're reading this book, more than likely you're interested in finding out more about codependency, or you've started or are ready to begin recovery. In this chapter, I discuss how important it is to focus on your recovery and make suggestions for getting started.

Recovery Is for You

From my personal and professional experiences, there are people in recovery who underestimate the time and attention involved in overcoming codependency and how it can sneak back up on them just when they are doing better. This book provides a comprehensive guide as to what's involved in recovery, but reading and even understanding it won't be enough. To change, commitment and effort are necessary. The commitment is to yourself and your recovery. You have to really want to change because the process won't always feel good or comfortable. There may be times when you ask if it's worth the effort. People complain that their partner isn't trying to change, and wonder why they should. It's important to realize from the outset that regardless of whether anyone else in your life recovers, recovery is for *you*. Burn that into your brain.

You're ready for recovery, but are you ready for change?

Before getting acquainted with codependency, you were in the dark about new possibilities for yourself and your circumstances. You may not have realized that healing is a path of personal growth that entails more than just changing your habits. Growth means trying new things, including new attitudes, behaviors, perceptions, and beliefs. When you come out of denial (see Chapter 5), you still may delay taking action, because:

- You may have adapted to difficult circumstances in order to survive, even when those circumstances were painful.

- You may be overwhelmed by the nature or gravity of your circumstances or by your attempts to control the uncontrollable.

- Maybe you complain about your situation and want things to change, or you want someone else to make you happy. It's typical for codependents to want others to change and not want to take responsibility for their actions, inactions, and choices.

- It's normal to be afraid of making changes because change may be seen as a threat. The bigger the decision or change, the greater the fear that accompanies it — fear of the unknown, abandonment, or standing up to intimidation.

- Good days provide relief, so you deny, minimize, and avoid the necessity to change.

Change requires you to take responsibility for your contribution to your problems. With it comes the awareness that today's choices are the seeds of tomorrow's change or stagnation, best described by Eldridge Cleaver, who famously said, "If you are not part of the solution, then you are part of the problem." Think about what has stopped you from taking action in the past or makes you hesitate now and what motivated you to read this book. See where you are in the following steps involved in making changes:

1. Thinking about the problem

2. Seeking answers, listening, and gathering information

3. Taking responsibility and realizing YOU have to change

4. Getting motivated

5. Planning and preparing for action

6. Attending meetings, counseling, and workshops

7. Using self-discipline to stay focused on your goal

8. Repeating action steps to achieve and maintain results

The spiral nature of recovery

The recovery process is not a straight path; rather, it is a cyclical, spiral movement forward, like a Slinky. Cycles are repetitions. Think of cycles of migration, the seasons, and planetary revolutions, but in healing you don't go back to the very beginning. Recovery spirals toward healing, meaning an improved state of functioning. If you've had an injury, you probably experienced improvement, setbacks, and gradual recovery. So, too, with codependency. There are times of confusion, stagnation, frustration, and slips backward, but most of the time, it's like steering a sailboat. In the beginning, you won't know how to steer or control the sails. You drift off course. In time, you merely adjust the tiller to sail in the right direction, mindful of the wind and your destination. The more awareness you bring to your recovery process, the more progress you experience. On the other hand, without mobilizing your will to recover, your functioning worsens.

Make recovery a priority

Many people begin recovery to be out of pain, to help someone else, or to save a relationship. These are fine reasons to start, but for change to last, you must be committed to yourself. The pain will lessen, the "someone" may or may not improve, or the relationship may end, but you're still left with yourself. When you make your recovery a priority, you reap the benefits. It's your life, and with recovery, you discover the keys to your happiness, which is your responsibility whether or not you're in a relationship. If you're depressed, given time, you'll be depressed in or out of a relationship — the same goes for other codependent traits. Codependency robs you of your vibrancy, contentment, health, and the ability to fully be yourself, which is the only thing that will make you happy in the long run.

Putting yourself first is difficult. You're used to making others a priority. That's the problem. To develop a new skill or build a muscle, you must exercise regularly, not when you get around to it. The same goes for new beliefs and habits. Act as if your recovery was the most treasured gift in the world — because it is. In time, you'll know that you're worthy of it.

Seeking Help and Support

Codependent relationships and families tend to be closed, meaning that you become isolated from outside information and the community. The best way to recover is to step beyond the family, because those relationships are restrictive for reasons more fully explained in Chapter 7. In cases where addiction is involved, often shame and fear prevent people from reaching out. In an abusive relationship, the abuser, like a dictator, maintains control, distrusts outsiders, and disallows external influence. It's important not to believe or give in to messages of distrust and fear. Instead, find out all you can and get help. Even if there's neither abuse, nor addiction involved, codependents need to open their minds, which have become fixated on another person and negative thoughts. The following are suggestions that have helped thousands of codependents. Some or none of them may feel right for you. Aim to suspend your doubts and give them a try. Utilize what resonates with you, and ignore what doesn't. Chapter 14 looks at spirituality in more depth. Chapter 18 discusses getting support in more detail.

Find support

You need information, guidance, and encouragement. Paradoxically, you need outside support to look inside of you. It takes self-discipline to not get dissuaded or distracted. Support is critical to help sustain your effort over time to make lasting change. It gives you hope and reminds you of your goals and what's possible. The biggest challenge is to stay focused on yourself. Change also entails discomfort — whether it's a new perception of reality or of yourself, fear of the unknown or people's reactions, or the confusion and incompetence of tackling something for the first time. You may feel guilty, awkward, and anxious. It's easy to become discouraged and swayed by old habits. Your codependent self will fight change tooth and nail to stop your progress. You need continual support and self-awareness to prevent slipping backwards. Perseverance pays off. The best help comes from people experienced with codependency, whether it comes in the form of a Twelve Step program, counselor, or psychotherapist. Other forms of support include family and friends, but often they have a codependent perspective and may have contributed to the problem in the first place. They may encourage your denial, or worse, blame you for your problems. Getting help from outside your family system is crucial in order to transform your beliefs and behavior. Online communities may be a good way to start, but beware that you may be getting wrong advice. It's preferable to find an online Twelve Step meeting.

Attend Twelve Step meetings

Attending Twelve Step meetings is the ideal way to begin recovery. (Specific meetings for codependency are discussed in Chapter 18.) Each has its own flavor. Some meetings have speakers, some review literature, and some are only participation, but you're not required to share. If you don't like one meeting, attend another. Here are some of the benefits:

✔ **Information:** You gain information both from the shared experience of long-time members and from the purchase of literature tailored to your problem.

✔ **Encouragement:** You may feel helpless when you first enter a Twelve Step program. You may have tried everything else, but nothing worked, and you no longer believe in change. Meetings can inspire you through success stories, real-life lessons, and from the experiences and strength of other members.

✔ **Personal guidance:** You make friends who understand what you're going through. They share their experiences, guidance, and offer telephone support. You can get a sponsor — someone to call for advice and support between meetings.

✔ **Motivation:** Perhaps you resolve to make a change or get excited about an idea, but soon lose interest or motivation. This is where a support system comes in. Listening to others can encourage and motivate you to continue on the path of change.

✔ **Anonymity:** Meetings are anonymous and maintain privacy.

✔ **Free:** Meetings are free. Donations are strictly voluntary.

✔ **Spirituality:** Meetings have a spiritual flavor, and members mention God or Higher Power; however, they don't discuss religion or require that you share their philosophy.

✔ **Meetings are daily:** You can find meetings to fit your schedule, generally from 7 a.m. to 8:30 p.m. every day.

Seek psychotherapy

Another form of support is psychotherapy, commonly referred to as therapy, with a mental health professional knowledgeable about codependency and addiction. Mental health professionals include licensed marriage and family therapists, licensed clinical professional counselors, licensed clinical social workers, who typically have a master's degree, and some have doctorates, and psychiatrists. Some states license other counselors who require a master's degree, such as alcohol and drug counselors. Psychologists have doctorates, and psychiatrists are medical doctors who can write prescriptions. A psychoanalyst holds a degree awarded by a psychoanalytic organization after intensive study. Ask any professional you consult about their credentials and if they are experienced working with codependency and symptoms you identify in reading Chapters 3 and 4. In addition to providing encouragement, personal guidance, and motivation, the benefits of psychotherapy include:

✔ **Individual consultations:** You get individual attention to address your particular situation, beliefs, and feelings. Your individual history, reactions, thinking, and behavioral patterns can be understood, examined, and replaced with new patterns.

- ✔ **Expert, objective guidance:** A trained professional is more objective and has greater professional knowledge and experience than a friend, sponsor, or meeting member. Also, psychotherapy can avoid confusion about Twelve Step concepts of *powerless* with helplessness, *acceptance* with passivity, or *moral inventory* with self-criticism.

- ✔ **Intimacy:** The personal and intimate nature of the therapeutic process enhances intimacy skills.

- ✔ **Privacy:** Some people are uncomfortable with sharing in a group setting, or they desire greater confidentiality.

- ✔ **Deeper issues can be healed:** A professional can address issues related to your family of origin, abuse, trauma, mood disorders, shame, intimacy, and low self-esteem.

- ✔ **Non-spiritual:** Some people are uncomfortable with the spiritual nature of Twelve Step programs and prefer counseling.

- ✔ **Couples counseling:** This is an opportunity to work on issues with your partner concerning intimacy, parenting, sexuality, and communication. You can get objective feedback about what's happening between the two of you. It also provides a safe place to say things you may not otherwise admit to each other.

If you're having suicidal thoughts or are currently in an abusive relationship, call a hotline and seek therapy. (See Chapter 18.)

Both therapy and meetings have different advantages and shouldn't be thought of as one in lieu of the other, but as additional forms of help. Your recovery will be easier and faster with greater support. Both psychotherapy and Twelve Step meetings address relationship, spiritual, addiction, behavior modification, and boundary issues.

Utilize coaches and unlicensed counselors

Some coaches and counselors have great skills and can provide motivation and support. They can hold you accountable when learning new behavior and achieving business and personal goals, such as assertiveness, meditation, dating, and weight loss. To be useful, they should be familiar with addiction and codependency.

They're not governed by the same ethical rules about boundaries that regulate licensed mental health professionals. Be alert to any behavior that causes you discomfort. A coach or counselor (or licensed professional, for that matter) may be violating your boundaries and thus be unable to teach you how to establish and protect your own boundaries. Keep in mind that they aren't trained to help you with emotional, intimacy, and trauma issues.

Understand constructive vs. destructive friendships

Friends can provide tremendous help or major harm to your recovery. Most people inject their own opinions and are unable to listen objectively. Helpful friends listen and don't judge you, but are able to gently point out when you're not being honest or kind with yourself or have unrealistic expectations. They encourage you and remind you of your strengths when you're too down to see them, and they celebrate your growth.

Beware of friends who gossip, have strong biases, abuse drugs or alcohol, envy or compete with you, or don't empathize and tell you to get over your problem. Some people are full of criticisms and "should's" for your life, even though they've had no experience with what you're going through. Codependents often do this. Despite their good intentions, it's no wonder you might leave their company feeling worse. Other friends may join the blame-wagon when you're upset at someone, which only fuels the fire, without really helping you.

Be Gentle with Yourself

In reading this book and beginning recovery, you gain self-awareness. You may feel overwhelmed by information, want to change quickly, or feel self-critical. You could think you're falling short of who you thought you were, who you'd like to be, or who you'd like others to see. Be patient and instead of judging yourself, act as if you're doing research — collecting data on your behavior. Even get excited when you find a shortcoming. Your awareness is growing, which is the beginning of change. Good parents don't criticize the baby for falling when he's learning to walk, but applaud his efforts. When you see yourself in your old behavior patterns, think about what you've learned, and tell yourself, "Next time, I'll have an opportunity to handle things differently." Remember that recovery is a process. It took a long time to become who you are, and it takes time to unlearn habits and beliefs that don't serve you. Former University of Southern California football coach Pete Carroll, named Coach of the Decade by *Lindy's Magazine,* attributed part of the team's success to the fact that when they made errors, he never flagellated them, but encouraged them to stay in the present, go back in the game, and play even better. He never tore them down, only built them up. Be like Carroll. Be a positive coach.

What If You're Not a Believer?

You may wonder whether they must believe in order to recover. The answer is, *No.* Some people who don't practice a religion or believe in God are turned off to Twelve Step programs. Some are atheists. They prefer to go to therapy, and they recover from codependency and addiction without religious beliefs or reliance on God. However, they miss out on many program benefits. Twelve-Step programs aren't religious, but are spiritual. In fact, discussion of religion is prohibited at Twelve Step meetings. No belief is required. Each person may define spirituality for him or herself, if desired. Faith in something — whether it's your sponsor, the future, the therapeutic process, or your body/mind's ability to heal — can aid your recovery, particularly when it comes to letting go discussed in Chapter 9.

Most codependents have been abused, betrayed, or disappointed and find it hard to have faith in or trust anything or anyone. The problem has been misplaced trust in untrustworthy people. Others blame God for their disappointments. Being able to trust again is part of recovery. In time, you'll learn to trust yourself.

Should You Tell the Addict or Your Partner?

Your recovery is for you, and you're entitled to privacy about your therapy, meetings, and anything else. Some people will not want you to get counseling or attend meetings in order to control you for some of the following reasons:

They are afraid you'll leave.

They are afraid you'll get stronger and challenge them.

They want to continue their addiction.

They're ashamed and afraid you'll make them look bad.

As you can see, their motivations are fear and shame. If you're worried that your partner will be abusive or undermine your recovery, wait until you're stronger and have the words and support to deal with an abusive reaction. You have more power than you realize. If you decide to tell the addict or your partner, you can reassure him or her that your recovery is for your problems, which it is.

Chapter 7

How Did You Become Codependent?

▶ Explaining how codependency gets passed on in infancy

▶ Discovering the breadth of family dysfunction in America

▶ Understanding the traits of healthy and dysfunctional families

▶ Defining types of abuse

▶ Describing the dynamics and roles in families with addiction

In this chapter, the psychodynamic view of early child development of a healthy Self is discussed. Frequently, the primary caretaker is the mother; it may be the father, grandparent, or other relative or combination of people, but for simplicity, I refer to the mother as the primary caretaker. When infant parenting is inadequate, it likely reflects dysfunction in the whole family, which further damages the growing child's emerging Self. Symptoms of dysfunctional families from the perspective of family system's theory outlined and compared to healthy families.

Mommy and Me — A Psychodynamic View

Children are born vulnerable, full of needs, and dependent on their caretakers for everything. To grow, they need touch as much as food — plus attention, empathy, nurturing, and security. Babies are so dependent on their mothers that they don't know their bodies are separate. The mother's every response or lack of response impacts her child. Because most of her actions are spontaneous and unconscious, who she is psychologically has greater influence than even what she does. For example, the way a mother holds, nurses, and touches her baby communicates her sense of anxiety or security, love or disinterest, impatience or attentiveness. The tone of her voice, facial expression, and tension in her body give her baby information about whether the environment is safe. Research shows that if the mother is expressionless while talking to her baby, the baby begins to fret. On the other hand, meeting a child's psychological needs allows the maturation of a secure, vital, and independent Self. When established, it can weather crises and losses, failure and success, and rejection and admiration.

Starting at four to six months and continuing onward, babies must confidently achieve separation from their mothers and establish their own boundaries. They must individuate, which is a long psychological process whereby a child and later young adult becomes an individual and develops a whole Self — an individual who is separate psychologically, cognitively, and emotionally, and owns and trusts his or her perceptions, thoughts, feelings, and memories. Verbal and nonverbal parental responses either help or hinder this developmental task. Self-confident parents accept their children's endeavors and striving without fear, pushing, repressing, or competing. To separate and learn self-trust, children must first trust their mothers to reliably meet their needs, including the need to separate. How parents respond determines how effectively their children are able to set boundaries as adults.

Here's looking at you, kid

Key to the separation-individuation process and the formation of a healthy Self is the mother's ability to mirror the child's feelings. She does this by empathically and intuitively matching her responses to her child's needs and ever-fluctuating feelings. She joins in her child's glee and remains calm and present with her baby's sadness, containing and diffusing intense feelings. She empathizes, names, and reflects her child's feelings back accurately, teaching it to recognize, trust, and respond to its internal feelings, perceptions, and thoughts because "all-knowing Mommy" has validated them. Healthy boundaries prevent a mother from personalizing her child's feelings. She's able to acknowledge that her child has perceptions, feelings, and needs different from, and even in conflict with, hers.

What Mama don't have

Generally, deficient or inadequate mirroring reflects a mother's incomplete Self, which is how codependency becomes generational. It results from the mother's emotional unavailability and lack of empathy. If her toddler cries over a broken toy and she's pre-occupied or dismissive, her child will feel abandoned. Faulty mirroring can occur even when a mother gives her child an extraordinary amount of attention if it isn't in response to the child's particular need but is instead a manifestation of the mother's need for mirroring that she never received as a child. For instance, a mother may talk excitedly to her baby in a way that's intrusive or over-stimulating. The mother's defective mirroring may be caused by her:

- ✔ Illness

- ✔ Grief

- ✔ Stress due to external events

- ✔ Mental or emotional deficits, including depression and narcissism

- ✔ Rigid boundaries — she'll be cold and unable to empathize

- ✔ Weak boundaries — she won't see her child as separate

Weak boundaries are typical of codependents. The mother's empathy will be inaccurate because psychologically she sees her child as an extension of herself — as an opportunity for her to feel needed, valuable, important, lovable, and complete. She unconsciously only reinforces her baby's responses that boost her self-esteem. When her child is upset, she's unable to contain and mirror him or her. She may be overwhelmed, frightened, or impatient with her baby's continuous crying, or feel wounded by her child's rebellious anger and react by withdrawing or scolding.

With inadequate mirroring, children learn that their needs, feelings, and thoughts are unimportant, wrong, and shameful. Repeated instances teach children that love and approval come with meeting their mothers' needs, and for survival they repress their needs and feelings and tune in to the mother's expectations and emotions. A child's Self becomes organized around pleasing and performing for others' approval in order to feel loved. Instead of developing a strong sense of Self and awareness of needs, feelings, and thoughts, the individual's worth becomes determined by others, and later he or she enters relationships based on need. If a mother is chronically unable to meet a child's needs, he or she feels lost and abandoned, since there is no object to validate the Self's existence. The child may become apathetic, depressed, or anxious, later leading to self-stimulating or over-stimulating behavior, such as compulsive masturbation, addiction, or dangerous risk taking.

Codependent mothers may unconsciously fail to support their children's emerging drive for independence. Instead, the mothers' needs and automatic responses cripple their children by keeping them dependent, and consequently codependent as adults. On the other hand, mothers who feel burdened by their children's needs may encourage independence prematurely, overwhelming the child due to its limited capacity to sustain itself. They may feel abandoned, fear separation, and become codependent. With enough faulty maternal interactions, instead of developing a harmonious and vital Self, these children's emotional functioning becomes distorted. As adults, they engage in futile and desperate attempts to control and/or please others in order to satisfy their own unidentified needs. Without conscious awareness and empathy with their interior Selves, they treat themselves and others as objects, and being alone or too much intimacy threaten them with nonexistence or dissolution.

It's a Dysfunctional World

Dysfunctional families are the new norm in America. That's because 72 percent have a family member who's an addict — according to the American Medical Association. The numbers nearly add up to everyone, when you count another 20 percent of Americans with a serious mental illness. Addiction is the leading cause of family dysfunction, along with chronic illness, abuse, and trauma. Society is addicted to legal and illegal drugs, as well as relationships, romance, sex, money, work, gambling, food, exercise, consumption, speed, tweeting, cell phones, and the Internet, among other things.

Another factor contributing to family dysfunction is the high divorce rate in America. One-third of children don't live with both parents. Divorce is a trauma that almost always exposes children to conflict, crisis, loss, and some degree of abandonment. Many of those spousal relationships were likely dysfunctional before divorcing. Moreover, increased stress due to economic and health concerns adds to greater conflict and instability, mental illness, and less attention given to children.

Healthy vs. Dysfunctional Families — A Family Systems View

Family systems theorists view families as living organisms. The health and behavior of the parts are dependent upon each other and the whole, and vice versa. Parents establish and enforce the rules and model behavior and communication. Cooperation between them is essential for optimal family functioning. Through interactions with your parents, you learn life lessons that include:

✔ How to identify needs and feelings

✔ Whether your needs and feelings matter

✔ How to nurture yourself

✔ Ways to get needs met from others (which may be dysfunctional such as whining, tantrums, begging, lying)

✔ How to meet your own needs

✔ Whether authority can be trusted

✔ What behavior is rewarded (some parents reward negative behavior with more attention)

✔ Whether your authentic Self has value

✔ How to resolve conflict by observing and interacting with parent

✔ How to solve problems and make decisions by thinking through feelings and consequences

Healthy families

The Cosbys are an example of a family you want to be around. They had sibling rivalry, disagreements, and disappointments, but they also had the following ingredients of healthy families.

An open system

Whether it's a country, an organization, a family, or a person, openness is a sign of health. This is because it allows for freedom of expression, flow of information, flexibility, and adaptability, which prolong survival. Healthy families can weather crises because they are receptive to new ideas, talk about them, and adjust to the new circumstances. An open family is not afraid of outside influences and is often active in the community. You can share outside knowledge and experiences with your family, including other aspects of your personality expressed in different environments — you don't live a double life or always act the role of "Mom" or "kid brother." Information also flows outward. You don't fear revealing family "dirty laundry" with outsiders.

In an open environment, you're free to express your authentic Self. You can talk about what you see, hear, feel, and think. There aren't forbidden topics, like sex or money. A parent's shortcoming or failure isn't hidden, but instead teaches human frailty and that parents aren't perfect. Dissent isn't silenced, and family decisions and values may be questioned and debated. Although all feelings are allowed expression, verbal abuse isn't tolerated, and not all actions are permissible.

General Electric's "Open Door" policy

Jack Welch, former CEO of General Electric, transformed G.E. from a closed system to an open one. He prided himself on having an "Open Door" policy and encouraged open communication among workers and management and between G.E. and other companies. Profits tripled, and employee self-esteem, motivation, and productivity surged.

Equality for all

Healthy families have an atmosphere of equality, respect, and fairness. Spouses treat each other as equals, setting an example for siblings. Although parents still make the rules, they're not authoritarian. The family is more egalitarian than hierarchical. Aside from age-appropriate differences, you're treated equally, and older siblings aren't allowed to boss younger ones. Chores are divided fairly between genders. Everyone is accountable, including the parents. If they don't want to be interrupted, they don't interrupt. They model the behavior they teach their children and demonstrate that it's alright to make mistakes by apologizing for their own and forgiving those of others.

Everyone is heard

Communication is honest, direct, assertive, and respectful. Parents listen and try to understand you and each other. You get a chance to be heard, without being ignored or criticized. Listening to you with understanding is a sign of respect. It builds self-esteem, honors your individuality, and conveys that you and what you say have value. You learn to acknowledge and express your feelings and needs and gain confidence in yourself and your opinions.

Reasonable, consistent rules

Every family has rules — some overt and some covert. If you've had a job where you didn't know what was expected, you know how stressful that can be. In healthy families, rules and punishments are expressed, consistent, humane, and reasonable. This produces a secure environment. You learn to internalize a safe, consistent environment, and thereby are able to calm and modulate your feelings. Rules are also flexible and rational and may be questioned and commented upon. They make sense to you, and you aren't blamed or shamed but told that you broke a rule. Punishments are fair and related to rule violations. They guide and persuade you to learn from your mistakes. You're not told you're "bad," nor is love withheld, which is cruel.

Sometimes when I ask couples to list family rules, each one comes up with a different list. One husband incorrectly thought his wife had a rule that they could only have sex at night. She was shocked to learn this. On the other hand, she believed that he expected her to work out to "stay in shape," but he explained that his only concern was that she not gain weight. They never would have discovered their misconceptions had they not discussed their rules openly. Think about:

- ✔ What rules are in your household?
- ✔ Are there subjects that are off-limits?
- ✔ Is the expression of all feelings, including anger, permitted?
- ✔ Who made the rules?
- ✔ Are you allowed to comment on them?
- ✔ Are they interfering or accomplishing what you want?
- ✔ What happens if you disagree on a rule?
- ✔ Are they up to date or do you need new rules?

Finding solutions

Key to positive relationships is the ability to problem-solve and resolve conflict. (See Chapter 11.) Rather than have recurring fights over the same problem, spouses are able to settle disagreements, solve problems, and involve older children in decision-making that affects them.

Parents also guide and teach you how to make decisions by being supportive and encouraging and helping you to think through consequences of your choices. Healthy parenting gives you options and allows you to make age-appropriate decisions for yourself. Too much or too little involvement handicaps your ability to make plans and decisions as an adult.

Loving relationships

In addition to respect, healthy families have an atmosphere of acceptance, trust, security, caring, and good-will. This begins with the spousal relationship, which is based on love and empathy, not control. Family members protect and help each other. It's a place where you get nurtured, encouraged, and supported when you're hurt or down. Inevitably, there'll be conflicts and anger, but because love isn't withheld nor undermined by abuse, peace soon returns. You can trust your parents and know that you're loved unconditionally — even when you make mistakes or disappoint them. You grow into a responsible, happy, and confident adult, accustomed to love and reliability and being treated with respect and kindness. You won't allow anything less.

Dysfunctional families

Many dysfunctional families look healthy on the outside, but the internal dynamics revolve around a family member's addiction, abuse, illness, or trauma. Other families are dysfunctional due to rigid control or lack of love, which can cause the children to become codependent. The strongest predictor of codependency is having codependent parents.

Codependency usually starts with the repression of feelings, needs, observations, and thoughts that is typical in dysfunctional families. You learn to numb your hurt, distrust your parents, and become self-sufficient. You hide behind a false or phony personality and/or develop compulsive behaviors to cope. The following are symptoms, but not all are necessary for a family to be dysfunctional. Families with drug addiction or abuse usually have more of the symptoms.

We vs. them

Dysfunctional families are closed to varying degrees. Some won't allow differing or new ideas to be discussed among members or with outsiders. They may not welcome guests or friendships with those of another race or religion. Remember Archie Bunker of "All in the Family." He was autocratic and intolerant of opposing views. Some families are isolated and don't interact with the community. Others do, but appearances are everything. The family may be respected in the community, but the truth isn't shared. Talking about the family to others is considered disloyal. At bottom are shame and fears of dissimilar ideas.

Denial

Family problems and crises, such as a member's absence, illness, or addiction, never get talked about. Parents think that if they try to act normal and pretend the problem doesn't exist, maybe it'll go away, and children won't notice or be harmed. (See Chapter 5 for more information on denial.) However, this pretense makes you doubt your perceptions because what you see and know aren't acknowledged by authority figures. You learn not to question or trust your parents nor trust your perceptions, feelings, or yourself, even as an adult. Denial conveys to children that they can't talk about something frightening — even to each other. Sadly, frightened children sharing the same bedroom, who overhear their parents fight, live in fear, but often hide their pain from each other. If you repress your feelings, observations, and reactions — not once, but on a regular basis, you become numb and depressed.

✔ What truths were dismissed or ignored in your family?

  ✔ How did your parents do that?

  ✔ How did it affect you?

Secrets

Closed systems have secrets. Some families hide a shameful secret for generations — whether it's addiction, violence, criminal activity, sexual issues, or mental illness. The shame is felt by the children — even when they don't know the secret. If you know the secret, but can't ask questions or talk about it, you feel different, damaged, or ashamed.

A genogram is a diagram that charts family relationships, patterns, and secrets (see Figure 7-1). It's guaranteed to be illuminating. Gather information by interviewing all your relatives and create a family genogram. The males, shown as a square, are to the left of females, represented by a circle, and the eldest child is on the left.

In this sample genogram, you were born in 1969, married Bea in 1996, and have a son and daughter. Your parents, Bob and Ana, divorced (the "//") in 1984 when you were 15. Ana married Ira four years later, but separated ("/"). Your father, now living with Meg (the broken "– – –" line), is an alcoholic, as was your great grandfather, Jim. In 1986, your father married Fay, who died in 2009. From that marriage, you have a half-sister Lea, born following a miscarriage, and a step-sister Mia. Your other half-siblings are Pam, Joe, and Jill. You're also an uncle to your brother Al's daughter Sue.

A genogram also reveals curious generational patterns. Perhaps you married or had a child at the same age as one of your parents. By creating a genogram, you can find answers to many of your family questions. In this example, Ana's father, Sid, and brother, Ted, are also alcoholics. As a codependent, she was primed to marry your father. Ana had twins, as did her grandmother, Nora. Ana's were fraternal, and Nora's were identical, indicated by the adjoining bar ("–"). Ana married at 19, like her mother, Ema. Both you and your uncle Max were born the year of both your parents' marriage, implying shotgun weddings. Also notice that both of your grandmas were the eldest of large families, suggesting they were strong women and caretakers.

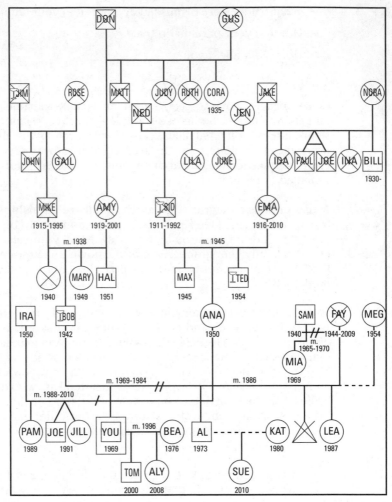

Figure 7-1: Your genogram.

Look online or make up symbols to indicate mental illness, adoptions, family violence, incarceration, and different types of addiction, including alcoholism, gambling, sex, and eating disorders. You can also track illness and disease, such as depression, addiction, heart disease, diabetes, and cancer.

- ✔ What secrets were kept in the family you grew up in?
- ✔ Are they generational?
- ✔ How did they affect your family?
- ✔ What rules and behavior kept the secrets hidden?
- ✔ Does it make you feel ashamed?

Individual and generational boundary problems

Good parenting requires having appropriate and flexible boundaries that respect your individuality and separateness. In healthy families, parents respect your emotional, mental, sexual, and physical boundaries. In dysfunctional families, boundaries are rigid, blurred, or a mixture. (See a discussion of boundaries in Chapter 3.) When boundaries are too rigid, family members are disengaged, emotionally and physically. There may be no feeling of closeness, nor affection showed. As adults, siblings are emotionally distant, and families don't often celebrate together. In other families, boundaries are non-existent or enmeshed. It teaches you that you have no right to set boundaries. Family members gossip and over-react to each other, give unwanted advice, and invade personal boundaries. Any form of abuse violates boundaries. Other families are mixed. Children may be enmeshed with a parent but distant from siblings.

Some controlling parents take over your decisions and control your hobbies, school courses, friends, and dress. Parents may also invade your boundaries by prying, reading your mail, questioning your friends about you, or ransacking or taking your belongings without permission. They resist your urge to separate because they want to be needed. Natural independence is seen as disloyalty and abandonment, and you may either rebel or feel guilty when you try to set boundaries with your parents and with others as an adult.

 Describe the boundaries in your family growing up in the following areas.

- ✔ Money

- ✔ Your personal belongings

- ✔ Physical touching and showing affection

- ✔ Sex and nudity

- ✔ Emotional — respect for your feelings

- ✔ Mental — respect for your thoughts and opinions

There're also generational boundaries between parents and children. Yours were violated if you were put in an adult role. This may have happened if one parent became overly close with you and used you as a companion, as a confidante to discuss your parent's relationship or personal problems, or as an ally against your other parent. That parent was using you as an emotional surrogate for the lack of intimacy between your parents and/or as an ally or pawn in their power struggles. After a divorce, generational boundaries are often disrespected when one parent uses a child to convey messages to the other parent.

Generational boundaries are also crossed when a child takes over parental responsibilities for an emotionally or physically absent or irresponsible parent. This can happen in single-parent families or if one parent is ill, in the military, or an addict. Some children as young as 5 are left to make their own meals. One child may assume the role of "little mother" or "little man" and take care of younger siblings or a needy parent. This is how many codependents learn to become over-functioning adults and caretakers. Some receive praise for doing so, and their role becomes part of their personality as adults.

Crossing generational boundaries is psychologically damaging. If this happened to you, you had to repress your needs and feelings in order to adopt an unnatural, age-inappropriate, persona (be "a little adult") and accommodate the needs of your parent. This separated you from your authentic child-self and undermines self-esteem.

Think about boundaries between generations.

- ✔ Did you have to perform adult tasks or assume adult responsibilities?

- ✔ Did a parent inappropriately confide with you?

- ✔ Did a parent ask you to talk to your other parent for him or her?

- ✔ Did you believe you had a special relationship with a parent who excluded your other parent?

- ✔ How did you feel in each of these situations?

Blame and shame — dysfunctional communication

In dysfunctional families, people don't listen, and communication is neither assertive nor open. It's used to control more than to understand. (See Chapter 11.) Typically, dysfunctional communication has one or more of the following characteristics:

- ✔ Indirect

- ✔ Abusive (defined in Chapter 3)

- ✔ Dishonest

- ✔ Contains double messages

- ✔ Disallows freedom of expression

- ✔ Invalidates reality and children's feelings and thoughts

- ✔ Blames

- ✔ Shames

- ✔ Engages in frequent fighting

- ✔ Scapegoats children

Double messages happen when a parent says one thing and does another or makes contradictory demands. Examples are a mother who says she's "Fine" while she's crying, a father who teaches "Never lie" but claims his 13-year-old is 12 in order to buy a cheaper ticket, or a mother who takes a child shopping and says, "Pick out whatever you want" but will only buy what she wants.

Sometimes there are walls of silence, or the communication is irrelevant to what's happening. Children learn not to ask questions or comment on distressing happenings. You feel abandoned and isolated from being forced to manage your feelings alone, which is more damaging than the actual events. You're afraid to express your thoughts and feelings and "walk on eggshells" because you're used to being blamed, shamed, ignored, or dismissed. Directly or indirectly, you've been told not to feel or think what you do. The result is that over time you repress your inner life and turn off internal cues that give you data about reality and yourself. As an adult, you no longer can identify your feelings and don't trust your opinions and thoughts.

In addition, you may have been shamed to feel unworthy of love, success, or anything good or pleasurable. When parents withhold love or blame and shame their children, the shame and fear of abandonment become internalized.

Make a list of shaming messages you heard in your family. Here are some common ones:

✔ "You're a sissy (bad), (dumb), (lazy), (selfish)."

✔ "Shame on you."

✔ "Be a man."

✔ "That didn't hurt."

✔ "I've sacrificed for you."

✔ "Act like a lady."

✔ "How can you do this to me?"

✔ "You're spoiled."

✔ "Grow up."

✔ "Act your age."

✔ "You're too sensitive."

✔ "Who do you think you are?"

✔ "You shouldn't feel ___."

✔ "We wanted a girl (or boy)."

✔ "You're driving me crazy."

✔ "If it hadn't been for you . . . ."

✔ "You can't do anything right."

✔ "You'll never amount to anything."

Conflicts between parents frighten children, who also often bear the brunt of their parents' anger. Children can become a battle ground for couples who don't communicate. Instead of fighting directly, parents scapegoat a child, by making their child the problem and center of their anger and dissatisfaction with one another. They argue about their child or parenting, and the child feels confused and torn between them. This also happens frequently before and after a divorce.

Rigid rules

In some families, parents are irresponsible, and rules are too lax. Their children lack guidance and don't feel safe and cared for. Other dysfunctional families have rigid, restrictive rules. A controlling parenting style can lead to codependency in the children. Rules often are unspoken, like prohibitions about commenting on what's going on, the family secret, and/or subjects deemed "inappropriate," such as death, the holocaust, grandpa's limp, or that father was married before. When rules expect perfection, there's no room for mistakes. Some families restrict the expression of anger, exuberance, or crying. There are religious families where you're always expected to feel grateful and forgiving and must deny your feelings of hurt, anger, and disappointment. To curb your feelings, you learn self-control and become overly controlled or controlling, all contributing to low self-esteem.

Make a list of restrictive rules that governed you growing up. Examples include:

✔ "Don't talk back."

✔ "Don't be direct."

✔ "Don't be honest. It's not tactful."

✔ "Be strong, perfect, and good."

✔ "Don't act silly — it's immature."

✔ "Don't express sadness or anger."

✔ "Never praise yourself. It's conceited."

✔ "It's selfish to consider your needs or desires."

✔ "Don't discuss feelings."

✔ "Don't mention problems."

✔ "I'm right because I said so."

✔ "Don't ask questions."

✔ "Only trust your family."

✔ "Men only want sex."

✔ "Masturbation is sinful."

✔ "Girls don't need to go to college."

✔ "Boys and men don't cry."

✔ "Children should be seen, but not heard."

✔ "Eat everything on your plate — like it or not."

✔ "Don't upset your mother."

✔ "Look at me when I talk to you (while being shamed)."

There're some very controlled families that are highly regimented. Order and discipline are valued more than feelings. If you had an authoritarian parent, your self-esteem became dependent upon that parent's mood, similar to alcoholic families. Studies show a correlation between codependency and having had a compulsive mother or an authoritarian father regardless of addiction, where there's control but little support for your feelings.

Arbitrariness and inconsistency

Arbitrary and inconsistent rules are worse than rigid rules. Rules that don't make sense feel unjust. You never know when you'll be punished. This is cruel and breeds confusion, feelings of helplessness, and unexpressed rage. You live in constant fear, walk on eggshells, and feel hopeless and resentful because of the unpredictability and unfairness. Arbitrary punishment undermines your sense of worth and dignity. You lose respect and trust in your parents and authority in general. When children are forced to comply, some act-out their emotions with rebellious or delinquent behavior, by doing poorly in school, or by using drugs. Problems also arise when parents don't get along or disagree on parenting. They often contradict each other. You may obey one parent and get punished by the other.

Unpredictability

Predictability creates safety. If you never know what mood Mom or Dad will be in, you can't be spontaneous and are always anxious. Some families have constant crises due to addiction, mental illness, or abuse. Instead of a safe haven, the family becomes a war zone from which you want to escape. Children may develop somatic complaints, like headaches and stomach aches. They become controlled to feel safe or act-out behaviorally.

The repetition compulsion

First identified by Freud, the repetition compulsion is a person's compulsion to repeat a previous trauma, usually unconsciously, as a perpetrator or victim in an attempt to master it or find a solution. The movie *Groundhog Day* had a similar theme, where Bill Murray repeated the same day over again until he learned a lesson about love.

Inability to problem-solve

Resolving problems and conflicts is key to a smooth-running organization. But in dysfunctional families, children and parents are blamed repeatedly, and there are constant arguments or silent walls of resentment. Nothing gets resolved.

Abuse

Abuse is common in dysfunctional families and may take the form of neglect or physical, sexual, emotional, or spiritual abuse. Abuse violates your boundaries and seriously damages your self-esteem. The abuser may be a parent, older sibling, or other relative. Sometimes, older siblings emulate a parent's abusive behavior and vent their unexpressed anger on a younger child. Abuse is usually random and unpredictable, adding to an atmosphere of anxiety or even terror. Abuse needn't be illegal or aggressive. Child abuse can be subtle, quiet, covert, and even pleasurable or disguised as play or jokes. Abusers commonly deny their abusive behavior and blame it on their victims. Victims also deny and minimize abuse they experience because they feel ashamed, even though they're not at fault. Only the abuser is responsible for his or her actions — never the victim. NEVER!

Adults who've been abused as children have particular difficulty when it comes to anger, safety, trust, and authority. Due to denial, many don't realize that they've suffered abuse. Unhealed, they have difficulty experiencing intimacy. Some enter into abusive relationships. Working through their past helps stop the compulsion to repeat it. (See Chapter 13 about healing the past.)

Neglect

Neglect may happen when parents are physically or mentally ill or abusing drugs. It's the failure of a parent to provide needed food, clothing, shelter, medical care, or supervision that threatens a child's health, safety, or well-being. Neglected children are robbed of a childhood and have trouble caring for themselves as adults. If they reverse roles and take care of a parent, they suffer the added effect of generational boundary violations.

Physical abuse

This includes not only violent acts, such as hitting, kicking, biting, choking, and burning, but also shoving, slapping, pinching, hair-pulling, throwing things, destroying property, and threats of physical harm. Corporal punishment that is done in anger or leaves a burn, bruise, or welt is also abusive. Most parents have been tempted to strike their child in frustration, but if the urge is acted upon, it's motivated by the parent's emotional need, not concern for the child. Corporal punishment doesn't teach correct behavior. It only instills fear and shame. Tickling or rough-housing by a parent or older sibling becomes abusive when you want it stopped but are overpowered or ignored. Continuing is domination by the stronger person over the weaker. It's humiliating and disempowering.

If you witnessed domestic violence or physical abuse of a sibling, you were traumatized as if it happened to you. You may feel guilty for not preventing the abuse. This is termed witness abuse. It includes witnessing a parent violently damage property — like breaking a door. The rage is what's terrorizing. You may enjoy watching your father tear down a room to remodel it but be petrified to witness it when your parents are arguing.

Sexual abuse

Sexual abuse can include any inappropriate touching, kissing, looking, nudity, flirting, pornography, peeping, exhibitionism, or sexual innuendo, stories, or jokes. When sexual contact with a child is kept secret, it's likely abusive, and the secret exacerbates the harm. Even if you experienced pleasure, inappropriate sexual contact is abusive because it's over-stimulating and a breach of trust because you're being used to gratify the abuser's needs. The age differential is an abuse of power. Victims of sexual abuse feel self-hatred and shame — especially if they experienced pleasure. As adults, they have problems with intimacy, trust, and sexuality.

Emotional abuse

Emotional abuse includes verbal abuse defined in Chapter 3. Emotional abuse can also take the form of withholding love or threatening or enforcing unreasonable punishment or chores, isolation, or deprivation. Some parents are cold and unaffectionate, and others are unresponsive, robotic, and ghostlike. As a child, it makes you feel unlovable and rejected and results in problems as an adult connecting emotionally. When parents controlled your activities and decisions or are possessive and jealous of your friends and lovers, you feel smothered or claustrophobic in intimate relationships. If your parents were hyper-critical, continually advising, criticizing, and improving you, you grow up to be hyper-critical of yourself and have low self-esteem. You believe that you're never enough — not doing enough, good enough, or accomplished enough to secure your parent's love or that of a mate.

Some parents with mental illness are cruel and sadistic. One father awakened his son each morning at 5 to pick up every leaf that had fallen the night day before. He later left his son at a gas station in a strange town. A mother killed her daughter's pet rabbit and gave away her son's athletic trophies.

Spiritual abuse

Spiritual abuse can occur in extremely religious families. Some parents neglect their obligations to understand, guide, and teach their children, and instead quote Bible dictum that a child can't understand. Others instill fear of a vengeful God or shame their children in the name of religion. This happened to many homosexuals. The reverse is also true where atheist parents forbid the mention of God or shame their children's spiritual curiosity and yearnings. Other families indoctrinate their children in cult practices that may also include abuse.

Drug addiction

As noted in Chapter 2, codependency was first observed by therapists studying alcoholic families. Not all children of addicts are codependent, but usually families with drug or alcohol addiction have all the above dysfunctional characteristics and more. Still, half of adult children of alcoholics remain in denial that they have an alcoholic parent. Instead, they live in shame and guilt. The majority has been abused and, like victims of abuse, has issues concerning trust and anger about the past.

Chaos and the merry-go-round of denial

The household of an addicted parent is monopolized by his or her erratic, irresponsible, and often tyrannical, abusive behavior, and the situation worsens as the addiction progresses. The addict acts like a little despot, denies that drinking or using is a problem, and decrees that no one may challenge it. Everyone's behavior organizes around the denial of the addict's disease. They try to maintain normalcy and protect and enable the addict. They repress thoughts, feelings, and observations in order not to make waves and live in fear of another binge, disaster, or blowup.

When the addict isn't under the influence, he or she is Dr. Jekyll, who is often loving and responsible. Dr. Jekyll makes promises, and the family is hopeful that sobriety will last. Soon Hyde returns, breaking the promises, trust, hearts, and hopes of the spouse and children who love him or her. This cycle plays over and over again ("The merry-go-round of denial," originally named by Reverend Joseph P. Kellermann) because, despite evidence to the contrary, the family continues to believe promises and hopes that the addictive behavior will end. Before the chronic stage of addiction, peace and normalcy return during sobriety but only add to the disappointment, desperation, and hopelessness when addictive behavior recurs — sometimes, without the drug.

The personality changes caused by addiction create an atmosphere of chaos. Parenting is unreliable, inconsistent, and unpredictable, even though it may be carried out primarily by the sober parent, who is highly stressed, trying to manage the household, irrational demands, and crises of the addict. Both parents are emotionally unavailable to the children. If both are addicts, they're both physically unavailable, too. As a child, you never have a sense of safety and consistency that you need in order to thrive. You don't invite friends over to avoid being embarrassed by your addict-parent. Your needs get ignored, and you learn not to ask rather than be disappointed. You become self-reliant and needless as an adult to avoid anyone having power over you again. Even when one parent is responsible, plans and rules are in constant flux due to the unpredictable changes of the addict's moods and drug and/or alcohol use, as shown in the following example:

The sober parent tells the children bedtime is 9 p.m., only to be undermined by the addict, who insists that they can stay up until 11 p.m. to watch a movie together. An argument between the parents ensues, and the children are suddenly punished by the addict for something trivial and sent to bed at 8 p.m. They distrust both parents, feel unsafe, guilty, betrayed, and alone, and are confused and angry at the injustice. Their feelings and needs don't count, and they have no one to talk to.

Role of the non-addict

Generally, the spouse of the addict will try everything from pleasing to threats in an attempt to control the uncontrollable situation of another's addiction. He or she may try to safeguard the children by keeping them away from the addict as much as possible. The non-addict parent's behavior depends upon his or her personality, coping style, and pre-existing codependency. It often begins by trying to help and protect the addict, and fluctuates between caretaking, scolding and blaming, and withdrawing emotionally as the drug addiction and codependency progress. The non-addict may eventually act-out with drugs, alcohol, affairs, or other irresponsible behavior. When both parents are addicted, a child may take this parental role.

These families tend to isolate from relatives, the community, and sources of help. You fared better if you had positive role models in relatives or others who helped with parenting. Studies show that it's harder on you if your mother is an addict and is devastating when both parents are addicted. Younger children are harmed more than older children, and boys are more vulnerable than girls. If the non-addict parent overcomes the pull of denial and codependency and confronts and holds the addict accountable, maintains friends, and seeks treatment, or attends a Twelve Step program, it brings more stability and health to the family.

Roles of the children

Like the spouse, the children adopt behaviors to relieve the family tension, which vary depending upon the child's personality and birth order. Sharon Wegscheider-Cruse and Claudia Black each identified four roles. Some children use aspects of more than one and play more than one role. Children in other types of dysfunctional families also develop these roles to varying degrees. Over time coping styles become defined roles that last into adulthood. Although they served a useful function growing up, they prevent you from being fully expressing yourself. You may be a rebel or a compliant, good student, but that role hides your true Self. Behaving differently from your accustomed role is difficult and frightening because it feels like your survival is still at stake — even after you've left your childhood family. Healing requires that you learn to value and express yourself in all areas of life.

The Hero

Often the oldest, you're responsible and the most identified with the parents. In a chaotic environment, you seek structure to create a sense of security. The Hero provides companionship to the non-addict parent, helps with family responsibilities, and may protect and help parent younger siblings. You know what's appropriate and do the right thing to be successful in school, socially, and at work. You develop leadership and organizational skills that are beneficial in achieving goals in school and into adulthood.

The Hero is used to carrying responsibility and being self-reliant, but has trouble trusting and receiving help. Any failure is hard to tolerate because of underlying feelings of inadequacy. You're serious, tend to be rigid and controlled, and lack flexibility and spontaneity. You may be uncomfortable playing or relaxing, and become a workaholic. Some use drugs in order to let go. One day, you discover that you have difficulty being intimate and open with your feelings and are anxious, lonely, and depressed.

The Adjuster

The Adapter is the child who doesn't complain and adapts to the family the way the wind blows. If you're an Adjuster, you survived in the unpredictable environment of addiction by not drawing too much attention to yourself in the family and at school. Unlike the Hero, you feel the effect of events and circumstances and are not in charge of your life as an adult. Your challenge is to take control of your life and pursue your goals.

The Placater

The Placater is more sensitive to the actions and feelings of other family members and is hurt more easily. You're the most caring and derive self-esteem from making others feel good. To survive, you tend to others' emotional needs, never learned to consider your wants and needs, and feel guilty when you do. You give more than you receive. Like the Adjuster, you need to discover your wants, feel worthy of receiving them, and pursue your goals.

The Scapegoat

The Scapegoat acts-out with negative behavior that takes the family's attention off the addict. As the Scapegoat, you were constantly in trouble at home and at school and have issues with anger and conflicts with friends and co-workers. Your behavior is an expression of feelings that you can't communicate, and because you neither comply nor withdraw, you attract even more punishment and abuse from your parents and authority figures. Many Scapegoats get arrested for delinquent behavior and begin using drugs and/or alcohol as teenagers. In doing so, this may bring the parents together, which may be their unconscious motive, despite the consequences to themselves.

The Lost Child

The Lost Child is usually a younger or the youngest child who withdraws from the family drama into a world of fantasy or books, the Internet, and computerized games. As the Lost Child, you find security in solitude and stay out of harm's way by being alone.

The Mascot

The Mascot is also often a younger or the youngest child, who manages fear and insecurity being cute, funny, or coquettish to release tension in the family.

Try to identify roles played by you and members of your family.

- ✔ Who were the over-functioners and the under-functioners? Which one were you?

- ✔ How did your role make you feel?

- ✔ What function did it serve in the family system?

- ✔ How did it affect your self-worth?

- ✔ What strengths did you derive your role?

- ✔ What did it deprive you of?

- ✔ Imitate another family role to see how it feels.

Chapter 8

Taking Stock of Who You Are

. . . .

In This Chapter

▶ Getting to know yourself

▶ Discerning the differences between your needs and wants

▶ Identifying your needs, wants, feelings, and values

▶ Being your authentic Self

. . . .

Codependents' sense of identity is impaired. They wonder "What's normal?" and "Who am I? They compare themselves to others, feel empty, and need someone else to feel incomplete. Discovering who you are is an ongoing process and the first step to wholeness.

Finding Yourself

Most codependents are so used to accommodating others' feelings, opinions, desires, and needs that they can't identify their own. You tuned them out because of your family's rules and denial, or even before you could speak — before you could recognize your instincts and biological and emotional impulses that are part of your sensory cues. (See Chapter 7.) This internal guidance system informs you about your needs and feelings, helps you make good decisions, and enables you to accurately assess other people and situations. Some of you may live your life disconnected from your body. The feedback loop from body to brain is not well connected, impairing your interpretation of information your body is telling you. Healing entails tuning into yourself and re-establishing this communication.

 Have you thought about what you like and dislike, about your beliefs and values, and taken the time to formulate what you really believe and think? Maybe you've been busy studying, working, raising a family, and pretty much going along with what your parents, friends, or partner want and believe. Others of you may know yourself better but are afraid to disappoint or disagree with people in your life. You decide that it's easier not to rock the boat and don't realize the high price you pay. Each time you do this, you abandon yourself, and your Self gets smaller and your voice gets weaker, like a candle about to die out. You may find yourself sleeping more, eating more, and losing interest in people and activities you used to enjoy. You've "de-pressed" all your natural vitality. Before you can expect to find happiness in a relationship, you must first discover how to make yourself happy. Your assignment is to become your own best friend.

Spending time with yourself

Getting to know someone and becoming friends require time together. The *real* you has been buried and may be shy and require patience and safety to venture out. You have to commit to spending more time alone to get acquainted with yourself and begin an inner dialogue. Later, when you're around others you can check in with yourself — that's harder because you may be tempted to get lost in someone else. You're beginning a journey of self-discovery.

Spending time with yourself doesn't mean reading or watching TV alone. (Even that may be difficult if you're in a relationship.) It means having NO distractions so that you can really focus on what's going on inside. It's harder if you have young children, but you can make it a priority. Making yourself a priority is new. It may feel unfamiliar and uncomfortable to be alone and quiet without distraction, but this is how you get to know yourself and discover rich and nourishing inner resources. Have no expectations about how well or how long you do this. Start with a few minutes at a time, and it will become easier. You're used to a lot of stress and anxiety, and it will take time to quiet down. Many breathing and meditation techniques are also helpful. (See Chapter 14.)

Building Self-awareness

Getting to know someone means learning their tastes, opinions, and feelings about things. Learning about yourself is just the same. Begin listening and watching, just as you may observe someone at work or school before you plan to spend time together. The following exercises help you gain self-knowledge.

Daily journaling

Buy a notebook to serve as a journal. Writing your feelings and thoughts in a journal helps you focus during your alone time. In your journal, write about how you feel every day, what you think, and what you want to do that day and in the future. Some people write whatever comes to mind when they first wake up or at the end of the day. If you can't start, begin a sentence with something like:

> ✔ "I have nothing to say . . ."
>
> ✔ "I don't want to do this, because . . ."
>
> ✔ "My mind is blank, and it feels like . . ."
>
> ✔ "Right now I'm feeling . . . because . . ."

Generally, when you think you have nothing more to write, keep going. You may have reached an awareness or feelings that you're blocking. You can begin jotting down your dreams from the night before and your feelings and associations about the images and people in them.

Self-awareness

Start paying attention to your conversations during the day. See if you can **listen** to yourself while someone is talking to you. Wonder about how you feel.

> ✔ How often do you agree when you don't know, or disagree, but go along to be polite?
>
> ✔ Do you listen when you don't want to?
>
> ✔ Do you talk to fill an uncomfortable silence? Notice what you feel.
>
> ✔ Do you ask questions instead of volunteering your thoughts and feelings?
>
> ✔ Do you deflect compliments?
>
> ✔ Do you apologize often?
>
> ✔ Do you out loud or silently blame or criticize yourself or others?

At the end of the day, write down all you recall, and think about how you present yourself to others. This should be done like research, **not** in order to judge yourself. Ask yourself:

> ✔ What do you know about yourself from your behavior?
>
> ✔ What did you really feel or think in interactions with others? If you don't know, think about it, and try to decide.
>
> ✔ Did you make a conscious decision not to reveal yourself or was it automatic?
>
> ✔ What stopped you from being real? What do you imagine would happen if you were?

The next step in getting to know someone is asking about him or her. Ask yourself what you feel like doing right now. Some of you won't be able to answer that. Don't be discouraged. Imagine yourself doing different things, notice what sensations or feelings are generated. Does one activity make you sigh in relief, bring a smile to your face, give you an excited, warm, or relaxed feeling? After you know what you want to do, **do it.** If you stop yourself, jot down the thoughts that stop you.

To get better acquainted, interview yourself. Start with simple questions, such as, "My favorite color is . . .," "My favorite foods are . . ." (You can break this down into fruits, vegetables, desserts, etc.), "My favorite movies are . . .," "My favorite subjects in school were . . .," and continue finding out about what you like and dislike in music, animals, fabrics, flowers, sports, hobbies, television shows, books, people, politicians, and so on.

Now you're ready to get more information. Draw five columns on a page (as shown in Table 8-1). In the first column, list topics, such as your job, buying a new car, this book, names of friends, co-workers, and family members. Then head the other columns "Like," "Dislike," "Why," and "Neutral." Ask yourself, "How do I feel about the topic" Answer what is it that makes you feel that way.

Table 8-1		Getting to Know You		
Topic	**Like**	**Dislike**	**Why**	**Neutral**
My job				
A new car				
This book				
My friends				
My co-workers				
My family				

You are formulating opinions and finding out about yourself and your feelings about your life. Dig deeper. Write a paragraph on each of the following questions:

- What gives me the most difficulty?
- What do I like most (and least) about myself and my body?
- What excites me the most?
- What was the most courageous thing I've done?

    ✔ What was the biggest risk I took? What did I learn from it?

    ✔ What nourishes me most?

    ✔ What did I do that made me the proudest?

    ✔ What was the biggest challenge I overcame? What did I learn?

    ✔ Who had the most influence on me?

    ✔ What kind of work do I enjoy the most?

    ✔ What was my most painful experience? Did I learn from it?

Listening to your body

Listening to your body will help reactivate the feedback system to your brain. There are athletes or dancers who know how to move and control their bodies, and whether it's doing what they want, but aren't aware of the internal emotional information it can provide. Some codependents have trouble accurately seeing their body and actually have distorted self-perceptions, often larger or thinner, or less attractive. Others don't pay much attention to their body.

Your body senses things of which you may not be aware. Try sitting quietly. Take slow breaths to relax. Bring your awareness into your belly or heart and notice what's going on. What sort of temperature, color, density, sounds, and movement do you notice? Relax until you receive feedback; then ask this area how you feel about an issue. Wait for a sensory response. Listen to your body with your ears rather than seeing with your eyes. You can also focus on an issue in your life and listen to your bodily sensations around it. You may get a word, a feeling, or an image. It may not be an emotion like anger or sadness but merely a physical sensation, often a vague and unformed precursor to emotion, like heaviness, lightheadedness, or nausea. You needn't be afraid. Something is trying to surface. Patience is important. Don't analyze or jump to conclusions. Just let the feelings and images speak to you. Try dialoguing with the sensation or image. Ask:

    ✔ "How long have you been there?"

    ✔ "What was happening when you started?"

    ✔ "What do I need to know about this?"

    ✔ "What is the worst thing about this issue?"

    ✔ "What do you need from me?"

Stand with your eyes closed and lean slightly forward then back. Imagine that leaning forward means "Yes," and backwards means "No." Now stand still and ask yourself a yes or no question. Close your eyes and see which way you sway. With practice, this can be a handy tool in making decisions.

Taking Inventory

Identifying your needs, wants, feelings, and values is a major step in building your self-esteem and honing the ability to care for yourself and live a happier, more fulfilling life.

Identifying your needs and wants

Codependents have problems identifying, expressing, and fulfilling their needs and wants. You may be very attuned to the needs and desires of others and are used to accommodating them instead of their own. Recovery means turning that around. It requires you to become responsible for yourself. (See Chapters 9 and 10 to read about taking responsibility for yourself and communicating what you need and want.) First, you have to find out what you need and want. This is an essential step in recovery, usually not addressed in Twelve Step programs.

My needs

Some people recognize wants but not their needs, or vice versa, and many get them confused. The reason it's important to have your needs satisfied is because you feel emotional pain when they're not. You may be in pain and not know why or which needs are not being met. After you identify your emotions and needs, you can then take responsibility for getting their needs met and feeling better. For example, if you're feeling sad, you may not realize you're lonely and have a need for social connection. Even if you do, many codependents isolate rather than reach out. After you know the problem and the solution, you can take action by calling a friend or planning social activities.

There are 20 needs listed in Chapter 5. In addition, more needs are listed under the eight categories in Table 8-2. Can you add to the list?

Table 8-2

Categories of Needs

Mental	Autonomy	Social	Emotional	Self-worth	Self-expression	Spiritual	Physical
Information	Independence	Family	Intimacy	Authenticity	Purpose	Contemplation	Rest
Awareness	Empowerment	Reciprocity	Acceptance	Honesty	Self-growth	Meditation	Shelter
Reflection	Solitude	Cooperation	Being understood	Self-respect	Goals	Reverence	Food
Clarity	Freedom	Justice	Safe to be yourself	Confidence		Order	Water
Discernment		Reliability	Affection			Gratitude	Air
Comprehension		Companionship	Support			Hope	Sex/Sensual Pleasure
		Communication	Caring			Faith	Health
		Connection	Enthusiasm				Medical check-ups
		Generosity	Grieving				Movement

When your needs are met, you feel happy, grateful, safe, loved, playful, alert, and calm. When they're not, you are sad, fearful, angry, tired, and lonely. Think about how you meet or don't meet your needs, and what you may do to start meeting your needs.

My wants

Your wants are expressions of your uniqueness. If they weren't mirrored in childhood (see Chapter 7), then you may have stopped wanting. Some parents give children material things, but they don't listen and nurture their children. Others shame their children for wanting something when they can't afford to or don't want to fulfill their children's needs or wants. They don't take responsibility and admit the truth. There are parents who give their children what they think they should have instead of what their children want. All of these painful experiences with wanting can result in the belief, "I shouldn't want." Rather than be shamed or disappointed, codependents shut down their desires. Many don't buy themselves what they want even though they can afford it. Others indulge themselves indiscriminately when they can't afford it in an attempt to fill an insatiable hunger for the love they've missed.

Assume you can do whatever you desire, regardless of physical, emotional, or financial limitations. Complete this sentence: "I really want to . . ." Be as wild and imaginative as you can. Have fun with this exercise and write as much detail as you can conjure up. One of your wants may become a goal.

Make a Want List of things you *can* do or get, such as:

- ✔ Get a haircut
- ✔ Go to the movies when the children are in school
- ✔ Join the choir
- ✔ Play basketball
- ✔ Take surfing lessons
- ✔ Go dancing
- ✔ Plant strawberries
- ✔ Buy a trampoline
- ✔ Learn Spanish

Start with the easiest and make it a goal to do each thing on your list. Listen to self-talk that dissuades you from doing what you want. Write them down and see if they remind you of parental messages. Then write arguments supporting your wants.

List things you *have to* do; then mark whether you also *want to* do it. Some *have to's* may be to meet essential needs, like grocery shopping, which is positive. Sometimes a "have to" is also a want. Can you change a *have to* into a *want?* State how. Table 8-3 is a sample list.

Table 8-3		Have To/Want To List
Activity	*Have to*	*Want to*
Work out at gym	X	Take a yoga class
Study for school exam	X	Study with friends
Buy gift for friend	X	X
Go to market	X	Go shopping at night
Return library book	X	X
Call mother often	X	Call once a week
Walk the dog	X	Dog walk with friend

Compare your Have To list with your Want To list. If you're not doing what you want, how much of your life is driven by what you think you have to do. Be aware that some obligations reflect deeper wants. "I have to go to the doctor" actually reflects a deeper desire to be healthy. Try integrating more wants into your life.

How do you feel?

Your feelings are your guide, and it's vital to pay attention and listen to them. They're part of your internal feedback system. Emotional awareness includes feeling them at the level at sensation, naming, and expressing them.

Many people generally say they don't know what they're feeling. You may have shut down and denied your feelings entirely (see Chapters 3 and 5) or feel something but can't name it. Perhaps you can name your emotions mentally but don't "feel" anything in your body. With practice, you can connect the dots.

Building your emotional vocabulary

Most feelings are variations or combinations of the following four basic emotions:

✔ Sad

✔ Glad

✔ Mad

✔ Fear

Guilt is a combination of anger and fear, and anxiety and irritation are milder forms of fear and anger, respectively. See how many feelings you can identify. Next time you have an emotion, feel into your body with it, using the self-awareness exercise described earlier in this chapter. Try to discriminate all the colorations of the emotion and accompanying sensations. Do you feel heat, trembling, skin crawling, or tightness? This will build your emotional database and ability to identify and communicate your feelings. You're learning what you missed and building body-mind memories that heal the feedback loop. When you have those same sensations in the future, you can to recognize the feeling.

Honoring your feelings

Even codependents who know what they feel or can identify a limited number of feelings often don't honor their feelings and don't share them, often to accommodate others. A common reframe is "What's wrong with me that I feel this way?" Rather than allow 10 minutes of letting your emotions flow, you may spend days judging and resisting feelings, becoming more unhappy and depressed. This is dishonoring yourself. Additionally, you may tell yourself that your feelings are unreasonable, weak, or dangerous. Although feelings aren't logical, they have a logic and intelligence of their own. Sometimes a feeling may seem irrational, but upon deeper inspection, there's a good reason for them. Try to feel the feeling that's under the surface.

Feelings aren't signs of weakness; they just are. Whatever you feel is legitimate, and you're entitled to feel it just because you do. The danger lies in ignoring feelings, which can lead to poor decisions and health problems. Although feelings without reason shouldn't control decisions, they often do when unacknowledged. Finally, honoring your feelings also means taking responsibility for them. No one makes you feel something — only you do.

Look at the list of your family rules and messages from Chapter 7 and see how they may have influenced your attitudes toward feelings. Many people adopt their parents' rules and beliefs without knowing it or ever questioning them. Take a survey and ask as many people as you can if they agree with your family's rules and beliefs. Find out other people's beliefs.

Make a list of new rules and beliefs for yourself. Here's a start:

- ✔ I have a right to my feelings.
- ✔ I don't have to defend them.
- ✔ All my feelings are okay, even anger and painful ones.
- ✔ No one can tell me what I "should" feel, even me.
- ✔ What I'm feeling will pass.
- ✔ My feelings have value and intelligence.
- ✔ Allowing myself to feel my emotions is healthy.

Allowing your feelings

Allowing your feelings means to go with them. Often clients ask, "Why should I feel (angry, hurt, sad), it won't change anything?" This is untrue. Honoring and allowing your feelings change you. Emotions ebb and flow. They pass, but resisting them makes them persist. If not expressed, they can get stuck in the body and cause more pain and problems in relationships. When you repress painful feelings, they can come out sideways, explode, and sabotage you. Good feelings, like enthusiasm and joy, shut down, too. You may even lose interest in sex or feel passionless

One reason codependents don't express their needs and feelings is because in the past they were shamed or ignored (the "why bother" argument). Don't assume all people will react the same way. Recovery involves discernment of who's trustworthy and not taking someone's reaction personally.

Try to open your heart to yourself. Put your hand on your chest, imagine your heart opening, and breathe. If you're angry, move, shout, stomp, growl, yell, pound. When you're done, write about it, and see if an action is required. (See Chapter 11 for healthy ways to express your feelings.)

Acting on your feelings is where reason comes in. Allow your feelings, think about expressing them and getting your needs met, and then take appropriate action. The consequence in turn will affect your feelings and tell you whether the action got the hoped-for result. This is how you learn from mistakes and successes.

Figure 8-1 shows the progression from a need to feelings, actions, and consequences, which generate new feelings. If you're unaware of your needs or feelings, your actions won't meet your needs, and more negative feelings are generated. The unmet need grows. When you meet your needs, you create positive feelings.

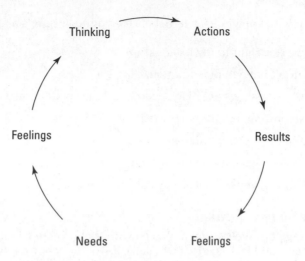

Figure 8-1: The cycle of needs and feelings.

Trusting yourself

If you grew up in a family where your feelings and perceptions were denied, you learned that you couldn't trust your internal cues — your observations, impressions, and feelings. As a result, your ability to trust your feelings and make decisions became impaired. By looking to others for answers, you give up living your own life. Additionally, if you're unable to discern situations and people that are dangerous or not good for you, you end up trusting untrustworthy people in relationships that damage you again, creating more distrust. Listening to yourself and honoring your feelings are the beginnings of trusting, loving, and protecting yourself.

Listen for that small voice you may have ignored in the past. Wait for it before making decisions. Notice what you think you "should" do versus what you want to do. Pay attention to how you feel when something feels "right, "off," or uncomfortable. This felt sense may be your first impression before you override it with logical reasons and ignore it, or it may require you to spend time in indecision and confusion or get more information about a situation or person in order to get clarity. That's okay. Don't rush. Also, be aware that your impressions and feelings change over time as you get to know someone.

In making decisions, ask yourself, "What would be the most loving thing to do?" and "How do I feel about it?" instead of, "What do I think about it?" Spend time with yourself deciding before asking others, and listen for your inner voice. It's especially important to wait when you're in an obsession or emotional reaction and feel compelled to act. (See Chapter 9.) If you receive others' suggestions, go inside again to see if it matches your internal cues. The more you do this, the more reliable and stronger that voice becomes, and you begin to trust yourself — your body, your choices, thoughts, and feelings — to make your life your own.

Listening to yourself is also the gateway to uncovering your passion (discussed in Chapter 17). Following your heart despite what others may say involves risk. Yet, this is how you build confidence. Only you can know what's right for you.

Your credo

Your credo is made up of your principles, concepts, and beliefs that govern your decisions and influence your feelings. You give more time and attention to the things you value most. Something that violates your values may make you angry or afraid. Being whole includes knowing what you stand for. This is part of your journey of self-discovery. It's important because when you accept others' behavior or behave contrary to your core beliefs, you undermine your integrity and self-esteem. *Integrity* means integration of your values, beliefs, and behavior — that you "walk your talk." Holding to your values despite opposition builds integrity and personal power. To identify your values, think about the following:

  ✔ What makes you the angriest about things in the world?

  ✔ Which organizations or charities do you, or would you, support?

  ✔ What mentors or public figures do you respect or admire? Why?

  ✔ Which religious beliefs do you agree and disagree with? Why?

  ✔ What are your political views?

  ✔ What book and movie genres do you most enjoy?

Choose ten of the following values, and rank them from 1-high to 10-low. You're influenced by the values of the nation, society, your family, culture, and religion. Think about which values you've adopted from others and which are your own?

Freedom	Religion	Health
Equality	Adventure	Achievement
Beauty	Charity	Easy lifestyle
Justice	Education	Service to others
Recognition	True love	Nature and planet
Friendship	Family	Truth
Wealth	Pleasure	Respect
Creativity	Harmony	Compassion

Now that you know your values, notice if your words and actions match your values. If not, re-evaluate your values and what influenced you to depart from them. If you did, how did it make you feel? One example may be if you spend most of your time doing things you don't value and not doing what you do.

Can You Just Be You?

Authenticity means being honest and genuine. It requires congruence or alignment between your words and actions, values, and motives. For this you must know yourself and gradually risk bringing the real you into the world by expressing and acting on what you know. This is a major part of overcoming codependency. People do this in therapy and in Twelve Step meetings when they risk revealing themselves and exposing their vulnerability instead of reacting.

You ranked your values, now make a list of virtues and qualities you want to have. Make a second list of qualities as you see yourself right now. How do they match up? Question yourself to see if your activities, goals, beliefs, and values are in alignment. Are you willing to be honest with qualities you dislike? This is a difficult, but a necessary step toward self-esteem and authenticity. Facing the truth is the beginning of change.

Your self-perception may be untrue if you're unable to discern the truth from labels given you in childhood.

The ongoing process of self-discovery challenges you to discover who you really are, to live from that truth, and to discard all of what isn't you, including those old, false beliefs.

Chapter 9

Nonattachment and Acceptance

· ·

In This Chapter

▶ Discerning the difference between codependent attachment and nonattachment

▶ Taking responsibility for yourself

▶ Understanding how fear and expectations underlie control

▶ Discovering the real reasons for reacting, worrying, and obsessing

▶ Appreciating the importance of acceptance

▶ Gaining tips and tools for nonattachment

· ·

Codependents become overly attached — not because they love so much but because they need so much. Attachment is based upon need — need for someone to be a certain way so that you can feel okay. This chapter is about changing your bad habits and erroneous beliefs that keep you reacting and attached in unhealthy ways. You can learn to enjoy your life despite another person's problems and behavior. Change begins with taking a look at codependent patterns of managing and controlling, reacting and worrying, and obsessing. They're all interconnected, but for the sake of discussion, this chapter addresses each separately.

Codependent Attachment and Nonattachment

It's normal and healthy to get attached to someone in your family or with whom you're intimate, but codependents' patterns of attaching cause them pain and problems. The antidote is nonattachment. Al-Anon and Co-Dependents Anonymous (CoDA) recommend "detaching." I prefer the *nonattachment,* which implies neutrality, because many people confuse detachment with physical or emotional withdrawal.

Codependent attachment

Codependent attachment is excessive. Instead of two people with separate minds and independent feelings, the boundaries between you and (call him or her "X") are blurred. You can spot it when:

- ✔ Your moods depend on X. You can't be happy if X isn't.
- ✔ You have strong emotional reactions to X's opinions, thoughts, feelings, and judgments.
- ✔ You worry and think about X's problems.
- ✔ You analyze X's motives or feelings.
- ✔ You ponder what X is doing, not doing, thinking, or feeling.
- ✔ Your attention to X prevents you from having time for or interest in your career, hobbies, activities, or friends.
- ✔ You only want to spend time with X and drop other activities if X disapproves or won't accompany you.
- ✔ You try to please X because you're afraid of rejection.
- ✔ You're anxious about doing things alone.

When you are codependently attached, you're myopic. Others are extensions of you and you of them. You try to control their opinions, feelings, and actions to get what you need and feel okay. You try to control them to avoid witnessing their suffering. You try to impress and please them, persuade them to agree with you, and react with hurt or anger when they want space.

Nonattachment

In the previous examples, if you're nonattached, rather than control others, you're compassionate and encourage them. Rather than manipulate others to like you, you're authentic. You have no need to argue or persuade others but are curious and respectful of differing points of view. You honor their need for space or silence, and meanwhile enjoy your time alone or with someone else. This may sound impossible, but the pay-off is rewarding. Nonattachment as used here differs from that in Buddhism. It involves three concepts:

1. Having appropriate boundaries
2. Accepting reality
3. Being in the present, not the past or future

Nonattachment is a way of separating the unhealthy emotional glue that keeps you fused in a codependent relationship. It involves letting go of your expectations and entanglements with other peoples' problems and affairs, of reacting to things they say and do, and of obsessing and worrying about things. You mind your own business. It doesn't take away your feelings and concern but channels them in a healthy manner. In practice, it's more compassionate and loving than codependent attachment.

Nonattachment doesn't mean neglecting family responsibilities or leaving someone. Physical proximity is irrelevant nonattachment, although physical space or separation may be useful as a means of centering yourself, but this is not what detaching means. In fact, some divorced couples are more emotionally attached and reactive to one another than most married couples. Someone living far away can push your buttons in a phone call, so that you dwell on the conversation for days.

Nor is nonattachment the same as being aloof, disinterested, emotionally shut down, or ignoring someone. When first practicing nonattachment, people often turn off their feelings or use walls of silence to refrain from codependent behavior, but with persistence, understanding, and compassion, they're able to let go with love.

Why let go of attachment?

Letting go reaps you profound benefits, not only in the relationship, but in personal growth, inner peace, and all areas of your life.

You learn to love

Being nonattached in a relationship is the most loving way to be present and practice unconditional love with someone. How is this paradox possible? When it comes to relationships, the underlying principle of nonattachment is honoring another person's separateness from a deeply felt place. Think of letting go as stepping back from your personal needs to see the larger picture. Imagine the reality that both you and the other person are two separate people with diverging needs, genetics, life experiences, and perspectives, both whole and capable. It takes time for this intellectual understanding to seep into your heart until nonattachment becomes a natural way of interacting. It's from this place of separateness that you can fully see yourself and others as the unique individuals that they are. This is honoring and loving them.

You gain peace, freedom, and power

Whatever or whomever you're reacting to or trying to fix or control, controls you. When you stop managing, judging, or helping someone else, your mind is free from worry. You're off the hook for their choices and the outcome of their problems. You're freer to be yourself, and you allow others to do so as well. When you take the further step of learning to let go of your reactions and are able to detach from other people's moods, actions, and words, you take back your power. Instead of a reactor, you become a self-determined actor in your life. You take charge of yourself and your thoughts and decide how you will act in that moment and every moment. You choose your behavior independently of others. This skyrockets your self-esteem. When off the emotional rollercoaster with someone else, your mind is at peace, regardless of how roiled up he or she is. You take back the power to control your mind, feelings, and self-esteem.

You gain time for yourself

When you let go of responsibility for someone else, you're no longer consumed with watching to see if he or she is meeting his or her responsibilities. You have that much more freedom and can live your life instead of living someone else's. This allows you to develop yourself, and your career, hobbies, interests, and friends.

Each person learns independence and self-responsibility

Nonattachment also allows both you and the other person to take responsibility for your own lives. Those whom you've been managing or controlling gain the opportunity to learn from their mistakes and to take responsibility for their choices. As a result, you both become more independent.

What Are Your Responsibilities?

It's natural to desire happiness for your loved ones and painful to see them suffer, but codependents make the leap of feeling responsible for others' pain and happiness. It's so upsetting that they try to change the negative feelings and solve the problems of people close to them. The fact is you can only heal your half of the relationship — yourself.

You're responsible for your thoughts, feelings, actions, and the consequences of those actions, and other people are responsible for theirs. (Chapter 3 discusses responsibility in relationships.) Taking responsibility isn't the same as blaming yourself. Codependents do too much of that already. The former is just an admission — an acknowledgement that "I said (or did)" something. Period! It doesn't make you a terrible person.

Cheering someone up occasionally or giving him or her more attention is not codependent. A benefit of a good marriage is that spouses nurture one another when one is troubled, but it's support, not codependent caretaking, and it's reciprocal. In contrast, when you consistently try to change others' moods or solve their problems, you're becoming their caretaker based upon the erroneous belief that you can control what's causing their pain. You're assuming responsibilities that are theirs, not yours. Sometimes codependent couples agree that one spouse has the obligation to make the other happy. This is an impossible task and leads to mutual unhappiness, anger, and resentment. The cheerleader is always failing. Whatever he or she tries won't be quite right or enough. If you assume responsibility for your partner's happiness, you're enabling his or her dependence, irresponsibility, and childish behavior and depriving him or her of the opportunity to grow-up and become independent. On the other hand, by taking responsibility to make yourself happy, you bring happiness to the relationship, and you're able to interact with your partner from an openhearted place.

Henry's wife was depressed. He loved her and tried everything to make her happy. Nothing helped for very long, and she continued to complain. Soon he was as resentful and as unhappy as she and had no love left to give. The unconscious bargain was that his wife be dependent, irresponsible, and needy, and Henry remain dependent, dutiful, and needless, ensuring she wouldn't leave him.

Another pitfall for codependents is that they take too much responsibility and blame for the problems in their relationship. They try to change themselves (the human pretzel solution) in order to make the relationship work. The belief is, "If I caused the problem, then I can learn what I did wrong, change myself, and then the problem will go away." This denies that each person in a relationship is responsible for his or her own feelings and actions.

✔ List the things for which you feel responsible. Include family and work responsibilities. Distinguish between responsibility to others and responsibility for others. What's the difference?

✔ List each responsibility you assume for others who can manage that responsibility. If the person is a child or teenager, is he or she old enough to take over that responsibility or learn to take it over? Talk to those individuals about assuming responsibility for themselves. (Shared responsibilities, errands, and chores aren't problems — unless there's imbalance and you resent it.)

✔ Review your list of needs from Chapter 8. For each one, write actions you can take to be responsible for meeting your needs.

✔ Create a plan to make time to meet your responsibilities and needs and let others manage their own lives.

Managing and Controlling

Managing and controlling behaviors, which include caretaking and enabling, violate others' boundaries. Managing someone's life shows disrespect. It sends the message that the person is incompetent and needs your help. Underneath are your fear and expectations about that person's life, as shown in Figure 9-1.

I'm uncomfortable so you have to change. What you do might hurt me, so I have to watch and control you. I'm responsible for you and have to make sure you make no mistakes (according to me), because you can't take care of yourself (according to me) without my help.

Figure 9-1: Knowing what's best.

In reality, you can't know what's best for someone else, given his or her individual background, experiences, and desires. Managing can start with little things, like giving advice on your husband's clothes, your teenager's diet, or your girlfriend's romance. Attempts to change, control, and give unwanted advice are codependent patterns that undermine the others' self-esteem. Perhaps you lend a sympathetic ear to their problems and suggest solutions. Soon, you end up in the role of fixer, counselor, or cheerleader and become increasingly entangled in their choices and upset that their behavior doesn't meet your expectations. You begin to watch their every move to see if they are doing the "right" thing. If you're wondering if you're managing, controlling, or enabling, here are some signs:

- ✔ You judge, advise, or nag to change X's behavior or beliefs.

- ✔ You repeat prodding questions.

- ✔ You follow, pry, or try to get information about X.

- ✔ You repeatedly do things for X that X is capable of doing.

- ✔ You enable X (defined in see Chapter 3).

- ✔ You do things for X that you don't really want to do.

✔ You meet X's needs or offer help without being asked or before there's any agreement about it.

✔ You do more than your share or give more than you receive in relationships.

✔ You try to fix X's bad feelings.

✔ You do X's thinking for him or her.

✔ You solve X's problems.

✔ You speak for X.

When it comes to children, teaching is different than control, which breeds resentment and rebellion. You naturally exercise appropriate authority over young children, but as they mature, good parents relinquish age-appropriate decisions and tasks to their children. Some parents control and enable their children too much, who then as adults they don't know how to be responsible for themselves.

Fear underlies control

Controlling behavior is based upon dependence and fear of the consequences that others' behavior has on them and on you. In a new relationship, you're accepting of, and maybe attracted to, differences in someone else, but as you get attached and don't want to leave the relationship, those differences may disturb you when you imagine how they may affect you in the future. You begin to have expectations and start making suggestions or comments with an eye toward changing the other person. As your lives become intertwined, there's greater attachment and dependence upon one another and greater fear of the impact the other person's actions will have on you. The urge to control accelerates when you see someone close to you behaving in a self-destructive manner. Your concern makes you try to help and control them that much more. Even if your advice is good, giving it is usually counterproductive.

What if you were asked to help?

This is a good and difficult question. The answer is, it depends. You may think, "I'm not interfering, controlling, or crossing a boundary if I'm invited to help." That's not necessarily true. Consider the following:

✔ You still may be interfering with the person's opportunity to find strength, problem-solve, and be more independent. Does it frighten you that you won't be needed?

✔ Once you start, you may fall into a pattern of taking over and controlling. You may want to get follow-ups and monitor the person's behavior and the outcome. Can you help and let go?

✔ If you have a history of helping the person and it's not reciprocated, you've assumed the Top Dog fixer role, becoming responsible for Underdog in a relationship that's out of balance.

✔ Are you reinforcing your controlling and caretaking habits?

✔ How may you offer support without caretaking?

A wiser loving course would be to listen to the person's own ideas and offer encouragement and support, letting him or her know you have confidence in his or her ability to handle the matter and that he or she knows more about it than you. Read about caretaking verses caregiving in Chapter 2.

Write about the following:

✔ Whom and what do you try to control, fix, or manage?

✔ Specifically, how do you attempt this?

✔ What are your motives in the situation?

✔ Do you feel any resentment or self-pity about helping?

✔ Are you "sacrificing" or taking care of your own needs?

✔ Does helping make you anxious, frustrated, or tired?

✔ Would you feel too guilty to say "No?"

✔ Do you think that you know what's best for the person?

✔ What's your worst fear if you stopped?

✔ How would you feel if you stopped?

✔ How do you feel when someone tries to change or control you?

✔ Are you able to listen to problems without offering advice?

✔ How would it feel to ask for help or emotional support?

✔ Do you give advice that isn't followed? How do you think it makes the other person feel? How does that make you feel?

✔ Do you ever feel used or unappreciated?

✔ When you do something for someone he or she can do, how does it make you feel about you and about the other person?

Expectations plant seeds of resentment

Having expectations is a prescription for pain. They create problems in relationships when you have an agenda about the kind of person you want your partner to become and how he or she should behave. They cause you disappointment and plant seeds of judgments, which grow into resentments. They spread like wildfire and burn any good feelings you have toward the person. No one likes to be judged, including you. If you have a cat, you don't expect your cat to act like a dog. You wouldn't expect a cat to swim and take a hike with you. If you do, you're going to make both you and your cat very miserable. Soon, you'd become furious and begin to hate your cat. Now, when you expect someone close to you to behave in a way that he or she doesn't want to or that's against his or her nature, you both end up resentful.

Jeremy was an organized accountant and found it intolerable that his artist wife, Kaitlin, was messy. He'd initially been attracted to her carefree spirit, but he didn't focus on how disorganized she was. First, he judged that she didn't hang up her clothes and that she had magazines and clippings on all of the tables and counter-tops. Everywhere he looked, he found more evidence of her flaws, until he was consumed with animosity. He cleaned up after her and complained, and she resented him and made little effort to change. To preserve his sanity and the relationship, Jeremy began practicing nonattachment and reminded himself of why he loved his wife. Although he didn't like the mess, it didn't bother him as much. He learned to accept his wife. He was no longer angry. They decided to hire a maid, which helped and encouraged Kaitlin to be neater.

Maybe you have a preconception of how your relationship should evolve or what marriage should look like — perhaps the way your parents behaved or the opposite, or what you imagine. This can create expectations in your mind that set you up for disappointment.

Janet's father always took care of her mother's automobile. When Janet got married, her husband Daniel assumed Janet would take care of her car. She resented her husband's lack of help, which she believed was a man's job, but never talked about it. She knew nothing about oil changes and almost ruined her car's engine by not getting them. Finally, she asked Daniel if he'd take care of her car's maintenance. "Why should I? It's your car," was his answer. Daniel had expectations, too — that Janet pick up and wash his dirty clothes, but Janet immediately refused. By talking about it, they each let go of their expectations and rules that their parents lived by.

Are your expectations unreasonable?

Your expectations may be reasonable and even desirable in general, but *unreasonable with respect to a particular person*. To determine whether they're reasonable, consider the facts of whether the person is capable and willing to meet them. How have your expectations turned out in the past? Were they met? What does this tell you about the other person and about yourself?

Look objectively at your relationship, and ask yourself what you've said and done to achieve your expectations and what has the other person said and done. Consider your motives and whether you've clearly communicated your desires without resentment, blame, or criticism. Don't expect someone to read your mind. That's an unreasonable expectation! Make sure you courteously ask for what you want. If you've asked someone repeatedly to make a change and he or she doesn't, it's unreasonable that more requests, manipulation, or nagging will make a difference.

Are you in reality?

If you notice that you have fantasies about your relationship or how you'd like your partner to behave, there's a good chance that you're denying your unhappiness in the present and are escaping into the future. (Read Chapter 5 to determine if you're in denial.) Consider which of your needs aren't being met now. Are you avoiding taking responsibility for your own happiness? Have you discussed your dissatisfaction with your partner and listened to his or her views? Don't argue, but listen because this is the reality.

What about reasonable expectations?

It's reasonable that each person contribute to a relationship and meet his or her own responsibilities. It's reasonable to be treated with respect and integrity, and it's actually a good idea to have expectations before you make commit to someone. Dating is an opportunity to evaluate whether the person is a suitable match. Is he or she a cat or a dog? Are you compatible? Can you live with the person's habits and shortcomings, as you see them? If you go into a relationship expecting someone to change, you're asking for trouble.

Nonattachment doesn't mean that you should accept abuse or behavior that goes against your values. Being responsible for yourself also means that you don't allow someone to treat you badly. You may need to have a frank conversation to resolve your conflicts and set boundaries if you're being abused. (See Chapter 11.) When you try to control your partner by pleasing or manipulation, you get more of the behavior you don't want. If neither approach is effective, think about why you want to continue the relationship and consider joining a support group and obtaining professional help. (See Chapter 18.)

When it comes to addiction

It's unreasonable to expect an addict not to practice his or her addiction. Acting surprised, disappointed, angry, or hurt that an alcoholic gets drunk is like being upset that the sun rises. Although it's painful to see someone you love hurting him- or herself, your expectations cause you more pain. If you've been trying to stop or control someone's addiction, you probably feel like Sisyphus in Figure 9-2 pushing a bolder uphill. Just when you think you're making progress, you have to start over again.

Figure 9-2: Do you feel like Sisyphus?

Nothing you say makes any permanent difference. You come to realize that your words and enabling actions are futile, and only breed
resistance. In fact, stopping addictive behavior is so difficult for
addicts that anyone attempting to influence them distracts them
from the problem of their addiction. You become the obstacle in
their mind. Controlling and enabling actually prolong an addiction.
(You can learn more about enabling in Chapter 3.) Addicts and abusers love to blame their behavior on someone else. They try to make
you responsible for their actions and addiction, which are abso-
lutely not your responsibility, and you can tell them so. Assuming
responsibility for them enables their addiction and keeps denial in
place so they don't have to be responsible for their actions.

It may be difficult to change your behavior and practice nonattachment. Before you can let go of control, you need to accept
that you're powerless over other people. Nonattachment respects
the addicts' choice to practice their addiction even though it's
self-destructive and even if you disagree with it. After you get out

of the way and stop controlling and/or enabling and protecting an addict from the truth, you prepare yourself to set boundaries. (Chapter 11 can help you find ways to set boundaries.) This allows the other person to experience the consequences of his or her addiction and take responsibility for his or her actions.

I experienced this firsthand. I began practicing nonattachment with an alcoholic and stopped reacting to his drinking. My entire attitude began to change. He noticed and remarked, "You're being so nice that I can't blame you for my drinking. It's making me look at myself." Nonattachment works!

Ask yourself:

- ✔ Do you believe you're powerless over people?
- ✔ Do you feel responsible for someone's addictive behavior?
- ✔ Do you believe you can convince him or her to stop it?

Getting Triggered and Reacting

Even when you're not controlling, it's easy to react and over-react to people and events. Codependents react to others' needs, feelings, judgments, behavior, and desires. Your thinking and feeling become based upon what's going on inside someone else. There are reactions and over-reactions, signaled by their intensity and duration. How upset are you and for how long in proportion to what triggered you? What you over-react to — your *"triggers"* — are unique to you. You're reminded of a painful interaction you've had with someone in your past, that you re-experience it in the present. In some cases the trigger may be innocuous. Common signs of being triggered are when your reaction is disproportionate to the incident. For example, someone cuts in line at the market and you blow up, you get very anxious when someone is 10 minutes late, or you hear something different than what was actually said.

Some people catastrophize everything. They over-react and make mountains out of molehills about whatever doesn't go their way. They're constantly overwhelmed and anxious, reliving the drama of their childhood. Others feel compelled to react by taking action and doing something about whatever arises in order to quell their inner emotions. Unfortunately, because the action is not thought through completely, it often makes matters worse. They need to learn to, *"Don't just do something; sit there!"*

In reactions, sometimes anger, compliance, or withdrawal cover up real hurt or vulnerability, blame covers up guilt, and self-blame covers up anger. Reactions both large and small steal you from your Self. With intact boundaries, you'd be able to see that the other person's actions and point-of-view are not a reflection on you, but express his or her unique perspective, experience, needs, and feelings. There'd be no need to react, only to listen and respond. You wouldn't blame or withdraw or be angry because your partner is and you wouldn't stop speaking just because he or she isn't speaking to you. When your Self is more whole and your self-esteem is higher, you can tolerate differing opinions and even negative feelings about you. (See Chapter 10.) You'd listen to your own feelings, think about the comment and decide for yourself whether you agree, and if so, determine whether you want to make some changes. You may communicate your thoughts or feelings about what was said by responding authentically, but that's different from an automatic knee-jerk reaction, which is *not* being real.

How you react is based upon your personality, culture, and prior experience. People react in many ways:

- Blamers ("It's your fault.")

- Placaters ("Whatever you say.")

- Apologizers ("I'm sorry you feel that way.")

- Distracters (Acting irrelevant, e.g., combing hair or joking)

- Seducers (Kiss and make up.)

- Computer style ("We were only 17 minutes, 20 seconds late.")

- Withdrawers ("I don't want to talk about it.")

- Attackers ("You lousy_*!#%!")

- Professorial ("My opinion is evidenced-based.")

- Martyr ("I can't do anything right.")

Arguments escalate when you react in one of the above styles. Blurred boundaries prevent you from really seeing each other. Instead, you're fighting battles that happened long ago in your childhood. When you stop reacting, you're able to respond and communicate assertively. (Check out Chapters 11 and 13 to learn how to effectively express yourself and heal past trauma.)

Randall asked his girlfriend to call more often and make him dinner, which he said would make him feel loved. She became very angry. She over-reacted because she heard his request as a demand — what she'd been used to from her father. As she worked on that relationship, she saw that she could choose whether she wanted to satisfy Randall, that doing so assured her of getting more of her needs met and that she could make her own requests of him.

Marcia was a nurse and was suffering burn-out from working long hours. Between shifts, she expected her boyfriend to give her attention and complained that she felt ignored. He wanted to please her but was also busy with work and began reacting to her phone calls by retreating in defiance. When Marcia recalled her yearning to spend time with her father after her parents divorced, she realized that her expectations of her boyfriend were unreasonable, and his withdrawal triggered her even more. When he saw that Marcia wasn't like his critical mother, he stopped reacting. He could both set boundaries and get closer to Marcia, who was able to take responsibility for her own self-care and set boundaries at work.

It's easy to react to the words and actions of someone intoxicated with anger, drugs, or alcohol, but your feelings and words won't be considered and possibly not even remembered. You may be upset long after the other person has returned to "normal." Imagine that someone is throwing you a ball of fire — his or her negativity. This is an attempt to shift responsibility for his or her using or drinking, bad moods, or other behavior. Attack and blame avoid self-examination. You can play that game in Figure 9-3 or drop the ball.

Figure 9-3: Choose not to play.

By catching the ball, someone sends you his or her pain. If you toss it back, your hands remain burned, and the flames build with each toss. You can always opt not to play. Answer these questions:

✔ Who triggers you?

✔ What behaviors trigger you?

✔ Write about each trigger and the feelings you experience.

✔ How do you react? Do you always react in the same way?

✔ What happens to the other person? Does he or she react back?

✔ Do your reactions help the situation?

✔ What past persons, events, and feelings do they remind you of?

✔ Try reacting differently and answer the above questions again.

Worrying and Obsessing

Have you noticed that worrying about what may come to pass or obsessing about a person is an attempt to control — even if only in your mind? Unfortunately, many people equate love and worry and would feel guilty not worrying, even though it causes stress and is counterproductive. Moreover, the worry you imagine generally doesn't arrive or at least not in the same way. Even if it does, worrying didn't change the outcome. Nor does it effectively prepare you to handle problems when they do arise, such as acquiring information and support and centering yourself with prayer and relaxation. Instead, worry and obsession drain you. They can also make you react in rehearsed or habitual ways that are inappropriate to the actual circumstances because worrying and obsessing take you out of the present. Nonattachment helps you to be more present and loving to yourself and others. Being in the here and now is the first step in finding solutions to all problems.

Acceptance in Baby Steps

Acceptance is a process. It doesn't happen in a day, a week, or a month but takes effort and proceeds in baby steps and missteps. As explained in Chapter 6, change starts with awareness. Notice whether your behavior and thoughts are achieving the results you want. Next, practice nonattachment using the ideas in the Tools section later in this chapter. These suggestions can help you develop an attitude of acceptance, which promotes nonattachment.

Facing powerlessness

If what you're doing works, by all means continue; but if your reactions and efforts to control and fix haven't helped, consider that you may be powerless to change another person or situation. It's hard enough to change yourself, even with considerable effort. Powerlessness doesn't mean that you're helpless. There are a multitude of actions — even inactions — that are more effective to deal with problems and create more peace, clarity, and a sense of control than reacting and fruitless efforts. More importantly, you reclaim your power over your mind and will.

✔ List all of the people and things over which you're powerless.

✔ List the things you've tried in attempting to change someone.

✔ Write your feelings about others' reactions to you.

✔ What feelings and beliefs prevent you from letting go?

Understanding acceptance

Acceptance is an acknowledgement of what is. There's a lot of confusion about what acceptance means.

✔ It's not resignation, which suggests a passive stance that emanates from hopelessness. Acceptance is a positive step toward taking charge of your life and responsibilities.

✔ It doesn't mean you approve of the facts. Rather acceptance is an acknowledgement that those facts exist — like them or not.

✔ It doesn't mean that you must accept abusive or unacceptable behavior. This is a common misconception. The fact is many people aren't aware that they're being abused and don't acknowledge it as such. Consequently, they don't confront it. With acceptance, you're able to change your behavior, seek safety and support, and set boundaries.

Why acceptance is important

Before you can choose to act differently, you must accept the world on its terms, and then consider your options. The alternative to acceptance is an eternal war with reality. It's a losing battle. In relationships, it places you in a disempowered position of being a victim and fixating on someone who is neither your responsibility, nor in your capacity to change. By being in opposition to what is, you're in a constant state of turmoil within yourself and in conflict with the person whom you're trying to control. It's a choice of having a mind at war or at peace.

There are deeper and deeper levels of acceptance. First you come to terms with the fact that you're powerless over others, that you're contributing to the problem, and then that *you* are the one who must make changes. Acceptance is a central empowering step that follows awareness and is a precursor to appropriate and effective action.

Acceptance of someone's addiction

It's important to realize that the addict didn't choose to become addicted. It's not a moral issue. Nothing you did caused it, nor can you control or change it. It doesn't mean that the addict is a bad person or doesn't love you. Addiction and codependency are considered diseases. Would you try to change someone's behavior associated with diseases like tuberculosis or diabetes? Would you blame the person, or have compassion and learn all you could about the disease and how to best deal with it?

Facing the fact that someone you love has a chronic, life-threatening disease is frightening and painful, which is why denial is so strong. Unfortunately, many people, including addicts, moralize addiction, creating an additional obstacle to acceptance and treatment that prolongs denial and perpetuates self-destructive behavior.

Tools for Practicing Nonattachment

If you believe you're codependent and recognize behaviors that you'd like to let go of, then you're ready to take action. Practicing nonattachment over time helps you gain acceptance. Support is essential. Additionally, the following tools can be very helpful. The more you utilize them, the easier nonattachment becomes.

Focus on yourself

It's hard to stop a thought or a habit without replacing it with a new one. If you get interested in your own life, you won't have time or energy to focus on someone else. Develop hobbies and goals that nurture and stimulate you. (See Chapters 14 and 17.) Doing so raises your self-esteem and separates it from someone else's actions.

Re-mind mantras

A *mantra* is a word or phrase that's repeated. Reminding yourself of these can change your thoughts, your attitude, and your behavior.

Live and let live

This is my favorite saying. Its meaning is very powerful. When you give yourself permission to do what you want, then you're able to give others that freedom. It defines correct boundaries. You're the only one over whom you have power, and only you are responsible for yourself. You discover that your actions create your happiness.

The four don'ts

Here are four don'ts to remind you not to focus on, have expectations of, judge, or spend your time thinking about others.

1. Don't watch.

2. Don't expect.

3. Don't judge.

4. Don't obsess.

Mind your own business

This is another reminder to focus on yourself when you're tempted to give advice or solve someone's problem. Ask yourself whether you've had the same experience with the exact circumstances facing the person you'd like to help, and further, whether you share the same desires, feelings, and concerns.

Let go and let God

You needn't believe in God or a higher power to let go, but if you do, it can be extremely helpful to put your concerns in God's hands, and allow God's will rather than your own to work out your problems. Imagine placing a person in God's hands. Encircle him or her in white light. Remind yourself that God knows what this person needs and let go. You can also surround the person in light and release him or her, whether or not you believe in God.

The three Cs

When it comes to someone else's addiction, the Al-Anon three Cs are helpful.

1. You didn't **C**ause it.

2. You can't **C**ontrol it.

3. You can't **C**ure it.

Prayer

Praying for the welfare of yourself and those you love can console your fears and fill the void left when you let go of helping and controlling. The Serenity Prayer is a prayer of acceptance and the perfect antidote for controlling behavior. (If you have difficulty with the word "serenity," try substituting the word "willingness.")

"God grant me the serenity to accept the things I cannot change, the courage to change the things I can, and the wisdom to know the difference."

Meditation and mindfulness

Meditation provides you many benefits. (See Chapter 14 for meditation tips.) It helps you to stay in the present when your mind wanders into obsessions about other people, the land of past hurts and resentments, or the dangerous territory of "What If's." Focus on sensations in the moment — what you see, what you touch, what you hear. Bring your awareness to the task at hand, like washing dishes or driving your car. By developing an ability to calm yourself and quiet your mind, you become more centered and less reactive to people and events. Meditation also builds self-awareness permitting you to think before you speak or act from your old habits. You're able to pause and choose your responses in conversations.

Time-outs

Time-outs are a great way to de-escalate arguments, emotional overwhelm, and obsessions. You may need to withdraw from what or who is triggering you. A change of scene, particularly if your attention is placed on something else, calms your emotions. If you're triggered by someone, you can explain that you need a little time to calm yourself and that you'd like to continue the conversation later (say when). A time-out can also be as short as taking five to ten slow breaths before you respond.

Journaling

Writing is especially useful when you've been triggered by someone. It can center you, allow you to vent, and help you discover the original source of your trigger. Write your current feelings, and let them take you to times when you've felt the same in the past.

Doing the opposite

Try new behavior. If you often argue, be silent instead. If you're usually silent, speak up. If you're always serious, tell a joke. It may surprise people close to you and even yourself. One man always argued with his verbally abusive, alcoholic wife. He got into the habit of saying, "Isn't it amazing that we still love each other." She was shocked. It made her smile, and she became affectionate.

Doing the opposite can also mean using a different part of your brain. Instead of obsessing, take a positive action toward solving the solution, which may be as simple as getting more information. When you're obsessing about a person, shift to your emotions to release pent-up feelings. You can also, "Lose your mind and come to your senses." Do something physical. Take a walk, put on music, sing, dance, make a meal, play a sport or with a pet, or do anything that changes your mental state. Passive activities, like movies or television, may not engage you enough to shift you for very long.

If you feel compelled to act, wait. Ask yourself what would be the consequence of waiting another day. Doing that every day may reveal that you needn't act at all. If it's a decision, can you postpone it? If postponing a decision is creating more problems, try getting more information and taking baby steps toward the solution.

Acting as if

This tip is basically, "Fake it 'til you make it." It's common for people to hide their feelings in certain situations — like at work. Many codependents do this in personal relationships far too much. Yet others are quick to react to someone's words with hurt, anger, or defensiveness. If that's you, try "acting as if" the remark didn't bother you. After a while, you may discover that by doing so, you aren't bothered and aren't taking others' words personally.

Removing labels

This is a great way to reduce expectations in close Relationships. Next time you're reacting, imagine how you'd feel if your partner were just a friend. Are you more judgmental of your spouse than your friends? Why not be as forgiving of your mate? This trick can apply to other family members as well. What would it be like to treat your family the way you treat your friends, or expect family to treat you like your friends do? What's the difference?

Visualizing

It's been proven that visualization is a powerful learning tool for new behavior. Mental rehearsals are nearly as effective as actual physical ones. Visualize yourself practicing nonattachment. See yourself being calm, centered, and confident, and not reacting to your partner's anger, addiction, or other words and behavior. Imagine what you may say or do. Picture how your life may be different by practicing nonattachment.

Having a Plan B

This is especially useful if your partner is unreliable — typically the case with addicts. Always have a Plan B, so you're never left in the lurch. In most situations, you can visit a friend, go alone to the movie, theater, or party, or go to a Twelve Step meeting. Even if you stay at home, instead of feeling angry and sorry for yourself, use the time to enjoy a hobby, catch-up on reading, or make a special meal. Take charge of your life, rather than feel like a victim.

What to Expect

If you're out of your comfort zone, you're changing. When you rock the boat, others are uncomfortable, too. Here's what to expect.

From you

Expect to feel guilty when you don't help others as you have in the past. It may be very difficult to change this pattern. Yet it's easier when you realize that your help isn't helping, but hurting in the long run. At other times, you have glimpses of feeling centered, peaceful, free, and empowered. Serenity and freedom need some getting used to when you're accustomed to feeling trapped and anxious.

Letting go of all the mental and physical activity of trying to control, help, and manipulate others leaves a void, which may be accompanied by feelings of emptiness, boredom, anger, depression, and fear. It's also a loss — loss of your role and illusions of control and expectations about someone else and the relationship. Additionally, it can be overwhelming to realize you or someone you love has a life-threatening addiction over which you're powerless. You may find yourself grieving the addict's death, the possibility of which you haven't faced. (See Chapter 13 for stages of grief.)

These transitional feelings diminish over time, as nonattachment and peace become more comfortable. You begin to feel freer and empowered. When you are more accepting of yourself and others, you become softer and more cheerful, open, and patient. If you have children, you're less irritable and more present and nurturing.

From others

Expect others not to like your changes. The Underdog may try to make you feel guilty and manipulate you into helping and caretaking.

Relatives and others may accuse you of not caring or being selfish or self-centered. They won't understand what you're trying to do and may want you to return to your old ways, which are familiar to them. They also may want you to take care of Underdog for their peace of mind or so they don't have to. This is another reason why a support group is very important.

Conversely, Underdog is pleased that you are no longer overseeing, judging or trying to control. He or she is impressed by your new cheerful mood and may begin to look at him- or herself rather than blame you. This leads to more peace in your home.

Chapter 10

Learning to Value Yourself

In This Chapter

▶ Meeting the Critic, Pusher, and Perfectionist and finding out how to work with them

▶ Building self-esteem through self-responsibility, honesty, and keeping commitments

▶ Identifying your assets and acknowledging yourself

▶ Letting go of guilt

▶ Discovering the elements of self-acceptance and self-love

*I*magine your self-esteem as a neglected garden, overgrown with sprawling weeds that invaded what was once natural and beautiful. The seeds of those weeds blew into your childhood and have taken over your psyche in the guises of a *Critic*, a *Pusher*, and a *Perfectionist*. To heal and regenerate your garden, you must pull the weeds, prepare and fertilize the soil, and sow new seeds. Your garden also needs sunlight and water for nourishment and regular hoeing to prevent weeds from returning. Chapter 3 explained that when it comes to self-esteem, it's what you think that counts. This chapter takes a closer look at your thinking and provides techniques for pulling the weeds of your self-destructive thoughts and behaviors that undermine your self-esteem. It suggests how you can plant the seeds of positive self-worth, self-acceptance, and self-love.

The Tyrannical Trio — the Critic, Pusher, and Perfectionist

Before pulling weeds, you must be able to identify them. They're hiding in plain sight — your inner dialogue. The Critic is the voice that judges you and criticizes you and what you say and do. The Critic is never satisfied, nor thinks you're good enough. The Pusher chimes in and pushes you to perform and improve yourself to meet the Perfectionist's illusory standards. The three work together — although they sound like one voice — your own.

Most people are not aware that these inner mandates run their lives. Without more awareness, this terrible trio tyrannizes you and limits, rather than promotes, your creativity and productivity. Becoming conscious of your negative self-talk is one way to loosen their pernicious control.

Taming the Critic

Everyone has an inner judge, a Critic who points out mistakes and shortcomings. What should be a healthy conscience can turn into daily self-criticism and majorly contribute to low self-esteem. The Critic undermines confidence and happiness and makes you feel insecure, inadequate, or vaguely not enough. If you're rarely content, have trouble pursuing goals, or if you're in an abusive relationship, your Critic is probably working overtime. It judges others, too, and can isolate you, but by far, it's harshest on you. It's your own worst enemy. Although it may have good intentions and try to protect you from hurt or failure, in some people it's a relentless faultfinder. In others, it's filled with contempt and squelches their joy. Your Critic can make you depressed, ill, and ruin your life.

To overcome self-criticism, you must tame your Critic by first shining a spotlight on it and recognizing its voice. Try the following exercises to chase it out of hiding:

- ✔ Sit quietly and notice your thoughts. You may hear yourself saying, "I can't do this. I'm not good at it." Listen to that string of putdowns!

- ✔ Make a list of all the things you don't like about yourself in each area of your life. To help you, complete the sentence, "I don't like myself when I . . ." Listen for criticisms as they pop up during the day and add to the list. Be alert when you talk to yourself using the words "should," "always," or "never," your Critic is at work.

- ✔ If you're feeling bored, frustrated, down, or having uncomfortable emotions, they may be symptoms of negative thinking. Trace back to a preceding event and thoughts you had about it and about yourself.

- ✔ Notice your Critic's voice — the tone, volume, and words. Do they remind you of someone who spoke to you that way in the past? Children emulate their parents' words and tones and internalize them.

When you discover how active the Critic is in your life, you can begin to make friends with it and tame it to become a friendly coach. Instead of being against you, transform it to be for you.

✔ Dialogue with the Critic on paper, writing questions with your dominant hand (usually the right) and answering with your non-dominant hand. Discover the Critic's name, function, role models, and motives. How does it really feel about you? (Your non-dominant hand has greater access to your unconscious.)

✔ No matter how mean the Critic is, be respectful. You're making friends. Ask it how it would like to improve your flaws, and specifically its motives and desires with respect to each. You may discover that the Critic has good intentions.

✔ Teach the Critic to be friendlier. Instead of putdowns, let the Critic know that it would be more effective to be a supportive coach, to speak to you in a cheerful, encouraging tone. Write examples of how you want your Critic to talk to you. See what the Critic says about this. You may need to insist that name-calling is off-limits.

✔ You must be vigilant in interrupting and taming your Critic, just as if you're taming an unruly dog. Each time the Critic starts in, tell it "Stop," and remind it how you'd like to be spoken to. If it slips one by you, old habits are reinforced.

When you become aware of the Critic, it's common to develop a Super Critic who criticizes you for being self-critical. Don't fall prey to this sneaky tactic of the Critic, trying to be helpful with more criticism. Tell it to "Stop!"

The Pusher — your slave driver

The Pusher pushes you into action to get things done. It likes to be busy. The problem is it can become a slave driver. The Pusher is always looking for ways to improve you, your partner, your environment, and your work. There's always too much to do in too little time. You can be resting or trying to relax, but the Pusher's call to action reminds you of a dozen undone things. It may even get you off the couch. The Critic teams up with the Pusher to make you feel guilty for all you haven't done and finds flaws the Pusher can correct. If the Critic thinks you're fat and need to exercise, the Pusher gets you into action, and together with the Critic harasses you for not doing enough to lose more weight faster. A strong Pusher won't let you miss work when you're sick or take a vacation without bringing work along to "catch up." Yet, you never catch up because the Pusher would be out of a job. If you're injured or physically limited in some way, the Pusher and Critic make you miserable for not getting things done. On the bright side, a Pusher can help you achieve your goals, but there are always more. It can hound you so that you never stop long enough to enjoy your successes, and it can lead to stress-related illnesses if you're unable to rein it in. Your Pusher must learn to let things go and do less so you can become a human being, rather than a "human doing." (Chapter 14 provides tips on relaxing.) To increase awareness of the Pusher, try this:

Make a list of all you need to get done. Include things in every area of your life, from health checkups to reading lists. Read it aloud. Write with your non-dominant hand (usually the left) how you felt listening.

To get to know your Pusher better, dialogue with it in your journal. Writing with your dominant hand (usually the right), write the following, and finish the sentences and answer for the Pusher with your non-dominant hand.

- ✔ You push me to accomplish more because . . .

- ✔ You won't let me relax because . . .

- ✔ What would happen if I took it easy and you (the Pusher) stopped pushing me?

- ✔ When did you first start pushing me?

- ✔ Complete this sentence for yourself, not the Pusher: If I gave myself permission not to do some things on my list, I'd feel . . .

- ✔ Complete this sentence for yourself, not the Pusher: Pushing myself to accomplish more deprives me of . . .

The Perfectionist — nothing's good enough

The Perfectionist has unreachable ideals concerning everything about you, your behavior, and the people in your life. It lives in a world of illusion. As discussed in Chapter 3, perfectionism is driven by shame. Although the Perfectionist may focus on mistakes, orderliness, your body, athletic ability, or creativity, at its core is the belief that you're not adequate in some way — attractive enough, good enough, smart enough, strong enough, and so on. Perfectionism is an escape from these painful beliefs. You may find it hard to complete tasks because your work is never perfect. The Critic judges you for not meeting the Perfectionist's unrealistic standards. The fact that there's no such thing as "perfection" is meaningless to the Perfectionist because it would be out of a job.

The antidote for perfectionism is self-acceptance. Remember that to accept something (see the explanation of acceptance in Chapter 9), you don't have to like it, only to acknowledge it — as is. Some things about yourself you can change; others you can't. Paradoxically, until you accept yourself, it's difficult to change at all because you're in conflict with reality. Try this:

Take a mini-vacation

Close your eyes and imagine that you're on a vacation, reclining and relaxing in your favorite environment. Pretend that there are neon letters on your forehead that spell out RELAX. They light up every time you exhale. Take ten slow exhales. Breathe in the fresh air at your vacation spot. Smell it and feel it on your skin. Listen to the sounds around you — possibly water, birds, or a breeze. Feel the ground under you. Are you on grass, forest leaves, or a sandy beach? You no longer have to support yourself up. Let yourself sink into the earth beneath you. Exhale and see the neon letters "RELAX." Notice what you feel. Do you become anxious? If so, allow it. See how long you let yourself just be. Do this mini-vacation once a day, even for 5 or 10 minutes. The main thing is that you're beginning to interrupt the compulsive hold of the Pusher.

Make a list of your beliefs about yourself. In what ways do you feel you're not enough? How do your beliefs affect your actions? Look in the mirror and say, "I unconditionally accept myself just as I am." Can you mean it — without choking? Do you like what you see? What objections come to mind? Oh, I forgot to look in the mirror *naked.* Maybe you avoid mirrors altogether. That in itself undermines your self-esteem. You're trying to avoid and deny what you already believe about yourself. Inevitably, there are some things you don't like. Maybe you think you look old, or your breasts are too small, your hips are too wide, or your legs are too short. You don't have to like what you see, only to face and accept the reality that this is you. Repeat aloud, "I accept myself uncon-ditionally, even though ____." If you can't, then state, "I accept my refusal to accept that I'm (fat)." Do this mirror exercise over a few weeks. Write your feelings in your journal. Notice any changes in your attitude as you progress.

Building Self-Esteem

Now that you've started pulling out the weeds, it's time to prepare and fertilize the soil and plant new seeds. This means introducing some healthy new habits that may feel uncomfortable — even self-ish or conceited. It's very difficult to remove a negative thought or habit without replacing it with a positive one, but if you don't, you'll keep focusing on the old thoughts, which only reinforces them. You also need to nourish yourself with sunshine and water to help the seedlings grow.

The buck stops with you

Taking responsibility for your feelings and actions is key to building self-esteem; otherwise you'll continue to feel like a victim and dependent upon others' feelings and behavior over which you have no control. This is a losing formula. If you go from one relationship to another looking for someone to make you happy or fulfill you, you forfeit the opportunity to grow into your wholeness and strength. Instead, your codependency grows. Until you accept responsibility for yourself, you cannot change your life — and that includes improving your self-esteem. When you do, your future is in your hands. (See Chapters 3, 6, and 8 for more on self-responsibility.)

Of course, you aren't responsible for everything that happens to you. There are random acts of violence, accidents caused by others, acts of God and nature, genetic diseases, and so on. Although some philosophies suggest you're responsible for everything in your life, I think that view is extreme and can overwhelm and disempower you with feeling helpless. The Dalai Lama agrees there are many variables over which we have no control.

Living responsibly may be easier to understand than to actually put into practice. It requires self-awareness of your feelings and needs (see Chapter 8), noticing when you don't take responsibility, and ending blame, excuses, and attempts to change or control others. Then you're ready to take action to fulfill your needs and address your feelings. There are areas of your life in which you take more responsibility and feel better about yourself than other areas where you don't.

For many of you, taking greater responsibility for yourself requires nothing less than a 180-degree reversal from how you've lived your life so far. If you're used to looking to others to make you feel happy and secure, it may feel daunting to realize that they won't. But everyone has to grow up. The buck stops with you. You may not want the task. If you're angry, go ahead and have a tantrum! You don't have to do anything just yet. Let this realization sink in. When you start to take responsibility for yourself, the change is profound. Begin by trying the following:

- ✔ Notice when you think about what someone else should be doing. Stop and ask what you need to do. (See Chapter 9.) For example, you may tell someone to exercise or get more rest when you need it.

- ✔ When you're feeling hurt, angry, or sad, do you want focus on someone else's behavior? Think about your contribution to how you feel and ask what you can do. For example, allow your feelings, write in your journal, talk to a friend, or go have some fun.

- ✔ When something goes wrong or plans go awry, do you blame someone else? Do you get frustrated in dealing with people on the phone or driving in traffic and start to criticize them? Take responsibility for your feelings. Breathe and relax.

- ✔ If you're late for an appointment or a deadline, do you make up phony excuses or expect concessions and extensions from the other person, rather than owning your tardiness?

- ✔ When you have a problem, consider how you can help yourself.

- ✔ How do you feel when you are self-responsible? When you're not?

- ✔ In the areas where your self-responsibility is low, write about what you can do to start taking more responsibility. If you're tempted to focus on why you can't make changes, look for ways that you can. If you have a disability, find things that give you pleasure and people to help you do what you're unable to do yourself. Notice what beliefs and feelings stop you.

Write a paragraph, completing these sentences:

- ✔ I'm passive because . . .

- ✔ I allow the behavior I don't like is because . . .

- ✔ If I accepted responsibility for my body, I'd . . .

- ✔ If I stopped blaming my spouse for my unhappiness, I'd . . .

- ✔ If it were totally up to me to get what I want, I'd . . .

- ✔ If didn't blame my parents for my problems, I'd have to . . .

- ✔ If I took responsibility for how I treat my family, I'd . . .

- ✔ If I took responsibility for my finances, I'd . . .

- ✔ If I stopped procrastinating about . . .

- ✔ If I stopped waiting for things to change, I'd . . .

The truth sets you free

Codependents are afraid to reveal themselves because at bottom they don't accept themselves. They're afraid that people will be angry at them and leave if they told the truth. If you act phony, then you always doubt the good feelings others have about you because you think that they don't *really* know you. In Chapter 9, you learned that authenticity is the key to overcoming codependency. What a challenge! Living authentically means that there's no discrepancy between the real inner you and what you show to others. What would it be like to go through your day, your week, your life, and express your true Self? Write a paragraph about the consequence if:

✔ You didn't worry about hurting people's feelings?

✔ You didn't just go along with other people's decisions?

✔ You didn't give up your time or listen when you didn't want to?

✔ You said no when you wanted to?

✔ You told people when they disappointed you or hurt your feelings?

✔ You were more honest about your opinions?

✔ You weren't afraid to show your anger?

✔ You admitted when you didn't know the answer or what to do?

Remember the movie *Liar, Liar,* where Jim Carrey was a trial lawyer who couldn't keep from telling the truth for 24 hours? I'm not suggesting that you tell a colleague at work, as Jim Carrey did, "Your hairpiece looks like something that was killed crossing the highway," or even, "Your slip is showing." Being more honest is about revealing you. That's a lot harder. In some relationships, particularly at work, revealing your inner Self may or may not serve your goals. The more intimate you are with someone, the more essential honesty is to the health of the relationship.

Write a story about an imaginary day where you tell the truth to important people in your life. Write how you would feel. What stops you from being more honest? How does it affect your relationships?

Being more authentic helps grow your self-esteem. If you are hiding secrets in your relationships, there's a good chance you're repeating the rules in the family you grew up in. Usually the fear that the truth harms or destroys someone is really a camouflage for your fear that someone will dislike or reject you. However, the effect of your withholding the truth is what actually creates damage, hurt, and walls between you and others. Revealing facts is one level of truth. It's more difficult to be open and honest with your feelings in the present. (See Chapter 16 on intimacy.) When you're not, you confirm your belief that you have to hide who you are.

Positive affirmations are helpful but must be backed up by positive actions. Living authentically and responsibly is a daily challenge. Strive to know and trust yourself, be self-responsible, and express yourself.

Giving yourself credit where due

You're always either putting yourself down or lifting yourself up. You can choose to be for yourself or against yourself. You saw how the Critic, Pusher, and Perfectionist sabotage you. Now you must

plant seeds of positive self-talk. It's up to you to encourage yourself, even when you're down or afraid. A positive inner dialogue
is also crucial to motivate you to take risks, make changes, and
become more independent. You can do what you believe you can,
and you can't do what you don't believe you can.

Acknowledge yourself

Everyone likes compliments, a pat on the back, and recognition
for a job well done. Why wait for the kindness of others? It's up to
you to acknowledge and praise yourself. Have you noticed how the
warmth of others' praise quickly fades? When you give it to yourself,
the afterglow lingers. Talk to yourself about your successes, as you
would praise a friend. You can repeat it and bask in it as often as
you like. Doing this actually changes how you think about yourself
and raises your self-esteem. It isn't the same as empty affirmations.
It's giving credit to yourself that's backed up by experience —
memories of positive actions that you can recall.

✔ Get into the good habit of listing three positive traits or
behaviors about yourself each day. List ten if you can; even
small things, like holding the door for someone or saying good
morning to co-workers to whom you don't ordinarily speak.

✔ List things for which you're grateful. Gratitude blocks negativity. It's hard to be judgmental and grateful at the same time.

✔ Go over your list of self-criticisms and write encouraging
statements to counteract each criticism. Think of what you
would say to a toddler learning a new skill. Be gentle and
patient with yourself. Tell yourself, "I love and accept you,"
"You're doing great," "I'm so proud of your progress." Remind
yourself of small, positive changes and how you've turned
things around in the past.

✔ Arm yourself against the Critic. Sometimes, when you do
something positive the Critic steps in to minimize or negate
it and looks for mistakes or reasons to tear you down. The
Perfectionist says it wasn't quite perfect or good enough.
Confront and argue with them.

Another tactic of the Critic is to attack you because you're
acknowledging yourself. It may say you're conceited or arrogant.
Some people grew up with religious beliefs that confuse confidence
with arrogance. They believe that positive self-regard commits
the sin of pride or is the work of the Devil and punishable by God.
These family rules can be difficult to overcome because being a
positive person entails a psychological break with your family or
even your religion. If it were bad to feel confident, everyone would
be doomed to having low self-esteem.

Confidence isn't conceit or arrogance

Confidence is feeling secure in yourself based upon real knowledge of your strengths and limitations. On the other hand, conceit is unfounded self-flattery or an exaggerated sense of self-importance, and arrogance is a false sense of superiority over others. Both compensate for low self-esteem.

Your assets

Authenticity and self-esteem require that you acknowledge all of your Self, not only your shortcomings. Generally, when self-esteem is low, you don't value your uniqueness. You take your assets for granted or have difficulty believing in your good qualities or accepting compliments. Some people shun praise and feel guilty admitting anything positive about themselves. They're so brainwashed by the Critic, they think "Big deal" or "So what."

- ✔ Make a list of your positive traits.

- ✔ Make a list of your skills and abilities.

- ✔ Make a list of things you've accomplished. (If you can't think of anything, start with this: you learned to read!)

- ✔ Notice how you feel when complimented. Start saying, "Thank you" — end of sentence.

- ✔ Write about whether and for what you received praise growing up. (In some families only negativity is allowed, and no one ever gets credit.)

Keeping commitments to yourself

It's typical of codependents who wouldn't think of breaking a date with a friend to consistently break commitments to themselves. "Tomorrow I'll start a diet." "Tomorrow I'll go to the gym." When you do this, you're abandoning yourself — unless, in some instances, it may be more loving to rest, rather than do what you planned. There's only choice and consequence, and you're responsible for your choices and actions. Try always to choose in your highest self-interest — which may not give you immediate gratification, but result in long-term benefits and improved self-esteem. This is the way you nourish your garden and keep it healthy.

The other thing about keeping commitments to yourself is meeting your own expectations. This is similar to practicing your values. If you expect yourself to file your taxes on time but keep putting it off, soon you're going to be fed up with yourself, and your Critic will have a field day.

Sometimes, you may not know which action is more loving — keeping a commitment or letting yourself off the hook. Do the listening exercise in Chapter 8 to see what your body wants. If there are legitimate reasons why you can't meet your expectations, then explain the circumstances to your Critic and tell it to stop haranguing you. Whatever your decision, accept it.

Self-Acceptance and Self-Love

As discussed in Chapter 3, self-esteem is a self-evaluation. It's raised by improving how you think about yourself and living in congruence with your goals, values, and beliefs. Self-esteem varies depending upon how you act and to a minor extent upon external events and health challenges. Acting contrary to what you believe lowers your self-esteem. In contrast, acceptance of yourself is steady and unconditional. You accept yourself despite flaws, failures, and limitations, as in the earlier mirror exercise. If you hold on to guilt, your self-esteem and self-acceptance suffer.

Self-acceptance

Self-acceptance means that instead of thinking about how you need to be different, you accept who you are. Catch yourself making comparisons to others — both positively and negatively. Perhaps you're comparing your insides to others' outsides. Stop and remember that you and everyone else have a singular, unique fingerprint. Imagine that it includes all your assets and flaws, all your talents and limitations. Say to yourself, "This is who I am, and it's okay." If it's helpful, tell yourself, "This is how God made me, and wanted me to be. God willed me to be as I am." Repeat the words of Walter Cronkite, "That's the way it is," and Popeye, "I am what I am."

This attitude of self-acceptance works magic. When you start accepting yourself, you stop struggling to present yourself as smart, strong, kind, sexy, or any other pretense. Self-acceptance allows you to be authentic. You can finally relax, and more of the inner real you comes forward. You have no shame or fear of revealing yourself when you accept yourself unconditionally. This attitude spills over onto others for whom you have more compassion and acceptance. You won't feel the need to control or change them or even convince them to agree with you.

Letting go of guilt

You are unable to accept yourself until you forgive yourself for any guilt about your past. Make a list of things you've done that you feel guilty about. Under each one, analyze these questions:

- ✔ What were my motives? Go deep with this. Was a deeper motive to feel secure or lovable? For example, childhood shoplifting may have been motivated by a desire for peer acceptance or adultery by a need for love or retaliation for hurt.
- ✔ What were the circumstances and my knowledge at the time?
- ✔ In what way was I trying to take care of myself?
- ✔ What made my choice seem the best at the time?
- ✔ Was anyone harmed by my actions?
- ✔ Do I need to make amends? To whom?
- ✔ What did I learn from this experience?
- ✔ How would I handle this differently today?

Write a compassionate letter to yourself, forgiving yourself as you would write to a child who'd made a mistake — a child that you love and want to teach and forgive.

In some cases, you may need to make amends to others, and although this may feel awkward at first, it's truly liberating and uplifting. You may be pleasantly surprised by the positive reaction of others. Remember not to justify your actions or blame the other person, but only apologize for harm done. In addition, you're not doing this for their forgiveness, but for self-forgiveness. Therefore, the other person's reaction isn't important; you're doing it for yourself. Finally, the point of this is to decide not to repeat your behavior in the future. People with high self-esteem learn from their errors, rather than castigate themselves.

Self-love

Whereas acceptance is an attitude toward yourself, love is a combination of both feeling and action. Many think self-love is egotism or narcissism, but actually egotists and narcissists don't love themselves at all. A "big ego" is compensation for lack of self-love. Codependents think too little of themselves, not too much.

Love for your Self is healthy. The Bible says, "Love they neighbor as thyself." You're a human being as worthy of love as anyone else. Contrary to the idea that self-love is selfish and takes away from your ability to love others, the opposite is true. The greater is your love for yourself, the greater will be your ability to love others. Moreover, you only allow yourself to receive as much love as you give to yourself.

Love involves understanding, respect, acceptance, responsibility, and compassion. These virtues are not compartmentalized, but are experienced for your Self and for others. Love is not divisible. As you develop these aspects in yourself, your ability to love yourself and others grows.

Although self-love is certainly an important goal, it's not easily attained, particularly in Western society with its many distractions and emphasis on speed and productivity. Love requires focused attention, discipline, and patience. In addition, loving includes empathy and compassion, which enables you to feel with acceptance, caring, and understanding what someone else is feeling and to extend this compassion toward yourself. Compassion is expressed with gentleness, tenderness, and generosity of spirit — quite the opposite of the tyrannical trio. Notice if when you're stressed, overwhelmed, or exhausted, you attempt to do even more, instead of caring for yourself. This is challenging if you didn't feel accepted or nurtured as a child. You have no role model to emulate, and treat yourself harshly or with indifference the way you were treated.

Self-love is very different from self-pity, which is a blend of fear, judgment, and anger about troubles that have befallen you. With self-compassion and empathy, you're present to your raw feeling experience and are able to allow it and comfort yourself with understanding and care. Self-pity implies, "It shouldn't be this way," but with self-love, there's compassion for and acceptance of what is, with no attempt to resist or fix it.

The ability to do this requires faith, just as love requires faith when you risk committing your heart. The faith required in self-love is what enables you to allow your feelings, without lapsing into anxiety or judgment. A centeredness and calmness contain and support your emotions and afford you some objectivity. You know that despite this, "I'll survive." This objectivity permits you to comfort yourself. Naturally, there are times when you have no objectivity and no faith, but you continue to strive for it. Spending time alone with yourself is essential, and a meditation practice is helpful in developing the ability to witness and contain your emotions.

Imagine a little kitten sitting on your chest. You're stroking, cuddling, and speaking lovingly to it. Allow your heart to open. Hear it purring, and feel the warmth of its body next to yours, as your chest rises with each breath. Listen to your heartbeat. Now imagine the kitten inside your heart, and continue stroking and speaking lovingly to yourself about all that you've suffered and all your burdens, conflicts, and worries. Let everything just be for a few minutes. You don't have to solve or do anything. Tell yourself, "At this moment, I'm safe." Ask yourself, "What is the most loving thing I need right now?" Practice this every day.

Practicing self-love

Loving yourself is a life journey and goal that starts with self-knowledge (see Chapter 8). It's the core of recovery and rewards you with enormous benefits — increased self-esteem, peace, well-being, health, and loving relationships with others. You can consider it a spiritual practice because it requires awareness, reverence, and kindness toward yourself as one of God's creations. Loving yourself for 10 minutes a day is a good start, but it's an ongoing process. You have opportunities to do so throughout the day — often moment to moment — in your actions and the way you listen and speak to yourself.

Working with the tyrannical trio heightens your awareness of your automatic negative inner dialogue. Then it's up to you to change it into a positive one. You may feel foolish at first but try saying, "I love you" to yourself and aloud in the mirror. It's nice to hear from others and even from you.

You may notice that much of your behavior throughout the day is routine — what and how you have your breakfast, check messages, get to work. Interrupt your routine and listen to your heart, mind, and body. Ask yourself several times a day, "What am I feeling?" What do I need and want?" and "What is the most loving choice I can make right now?" Wait for answers, and give yourself what you need, including rest, healthy food, joy, compassion, and socializing. Choices made out of fear, anxiety, or guilt are usually not in your highest interest.

Loving parents gently discipline their children. Self-love requires curbing your automatic behavior that's self-defeating or unhealthy. You may need to set limits on procrastination, gluttony, sloth, tardiness, or the opposite, working, playing, or exercising more than is healthy. When you want to reach for second dessert, try being with yourself quietly. See what you're feeling — perhaps anxiety or restlessness. You may need to calm or comfort yourself or may find deeper feelings to explore.

Self-love also means having good will toward yourself. Try seeing yourself through compassionate and understanding eyes, as you may see a child, pet, or close friend. Look for the positive motive behind your actions — it's usually self-preservation — and that's okay. Your actions are a result of what you've learned from your parents and experiences to date. By compassionately observing and thinking about your behavior, you increase your opportunities to change it in the future.

Part III

The Skills: Taking Action

The 5th Wave   By Rich Tennant

ATTEMPTING TO REDUCE THE STRESS IN HIS LIFE, WALDO "WHIP" GUNSCHOTT GOES FROM BEING A WILD ANIMAL TRAINER, TO A WILD BALLOON ANIMAL TRAINER.

In this part...

Part III is all about action. Here you put into practice your improved self-esteem by expressing yourself more assertively and finding out how to set boundaries. There are suggestions on how to deal with your relationships, including sex, dating, and codependency phobia. If you want to go deeper, there's information about healing the underlying pain of codependency. This part emphasizes the importance of creating balance with a spiritual practice, recreation, and fun. Finally, the subject of relapse is discussed.

Chapter 11

Finding Your Voice

Communication is so important that it can make or break a relationship and is critical to success. It reflects your self-esteem to listeners — for better or for worse. Codependents suffer from dysfunctional communication habits learned in their families growing up (see Chapters 3 and 7). In most dysfunctional families, one or both parents are passive or aggressive and rarely assertive. Codependents usually copy these styles. Some avoid conflict and choose peace at any price. They feel anxious as when they were dependent on their parents for survival. Others blame, tune out, or react (see Chapter 9) to protect themselves but aren't assertive. Both of these styles perpetuate disharmony in relationships.

Expressing Yourself

You've begun to identify your feelings, needs, and values, and not to control, care take, or react. Putting into action what you've learned and expressing yourself is where the rubber meets the road. Learning how to express yourself effectively builds your self-esteem. It takes practice and courage.

When you stifle your feelings or ignore your needs, the relationship suffers and you dishonor the Self you're trying to develop. If your motive is to control, manipulate, or fix someone, your words communicate these codependent attitudes; but when your motive is to express your Self, your words convey that the focus is on you not the other person, whose reaction becomes less important.

Communication involves more than your words. You relay information with your entire body, including through:

- **Eyes:** Eye contact, movement, moisture, expression, and focus
- **Face:** Expression
- **Body:** Voluntary and involuntary movement, including posture, gestures, and muscular tension
- **Skin:** Color (such as blushing) and perspiration

Additionally, your voice communicates through:

- Volume
- Pitch
- Cadence
- Tone and emphasis
- Fluidity
- Enunciation

Being assertive — the six Cs

Assertive communication commands respect, projects confidence, and inspires influence. Communication is learned, and you can learn to communicate assertively. Learning assertiveness takes practice, so be patient.

Assertiveness means stating clearly and politely what you think, feel, need, or want. Most communication comes down to those four essentials. You can also explain why. The speaker's intent is to communicate about him- or herself. Assertive communication is respectful, direct, honest, open, nonthreatening, and nondefensive. It's not demanding, aggressive, rude, unpleasant, selfish, or manipulative. Assertive communication is comprised of six elements; I call them the six Cs.

- Congruency
- Courtesy
- Conciseness
- Clarity
- Cognizance
- Claim yourself

Congruency

Congruence means that you honestly express and manifest how you feel inside. It's key to effective communication. Truthfulness is about facts. Honesty has more to do with intent and feelings — that you say what you think or feel and mean what you say. When your words don't match your insides, you're sending a mixed message that your body reveals. Dishonesty is more common than you may guess. I'm not referring to overt lies, but about times you outwardly agree but inwardly don't. This is common among codependents. For example, when you say you're fine, but your body language reveals that you're unhappy — or, the opposite, you smile while imparting a sad story. In either case, your listener is confused and doesn't know how to respond and/or may not feel that he or she can trust you.

Fidgeting conveys anxiety and is a distraction to the listener. If you tell someone you feel comfortable or confident but make nervous movements, others believe your body. Eye contact is a learned habit and an important form of connecting in intimate relationships. Lack of eye contact signals low self-esteem. If this is a problem for you, practice looking around the person's head, hair, or ears.

Courtesy

The purpose of communication is to impart information and feelings, not to vent, avenge, or scold. If you're discourteous to listeners, you lose them. To be effective, you want to engage your listener. To do so, treat him or her with respect. Your listener is more likely to hear your criticism if it's constructive and delivered assertively.

Conciseness

Your impact wanes with words. Your listener wants you to cut to the chase and hear your point. When you're nervous or afraid and try to express yourself, you may make a disclaimer or beat around the bush to prevent your listener from getting upset, but that's the unintended consequence. Sort out the reasons why you're fearful, practice what you plan to say aloud, and weigh the long-term repercussions of saying nothing. Other reasons for wordiness are:

- ✔ You're talking to get attention.
- ✔ You're needy and don't know what you want.
- ✔ You have nothing to say, but are trying to fill a silence.

Clarity

Clarity means being direct. Codependents don't like to be direct. Directness means taking responsibility for your feelings and opinions, which can cause confrontation or rejection. Do you make camouflaged requests, such as:

"There's no food in the house."

"There's a new movie out."

"It would do you good to get out and see a movie."

"There's no gas in the car."

Don't ask questions, give hints, or speak abstractly. Don't say, "Do you want to go to a movie?" which is ambiguous as to whether *you* want to go, take a position (taking positions is explained later in this chapter) and say, "I'd like to see (name it, or) an action movie."

Don't assume things. People attribute different meanings to the same words. When the other speaker is indirect or unclear, ask for clarification. Restate what you heard and ask for more information.

Cognizance and listening

Cognizance refers to being aware and giving attention to your listener. It's essential. Communication is a two-way street. You must hear in order to be heard. To be an effective communicator, listen with attention and respect to what others say. Genuine listening engages them and helps you attune your response. Regard differentness as an opportunity to learn, rather than a threat you have to push away. Attentive, active listening includes paraphrasing and repeating what's said to you. This is responsible feedback because it shows that you care and are interested. Others are more receptive when they believe their feelings and opinions matter to you. Even when you hear all that is said, your listener doesn't know it, which is why reassurance is necessary. In addition, their meaning may be different from what you understood. Repeating what you heard provides that opportunity to get clarification.

Cognizance also implies that your knowledge and perceptions of others are accurate and not seen or heard through a lens of past experience or trauma — meaning that you're functioning in present time and not threatened by differences between you and the other person. You're able to really listen to them because you aren't reacting. This is huge growth in self-esteem.

Timing is critical. Don't start an important conversation in the car or when the other person is watching TV, on the computer, or is otherwise occupied, without permission. You're being impolite and interrupting the person's attention. You're setting yourself up for an argument and will be disappointed that you're not being heard.

Claim yourself

Being able to claim yourself is the hardest element. Taking responsibility for your opinions, actions, thoughts, feelings, and needs means you don't deny your feelings or actions, or blame or give others advice. Don't talk about them or quote some expert. Using "I" messages, as later discussed in the following sections, claims what you think and feel. It also means making statements rather than asking or avoiding questions.

Communicating feelings

It's very common for people to confuse thoughts and feelings in speaking. For instance, let's say you are annoyed that your friend ignores your request to call if he will be late for dinner. You say, "I feel you were (inconsiderate, etc.)" in explaining your feelings. This statement violates the sixth C, to claim yourself. It judges his behavior, without revealing how you feel or how his behavior affects you. A rule of thumb is this: if you can substitute the word "think" for "feel," then you've expressed your thoughts or opinions, which are often judgments about the other person. Applying this rule, you may say, "I felt disregarded (or "unimportant" or "hurt") when you didn't call me," or "I don't like it when you . . ." When you state your feelings or take a position, others won't feel the need to defend and justify themselves because you're only talking about yourself. The more vulnerable you can be in expressing your feelings, the more receptive your listener will be. Your initial feeling may be anger or resentment but try to identify your deeper feelings and express them. This is particularly difficult to do when you're emotional. It's helpful to wait and think about what you feel and what outcome or behavioral changes you want. To be assertive, practice phrasing it before having the conversation.

Beware your "I" statements aren't implied judgments, which will make your listener defensive, such as "I feel used," or "I feel I can't trust you." Instead, try, "I feel hurt — that I don't matter to you," and "I don't feel safe with you," which are disclosures that are more vulnerable.

It's perfectly fine and often helpful to the listener to describe his or her behavior, rather than generalize. Say, "When you leave dirty dishes around the house, I feel . . ." It takes time and practice to be able to identify your feelings. If you're in the middle of a conversation, it's okay to say, "Let me think about how I'm feeling. Hmm . . . It's not exactly angry . . . or hurt . . . more like unimportant. When I've asked you to put your dishes in the sink and you continue not to, I feel like my feelings don't matter to you, and then I feel unimportant." The point is to communicate the impact on you, not vent or punish the other person.

Communicating needs

Most codependents don't communicate their needs. They fear rejection or humiliation because they weren't listened to or were shamed in childhood. After you've identified what you need and want, the best approach is to directly ask for it. This can be frightening when you're not used to it. To avoid communicating their needs, many codependents believe others should be able to read their minds, and they devalue receiving something if they've asked for it, saying, "It doesn't count because I had to tell you," or "You should have known without my asking." This puts their partner in a double bind — wrong for not meeting the need on their own as well as for meeting it after they're told what it is. Another dysfunctional tactic that codependents use to avoid asking anything is to blame and criticize, which only leads to arguments and less likelihood of getting needs met.

Don't say: "You never do _____" or "You always do _____."

Say: "It's important to me that (or "I'd really appreciate), you __."

Let the person know the positive effect of filling your request. This is persuasive motivation: "If you told me more about what's going on at work, it would make me feel closer to you."

You can also add a feeling statement about the consequence of the opposite behavior: "When you don't tell me what goes on at work, I feel left out and excluded from a big part of your life."

Taking positions

Assertiveness entails taking positions that are direct. A position is a statement about what you will do or won't do, what you like or dislike, what you want or don't want, and what you're willing to tolerate or not. Instead, codependents react and are indirect. They conceal themselves and ask questions to avoid conflict, rejection, and criticism. If you don't take a stand, you can argue but can't negotiate conflicting needs or positions. Nothing gets resolved. Here's a typical codependent conversation:

> **A:** "I have to go downtown to the doctor. Do you want to go with me?"

(Non-I statement, designed to make B responsible for going)

> **B:** "Going downtown is not my favorite way to spend a Saturday. Do you want me to go with you?"

(Reaction + Clear question to get A to take a position)

> **A:** "Last weekend I went with you to get your office furniture, but if you don't want to go, I'll get someone else to go."

(manipulative reaction and avoidant non-answer)

B can react or respond assertively to **A**'s manipulation.

> **B-1:** "You went with me only because you didn't like what I'd picked out."

(reaction to **A**'s manipulation)

> **B-2:** "I'll go with you."

(position, not commenting on **A**'s reaction)

When codependents react instead of taking positions, it escalates conflict. **B**-1 reacts and attributes intention to **A**, which will lead to an argument, but **B**-2 takes a position. The goal is to be able to allow the other persons reaction without reacting to it, and respond with a position, as follows:

> **A:** Position + **B:** Position → negotiation
>
> **A:** Reaction + **B:** Reaction + **A:** Reaction → escalation and argument

Many people think it's pointless to express themselves if the other person wouldn't agree or accept their position. That is not the purpose of speaking up. You're doing it for you to change your submissive behavior, not to change someone else's opinions. When you speak up, you feel better about yourself and the relationship just for having expressed yourself. As your self-esteem grows, you're more comfortable with differing beliefs and opinions. You may want someone to behave differently by setting a boundary (as described in "Setting Boundaries" later in this chapter), but even in that case, the person doesn't have to agree with you, only to respect your request.

Codependent lingo

There are some common codependent speaking patterns designed to avoid confrontations — often by manipulating the other person. Here are some red flags to watch for. If you're guilty of them, write down some alternative ways of speaking to help you practice improved communication.

- ✔ **Victim talk:** "You're making me feel guilty," "Why don't you ever help around the house?", "You're giving me a headache." The speaker isn't taking responsibility for his or her own experience in these statements. It would be more effective to describe your experience, feelings, and needs.

- **Generalization:** "You never remember my birthday." "We always do what you want." If you say "always" or "never," you immediately lose your listener who feels judged and attacked. The other person will come up with at least one time when your statement was untrue. Then you argue about whose memory is correct, rather than the point you're trying to make. It's better to ask for what you want.

- **Empty apologies:** Codependents say, "I'm sorry" all the time. It can be annoying. Sometimes they even apologize for other people's behavior, which makes no sense to the listener. Because of irrational guilt, they apologize for something that doesn't matter; for example, if you're 5 minutes late and spend another five apologizing and excusing it. More often, codependents apologize to take the heat off themselves and end a conversation. They usually aren't sorry. Sometimes, they may not even understand why the other person is upset. When you're not sure if you owe an apology, you can always say, "I'll think about what you've said to me." This makes the other person feel heard and taken seriously, which is more helpful than an empty apology. A true apology is heartfelt, with understanding of both your behavior and its impact on someone else.

- **Justifications:** It's exceedingly hard for codependents early in recovery to take responsibility for their feelings and actions, and just say, "You're right," or the opposite, "No, I don't see it that way." Period! Notice if you use language such as, "I was just . . .," or "I only meant . . ." These along with other explanations and justifications convey guilt and low self-esteem and provide the other person ammunition to continue arguing. Explaining yourself gives someone else the right to judge your motives and what's best for you. Do you really mean to do that? Remember from Chapter 8 that you're entitled to your feelings. It's enough that you want or don't want something, without explanation.

- **Changing the subject:** Codependents change the subject to avoid confrontations or revealing themselves. It's better to directly respond and set a boundary, stating, "I rather not discuss that." Again, no justification is required, only that you don't want to talk about it.

- **Blaming:** Another avoidance tactic is to focus on the other person, and blame him or her for something to avoid taking responsibility for your own actions. Low self-esteem makes it hard for codependents to admit anything. If you made a mistake, it's better to admit it, but that doesn't mean you have to allow anyone to criticize or punish you for it.

- **Waffling:** Instead of saying "Yes" or "No" to a question, explanations to avoid taking a position are annoying to the other person, who generally doesn't care about your reasons.

- **Kicking the Can:** Due to fear of saying "No," codependents postpone meetings and conversations. Then when the time arrives, they feel more guilty and obliged, and it's even harder to say "No," or do what they want.

- **"Should-ing":** Using the word *should* is a red flag that you're crossing someone's boundary and probably giving advice or trying to control.

Communication tips

Here are some tips to remember:

- Codependents have a hard time finding and holding their position under pressure. When you're unsure, take time to gather your thoughts and feelings by yourself. Say, "Let me think about it," or "I'll get back to you on that."

- "No" is a complete sentence. You needn't justify or explain your feelings and thoughts. If questioned, use the broken-record technique and keep repeating, "I'm not comfortable with it."

- You may have to be persistent. Use the broken-record technique, and be careful not to waffle, or you undermine all the courage it took to repeat yourself. Eventually the listener will get tired of asking. Practice with strangers, like telemarketers.

- You don't have to answer every question asked you. You can say, "I'd rather not answer that," or "I don't want to discuss it." You may find answering all questions is a compulsive habit that is hard to break. Most people feel like interrogated children. Use the broken-record technique and repeat your statement.

- You have a right to change your mind without further explanation.

- Notice whether you continue talking when the other person has tuned out. If this is the case, stop and ask when would be a good time to continue the conversation. You can also say, "I think I lost your attention."

- Prepare ahead for difficult conversations. Think about your feelings and how to express them; then state what you want.

Setting Boundaries

After you've begun to connect to your body and can tell what feels good and bad and what you need and want, you're ready to set boundaries. Setting boundaries draws a line between you and someone else. It often requires that you say, "No," "I don't want to . . .," I don't like that . . .," "I'm not willing to . . .," or "Stop it." It's an advanced level of stating an "I" position. This can be difficult because even when you can express yourself, you may not believe that you have a right to say "No." All the reasons you may hesitate to take an "I" position are intensified when you stand up for yourself. Setting boundaries feels confrontational — although it needn't be, but it takes practice, practice, and more practice.

Why set boundaries

Boundaries indicate respect for others and for you. Setting boundaries shows that you're taking responsibility for, caring for, and protecting yourself. Don't advise or tell others what to do, and don't let them tell you. Don't blame them, and don't let them blame you. Respect others' bodies, beliefs, thoughts, feelings, and material things, and require that they respect yours.

Your feelings

Practice tuning in to yourself during conversations and listen to your body. Are your muscles tightening, heart racing, or mind blurring? Your body may be preparing to fight or flee, indicating an attack. You may not be aware of anything in the moment, but hours or days later have feelings traceable to the conversation. An indication that you may need to set limits is that you're feeling frightened, smothered, angry, low self-esteem, depressed, or resentful. Either someone may have violated your boundaries or you have given too much and feel used or taken for granted. Fear or anger means you may need to take an action to protect yourself or correct something.

You may need to set limits with yourself. For example, to work more or less, spend less time on the phone, or stop volunteering your time and energy. When you're tempted to blame someone else, ask yourself whether you need to set a boundary concerning that person's behavior or your own.

Trust and safety

Codependents look to others to make them feel safe. You may not realize that you're feeling unsafe because you don't trust yourself to set boundaries. When you prove to yourself that you can say "No," then you feel freer to say, "Yes" and allow more intimacy in your life. You trust yourself and feel safe because you know that you won't get close to someone who's violated your boundaries.

Self-esteem

You derive two, immediate benefits from setting boundaries. You get the behavior you want and get the added boost to your self-esteem from honoring your needs and standing up for yourself. Each time you do, you get stronger, and it gets easier. You can let go of control and be more spontaneous to say, "Yes" and "No." You realize that saying "No" to someone is saying "Yes" to you. You won't control others or allow them to control or abuse you. You receive more respect and your self-esteem and sense of freedom and power grows and grows.

- ✔ Practice saying "No" once a day for a week. Remember that "No" is a complete sentence.

- ✔ Practice not answering questions.

How to set boundaries

In setting boundaries, you have to think and not react. You won't be able to set them until you're ready and clear about what you want. Nagging, yelling, blaming, and complaining are reactions that focus on the other person and aren't boundaries. Until your words match your actions, you're not setting a boundary, and I guarantee you, you're going to be ignored. An ultimatum given in desperation is also a reaction, and often not taken seriously. So take your time, and don't pressure yourself or feel self-critical for waiting. If you set them before you're ready and later undo the boundary, it undermines your credibility — like "The Boy who Cried Wolf."

Your bottom line

To set limits, you need to know your bottom line. Think of two boundary-setting situations where:

A. You are asked to do something you don't want to do.

B. Someone else's behavior bothers you.

Then complete the exercise by following these steps. Think about and write down the following:

1. Describe exactly what it is that's bothering you. Try to figure out what about it really upsets you and why.

   Were you asked to lend money or drive a friend to the airport and don't want to — why? Are you angry that your husband is on the computer too much, or really because you feel that you don't matter? Is it that your wife spends a lot of money or that you want her to appreciate how hard your work?

2. How do you feel?

   A. Describe how you'll feel if you comply with the other person's request and if you don't.

   B. Describe how the person's behavior makes you feel. How will you feel if you don't set a boundary?

3. What needs to change?

   A. Is it possible to modify your compliance with the request in a way that feels comfortable?

   B. Describe what you want the person to do differently. Think about the consequences.

4. How will you feel about the other person and the relationship?

   A. Describe how it will make you feel about him or her *and* your relationship if you honor the request and if you don't.

   B. Describe how it will make you feel about him or her *and* your relationship if he or she honors your request or doesn't.

5. What's your bottom line?

   A. It may be a compromise with limits, such as, "I'm willing to drive you Tuesday before work," or your bottom line may be a simple "No" or "I rather not." Remember you don't need to explain or justify. Expect to receive pressure in some cases and repeated requests. The person is then not listening and ignoring you. Repeat yourself, if necessary. You may need to be prepared to set a second boundary about being nagged, such as, "I'm not willing to discuss this further."

   B. Decide your bottom line concerning the other person's behavior. What are you willing to accept? What is non-negotiable? Consider a consequence if he or she ignores your request. It may be how you're going to feel, an action you can take, or the natural consequence of the person's failure to listen to you. For example, "When you leave your dirty clothes on the floor, I feel that my needs don't matter to you. If it happens again, I won't feel like being close to you," or "I'm going to hire a maid," or "They'll stay where you left them." If it's an action or inaction, *you must be willing to follow through,* so it's important to move slowly and choose a reasonable consequence that you can comfortably carry out and stay connected to the person, unless you're willing to end the relationship. It's imperative that you don't make empty threats. Maybe you've done this in the past. That encourages the unwanted behavior by the other person. When you are certain about your boundary, others will listen.

Setting boundaries

After completing the exercise in the previous section, you can practice role-playing difficult boundary situations with a friend or in the mirror. If it's a request of you, you can state your decision and, if necessary, a brief explanation. If you are making the request, state the following five elements:

1. The *behavior* you don't want. Describe the behavior without judging it. Instead of "inconsiderate behavior," say "being late."

2. How it affects you.

3. The bottom line behavior you want *and* don't want. Be specific.

4. The positive consequences if the person complies.

5. The negative consequences if the person doesn't.

When you're ready to set your boundary, you needn't raise your voice. You can be calm, kind, and respectful and still be heard. Your resolve's communicated. The hardest one to convince is you. When you really know your limits, others sense it and won't violate your boundaries. Follow the do's and don'ts of setting limits, as shown in Table 11-1:

Learning to set boundaries

A young mother had a problem with her 8-year-old daughter who frequently missed the school bus and the mother had to drive her to school. Every morning she nagged her daughter to hurry and get ready, while her daughter dilly-dallied around. One day, the mother had had enough, and told her daughter that the next time she was late, she'd have to stay home all day with the housekeeper. The mother stopped nagging and scolding her daughter, and soon that day came. The child panicked and begged for a ride to school, promising it would never happen again. The mother calmly said, "No, I'm sorry, but I warned you," and continued to get herself ready to go to work. She was fully prepared to let her daughter stay home. After a half hour passed she was about to leave, but could see her daughter was very scared and remorseful, and drove her to school. Because of the mother's tone, even though she didn't enforce the consequence, the child was never late again. They both learned an important lesson about limits. Nagging, scolding, and complaining are not limits. The daughter learned to limit her own behavior after that, which helped her in school as well. Boundaries improved their relationship and self-esteem.

Table 11-1	Do's and Don't's of Setting Limits
Do	**Don't**
Be calm	Apologize, ramble, or waffle
Use "I" statements	Blame, scold, nag, get angry
Make eye-contact	Bring up the past
Be direct and frank	Justify and explain
Speak firmly and naturally	Be sarcastic, cold, superior
Be warm	Fidget
Relax	Use a loud or soft, wavering voice
Listen	Say "You know" or "I mean"

Confronting abuse

Emotional abuse may start innocuously but grow as the abuser becomes more assured that you won't leave the relationship. It may not begin until after an engagement, marriage, or pregnancy. If you look back, you may recall telltale signs of control or jealousy. (For a definition and examples of emotional abuse, see Chapter 3.)

A rule of thumb is that you only accept a little less abuse from others than you accept from yourself. Growing your self-esteem in the ways discussed in previous chapters is necessary before confronting abuse. Abuse is a manipulative tactic used to carry out the abuser's intent to control you and evade meaningful conversation. Notice the abuser's defenses — how he or she parries your attempts to communicate and puts everything back on you to deflect responsibility. When you focus on the content, you fall into the trap of trying to respond rationally, denying accusations, and explaining yourself. You lose your power. The abuser has won and avoided responsibility for the verbal abuse. You must first address the abuse. Prepare to confront the abuse by doing the following:

✔ Start to recognize instances when you're emotionally abused. Watch the abuser's tactics and write them down. Think of it as research data, rather than taking it personally.

✔ Pay attention to how you feel in your body and your feelings at these times. A knot in your stomach or a change of mood indicates that the interaction is making you feel badly. Identify your feelings. (See Chapter 8.)

✔ You must first feel that you're entitled to more respect. Do the exercises in previous chapters.

✔ Practice saying "No" and setting limits with strangers, then with nonthreatening acquaintances and people in your life. The more you value the relationship, the more anxious you are. Work up to doing this with the abuser, where you can expect a reaction.

✔ Work on childhood issues of abuse to help you handle conflict.

✔ Take an assertiveness class.

✔ Join a Twelve Step program and/or get counseling to help you both raise your self-esteem and deal with an abuser. It usually takes the support and validation of a group, therapist, or counselor to be able to stand up to abuse consistently. Without it, you may doubt your reality, feel guilty, and fear reprisal or loss of the relationship.

Rather than giving an ultimatum about verbal abuse in general, I believe it's preferable to practice reacting differently and then set limits each time verbal abuse occurs. Avoid defending or explaining yourself, which fuels abuse. There are other effective ways to respond shown in the following examples:

✔ Start by asking for clarification. Say, "Would you please repeat that?", or "Would you please explain what you mean when you call me a jerk?"

- ✔ State your feelings. "Do you realize that calling me names hurts my feelings?" You may soon discover the abuser doesn't care.

- ✔ State an observation. Casually, without blame, comment, "You seem to like putting me down (interrupting me, giving orders)."

- ✔ Imply boundaries. "You're entitled to your opinion," or "We disagree," or "I don't see it that way," and add, "I'll think about it." Reply to blame with, "I don't take responsibility for that."

- ✔ Try humor, which defeats the abuser's motive of having power over you, but don't be sarcastic.

- ✔ Agreeing with the criticism surprises the abuser and stops the criticism: "It was really dumb of me to forget to mail that letter." or "I'd win 'slob of the month' award." or "I guess I'll never be a good enough son." You can qualify your agreement with, "You may be right."

If these tactics don't work, you may want to confront the abuser and set a boundary directly. When you're ready, be direct and firm with statements, such as, "Stop it," "Don't talk to me that way," "That's demeaning," "Don't call me names," "Don't raise your voice at me," "Don't use that tone with me," "I don't respond to orders."

The abuser may respond with, "Or what?", and you can say, "I will not continue this conversation." Another retort from the abuser may be, "How dare you raise your voice (or tell me what to do)." This is why it's important to be calm and not react, which escalates conflict. Be prepared with a bottom line and consequences discussed earlier. State that you aren't telling the abuser what to do, but stating what *you* will do. Frequently, a verbal abuser becomes more abusive when confronted, in which case, you continue to address the abuse in the same manner. You may say, "If you continue, I'll leave the room," and do so if the abuse continues.

If you keep setting boundaries and carrying out consequences, the abuser will get the message that the abuse isn't getting the desired effect and will stop. If not, reconsider your bottom line and more consequences. You also need to set boundaries to address emotional abuse that is behavioral, such as withholding love, communication, support, or money, which are methods of maintaining power, as is behavior that controls where you go, to whom you talk, or what you think. It's one thing to say, "If you buy the couch, we cannot afford a vacation," versus cutting up your credit cards. Spying, stalking, invading your person, space, or belongings are also abusive and disregard your boundaries. Remember that an abuser may not be interested in your feelings but will respond to your actions.

The relationship may or may not change for the better, or deeper issues may surface. Either way, you're building your self-confidence and self-esteem, learning important skills about setting boundaries and taking back your power. When you do, you won't allow someone to abuse you.

Recognizing domestic violence

Domestic violence means physical abuse, which includes damaging property or your belongings, hair pulling, kicking, slapping, hitting, bruising, burning, shoving, and blocking with a weapon. Violence is about control and always begins with emotional abuse, although emotional abuse doesn't precede physical abuse. If there's physical abuse in your relationship, it will likely be repeated. Promises that it won't happen again occur after an incident when the abuser is remorseful. Victims are dependent on their partners and continue to stay with them, hoping and believing the abuser's promise.

Living with domestic violence destroys your self-esteem. In time, your sense of personal power diminishes as the abuser increasingly takes over control and isolates you from family and friends. You're entitled to feel safe with the person you love. The abuser will try to make excuses and blame you for his or her behavior. You're not responsible for anyone else's behavior. As with alcoholism, you did not cause the abuse, you can neither control it, nor cure it. Abusers can control their impulses, despite what they say. They don't hit their bosses even when they're angry because they know there are serious consequences. Legal repercussions are also consequences that deter violence once it's been reported.

 Studies have shown that negative communication styles and the inability to resolve conflict are leading risk factors for violence. If you tend to withdraw as a defense to emotional abuse, this also increases the chances that abuse will escalate. Typical of codependents, victims of abuse put the needs of their partner before their own. The safety of you and your children should be your number-one concern. What can you do?

- ✔ Improve you communication skills.

- ✔ Build your self-esteem.

- ✔ Join a Twelve Step program and enter individual therapy. This may be more helpful than couple's therapy.

- ✔ Practice setting boundaries to emotional abuse.

- ✔ Don't enable the abuser by maintaining secrecy about the violence or addiction. Secrecy isolates you from help and support and increases the abuser's control over you.

- ✔ Learn all you can about domestic violence (which is beyond the scope of this book).

- ✔ Be prepared to leave quickly. Plan how to exit in advance.

- ✔ Alert neighbors to call the police if they hear loud disturbances.

- ✔ Arrange a place to stay with a friend or relative. Have a bag in your car and/or at your safe place with extra medicine and keys, jewelry, cell phone, address book. Pack children's clothes.

- ✔ Keep the numbers of a local shelter and hotlines handy. (See Chapter 18.)

- ✔ Copy and pack important legal documents, such as birth certificates, court orders, passport, and bank, home, and car ownership records.

- ✔ Open credit card and bank accounts in your name; be sure to pack credit cards, checkbooks, and cash.

Coping with boundary setting

Setting boundaries with others may make you feel anxious and guilty. When you take an emotional risk, it's normal to have anxiety about what may happen or self-criticism about what you said or should have said. This is the old you who's terrified because you're challenging old rules and may fear retaliation or abandonment. These feelings pass, and each time you set a boundary, it gets easier. If you allow feelings to stop you, you continue to feel powerless and resentful, which undermine the relationship and your self-respect.

When you begin setting boundaries, you may feel stiff and be inflexible about them. This is a normal reaction to having had no boundaries and the fear of not being able to maintain them. When you trust yourself and discover that others respect your boundaries without jeopardizing the relationship, you become more flexible. You feel empowered and free to allow others to say "No" to you.

Handling Conflict

Conflict in relationships is inevitable. It's natural that two people will have miscommunications and different desires and needs. In fact, it's said that in every misunderstanding, there are six people involved: the couple and two sets of parents. This is because what you witnessed while you were growing up in your family influences your values, perceptions, and expectations. Knowing this is different than accepting it. Think about your differences, realize that they come with any relationship, and try to accept them, unless they violate your bottom line and are non-negotiable.

There are no villains and no victims

In relationships, there are no victims and no villains — only colluders and collaborators. It takes two to fight. If you don't react and instead respond with positions, you avoid escalating arguments. Be responsible for assertive communication, including setting boundaries. Difficult compromises require a deep understanding of each other's feelings and triggers. Express yours and listen.

Approach problem solving with good will from a win-win perspective. Think of the common welfare, not just your own. Realize the other person's happiness is important if you value the relationship. If he or she is unhappy with the solution, you both suffer. Start with the premise that you're committed to the relationship, that "we" have a problem, and that "we" can and solve it. Begin negotiation by brainstorming together. You can still be assertive, but listen to your partner's ideas as well. This shows that you value your partner, who is more likely to go along with solutions that he or she suggests.

Rules of engagement

To manage conflict in your intimate relationships, together establish and write down rules to govern arguments, such as not bringing up the past, changing topics, or settling disputes late at night or in the bedroom. Allow each other to call time-out and have time-limited talks to give you space in between to think things over. Repeating and even role-playing each other's position can be very helpful. If conflict continues without resolution, consider couples counseling.

Chapter 12

Recovery and Your Family, Friends, and Lovers

....

In This Chapter

▶ Dealing with reactions from your partner and family

▶ Living with an addict before and after sobriety

▶ Visiting your family

▶ Managing change in your friendships

▶ Understanding codependency and sex

....

This chapter discusses your relationships with family and friends after making progress in recovery. It discusses some of the problems that may arise in your family, dating, and how to set boundaries with other codependents.

Some people may be pleased that you're more assertive and glad to honor your boundaries. However, when you change the status quo in close relationships, you often get resistance because people get used to the old ground rules and change can be hard.

Your Partner

Couples do a dance — a pattern of relating. When you change the steps, your partner may be confused and not know what to do. He or she may follow your lead, but you can expect any new limits you set to be tested, so be prepared to enforce them.

Reactions to expect

Your partner may have tantrums, ignore you, or pressure you to return to the old routine. You may need support to keep from wavering until he or she adjusts to the new status quo. The more consistently you assert yourself, the sooner your changes are accepted. You may have to be a "broken record," but be assertive without justifying, blaming, or criticizing (see Chapter 11); otherwise, you fuel an argument and end up on the defensive.

Setting a boundary may lead to a negotiation, but know your bottom line so that you're not persuaded to accept something you can't live with. This is not selfish. It's self-respect and self-love, and when you do it with kindness, you gain the respect of others — even if they don't like it. Remember that the change is for your benefit.

You may get complaints that "you've changed" or "you're "selfish." You can agree, "Yes, I have changed," or "I am thinking of myself more. What's wrong with that?" These attempts to undermine your resolve eventually pass. If the other person hasn't listened to you or changed his or her behavior, be sure you've specified and carried out consequences. When you're serious, you're taken seriously. In addition, remember that boundaries aren't intended to control someone but are for your comfort. Consider actions you can take.

Dealing with an addict or alcoholic

Living with a practicing alcoholic or other drug user is challenging. You've noticed the mood swings and "Jekyll and Hyde" personalities. It's a mistake to take personally anything said to you by Mr. or Mrs. Hyde because it is largely drug-induced. It's helpful to remember the addict has a disease that affects moods and thinking. Try not to let blame or belittling affect your self-esteem. Instead, practice nonattachment (see Chapter 9).

Whether your style of reacting is to blame and criticize or suppress your feelings and complaints, these strategies (and reacting in general) are ineffective and unconstructive. Blame and criticism invite a defensive reaction. Brushing things under the rug doesn't help you feel better and enables the addict to continue his or her drug use as if it isn't causing problems. Calm assertiveness with a loving, or at least friendly, attitude is best. When discussing problems, take care to not give advice or dictate solutions. State the facts and be receptive to hearing new solutions. People are more likely to follow through on their own ideas. If you disagree or none is offered, you're in a better position to propose your solution. Calmly communicate to Dr. Jekyll what you want.

Although not reacting to an addict is wise, it's not easy. Emotions aren't always manageable. It's natural to be frustrated and angry with someone who is self-centered, abusive, and/or unreliable. Suppressing your anger or taking it out on your children or others creates more problems. Instead, write it in your journal, share at a Twelve Step group and in therapy, garden, run, dance, or hit some tennis or golf balls. Vigorous exercise is a great tension release, and so is yoga and meditation. In meditation (see Chapter 14), you quietly observe and feel your anger, and in so doing, it dissipates.

The problem of the addict's addiction belongs to the addict. It's best to invest your energy in yourself, children, work, supportive friends, interests, and hobbies. By not enabling and controlling, you become more independent and less subject to being controlled. This both affords you greater freedom and happiness, and allows the addict to deal with his or her addiction.

After sobriety

There's often a honeymoon period during new sobriety, but guilt, anger, and fear about the destructive past haunt the relationship and still need to be dealt with. The non-addict spouse usually has great hopes and expectations for a normal relationship after having felt deprived for so long but may be disappointed and resentful that the addict is now spending time away from home in Twelve Step meetings and talking intimately with other members. The spouse remembers all the hurts, insults, and disappointments, which the sober addict has denied or would like to forget. Alternatively, the spouse may bring up the past, which leads to more conflict because the addict either truly doesn't remember or feels too much shame to discuss it. Another problem is that the spouse is still anxious and on eggshells, unsure whether Hyde will return at any moment. When they both have more recovery, the spouse learns to forgive and let go of resentment about the past, and the addict takes responsibility and makes amends.

If the sober addict continues in recovery, problems may persist unless the non-addict spouse also finds recovery. This is because the couple's dynamics are changing, and a corresponding change in the non-addict is necessary to bring the relationship into balance. Top Dog (discussed in Chapter 3) has to give up control as the newly sober spouse assumes greater responsibility in the marriage and as a parent. Sometimes the issues of the non-addict become more self-apparent if he or she won't relinquish some control or is still unhappy even though the yearned-for sobriety has arrived. Deeper problems in the relationship that addiction masked and in each individual begin to surface, and they require work and healing.

Your Family Members

It's usually harder not to react to your parents than to your friends and partners, with whom you're on footing that is more equal. You may find it impossible to hold on to healthy behavior when you're around your parents, or you may be fortunate to have a mother and father who support your changes and boundaries concerning your personal relationships.

Many adults, who are parents themselves, feel like children around their own parents and that their parents are still telling them what to do. Psychiatrist and family expert Murray Bowen coined the term "undifferentiated family ego mass," which loosely means, when you're around your family, you lose your mind. That's because in dysfunctional families, it's as if there were just one ego. Whether or not your family is involved in your adult life, where the boundaries are weak or nonexistent, you may have trouble setting boundaries with them. Even if you moved as far away as you could, remember that physical distance is irrelevant. (See the discussion about nonattachment in Chapter 9.) Reactivity is what counts. In families that have "no talk" rules, you may feel uncomfortable talking about feelings or forbidden subjects. This is still a reaction.

Home visits

Your family, especially parents, may test and challenge your new boundaries. Perhaps you have a mom who calls every day or a sibling who wants to borrow money or is abusing drugs. Confused, they may blame your new limits on your partner or therapist.

You may need distance from your parents to create the boundaries that you're unable to make verbally. Some people cut off from their family for the same reason or because of unresolved anger about their childhood. Although cut-offs reduce emotional tension, the underlying problems remain and affect all their relationships. Bowen thought the ideal way to become independent from your family was to work on yourself in therapy, then visit your parents and practice what you've learned. I've witnessed clients who felt uncomfortable returning home do this. They gradually transitioned from staying in their parents' residence during visits, to becoming comfortable declining invitations home, to staying in a hotel or with friends without guilt. Their relationship also improved significantly.

When you visit, notice the rules and boundary and communication patterns, and then try acting in a way that's different from the role you played growing up (see Chapter 7). Pay attention to the habits and defenses you use to manage anxiety. Ask yourself, "What am I afraid of?" Remember that although you may feel like a child with your parents, you aren't one. You're now a powerful adult.

Where active drug addiction and abuse are occurring, consider what boundaries you require in order to feel comfortable. Is it a one-day or one-hour visit or a phone call? One newly sober mother told her children that she couldn't be around them until they stopped using drugs. You may have siblings who pressure you to rescue a parent, or you may be tempted to do so. With difficult family situations, it's helpful to talk with a therapist or other people in recovery from codependency.

Healing your family relations

Healing a relationship begins with you — your feelings and attitudes. Sometimes working on yourself is all it takes (see Chapter 13). Sometimes forgiveness is necessary, or a conversation is required. In many cases, the parent is dead, but this doesn't mean you can't heal the feelings you have about the relationship. Here are some things to think about when it comes to your family:

✔ Your parents don't have to heal for you to get well.

✔ Cut-offs don't heal.

✔ You don't have to like your parents but you probably love them   even though you may not feel it.

✔ Active addiction or abuse by a parent may trigger you. Set boundaries and practice nonattachment covered in Chapter 9.

✔ You can't change or rescue family members.

✔ Indifference, not hatred or anger, is the opposite of love.

✔ Hating someone else interferes with loving yourself.

✔ Unresolved anger and resentment hurt you.

Your Dysfunctional Friends

Your codependency symptoms (see Chapter 3) also show up in friendships but to a lesser degree because of less intimacy. As your self-esteem and assertiveness grow, you may observe new things about your friendships. Do you go along with a friend most of the time or do the opposite, take control. Do you have a relationship that feels one-sided or with someone whom you have trouble getting off the phone? Are you able to share your anger or disappointment about a friendship with your friend? Do you have a friend who persistently thinks like a victim? Notice if you cross boundaries with unrequested advice or help and then feel frustrated because your friend's problems don't change? The Twelve Step programs suggest not to advise other recovering members, and instead, to share your recovery, experience, and hope. You can let them know that you care but have no answers, and, if fitting, that they attend a Twelve Step program or seek therapy. This is the best response.

With some friends, you may need to allow them to see more of you in the relationship, and with others you may need to set boundaries. If you're irritated or don't want to speak to someone, ask yourself whether you need to set boundaries. Resetting boundaries with friends may be rocky at first, as with all intimate relationships, because they're used to the old dynamics and may feel hurt. You can lovingly explain your reasons and feelings. You're learning to give more to yourself. Some friends may not understand, or you may find that you feel criticized, not listened to, or controlled by them. Think about whether this friendship adds to your life.

Codependents tend to share their problems — the old saying applies, "Misery loves company." As you change, your friends change as well. You may discover that you prefer to be with people who are more assertive and happier in their lives. You may decide to leave old dysfunctional friends or limit your time with them.

Codependency Phobia

In recovery, you discover new fears and problems. Now that you've experienced more independence, you fear returning to your old ways. It's natural to be protective of your newfound autonomy and cautious about losing yourself in a relationship, but often, codependents go from weak or no boundaries to rigid ones. They're counter-dependent, wanting never again to be dependent upon someone after leaving an unhealthy relationship. They become inflexible about compromising or put up walls to feel strong and are self-sufficient, making it hard to get close. They think dependency is "weak" or unhealthy, not realizing it's part of the human condition and nothing about which to feel ashamed. They've probably never had healthy dependency in an enduring, nurturing relationship. This creates problems when their autonomy needs conflict with someone else's intimacy needs. For example, they'd never miss a regular Twelve Step meeting to spend time with a close friend or partner or use work, sports, illness, or pain as an excuse to avoid togetherness.

If growth continues, this boomerang period precedes healthy "interdependency," where two autonomous adults allow themselves to rely and depend on each other (see Chapters 2 and 16); however, some codependents are stuck here and are afraid of intimacy and/or commitment. Following the suggested exercises in this book to identify and express your needs and vulnerable feelings, along with practice in self-care and setting boundaries, can help you trust yourself and feel comfortable with intimacy and dependency.

Codependency in the Bedroom

Sex is a form of intimate communication. The problems codependents have with communication also show up in the bedroom. When there's a lack of emotional intimacy or other relationship troubles, sexual pleasure is usually the first to go.

Sexual passion makes you feel vulnerable, out-of-control, and dependent. It's a human need that's dependent upon cooperation of someone. Insecurity or religious beliefs can make you anxious about discussing your sexual needs and preferences, but it's important to share your fantasies, needs, desires, and dislikes. Yet, codependents find it difficult to talk frankly and honestly with each other about anything controversial — especially sex. Their tendencies to deny needs, hide feelings, seek control, and blame each other or themselves all contribute to sexual problems; therefore, it's best to consider a sexual problem as a relationship issue, which it is, even if it starts as an individual problem. Difficulties vary from impotency, frigidity, and inhibited sexual desire to sexual addiction. Sex addiction, like food addiction, crosses the line from a need to a compulsion, and sex or certain types of sexual acts like a drug that becomes a habit despite negative consequences.

If you're in a relationship where the sex was good but you've lost interest, it may be because you're passively expressing anger. Assertive expression of your anger can help you reconnect. If you're withholding anger because you're afraid of receiving verbal abuse, this communication problem must be addressed first to clear the air before sex can feel safe and satisfying. For sex to be healthy and gratifying, each partner must have self-esteem, boundaries, the ability to give and receive, and mutual respect for each other's differences — keys to healthy relationships. (See Chapter 16.)

Self-esteem

The inability to relax is a major factor in performance anxiety. Shame may restrain you and lead to worries about your appearance and/or performance. Self-esteem allows you to be uninhibited and expose yourself emotionally and physically. Practice meditation and mindfulness (see Chapter 14) and negotiate with your Critic (see Chapter 10) to stay out of the bedroom. This can help you be less self-conscious and let go and enjoy yourself — as sex should be.

As your self-esteem grows, you become more assertive about intimacy, which is essential to satisfying sex. Often problems derive or continue from an inability to talk about what you want sexually, what you need, and what you don't like. Instead, you don't enjoy sex or may withdraw. Try talking about your fantasies and what you like in bed, which may be easier than saying what you don't like.

Boundaries

Boundaries allow you to feel safe and be close without fear that you may lose your autonomy and freedom, be hurt, or feel smothered. Such fears can lead to impotency, frigidity, and loss of interest. You may avoid sex altogether because you're uncomfortable setting boundaries in or outside the bedroom. If you're feeling controlled, disrespected, or degraded, or experiencing emotional or physical abuse, there's a good chance it's affecting the sex due to a lack of safety and trust. Think about setting some limits. (See Chapter 11.)

Giving and receiving

Healthy sex involves both desire and wanting to be desired and the giving and receiving of pleasure. Some codependents deny their desire and perform sex as a duty without emotional involvement. Pleasers or caretakers often play those roles during sex. They're only comfortable giving because receiving makes them feel too vulnerable, exposed, and out of control. Giving helps them stay in control and focused on their partner.

Accepting differences

To become close, you must be able to respect each other's differences. Idealizing someone early in a relationship before you know each other well sets you up for disappointment and difficulty accepting him or her as you face reality. Sex suddenly becomes mundane or you just lack desire. Some couples keep it exciting by fighting, drama, and insecurity in the relationship. Relationships, including sex that's satisfying to both, require acceptance and sometimes negotiation of each other's preferences.

Addiction and sex

All of the problems mentioned so far in this section are exaggerated and complicated by addiction. Often addicts aren't emotionally present during sex. Alcohol may impede a man's ability to perform, leaving both partners frustrated. Repeated failures undermine the relationship and may cause both partners to avoid sex. The alcoholic's mate may be turned off by drunkenness and refuse sex or comply out of fear or a sense of obligation, which leads to resentment.

Another dynamic is that the Underdog addict (see Chapter 3) looks to the Top Dog spouse as strong and steadfast to lean on, like a parent. The addict may idealize Top Dog as saintly compared to his or her own self-loathing and provoke Top Dog's scolding or punishment to alleviate guilt. Even if Top Dog doesn't scold, the addict still believes he or she is being judged and may avoid sex due to feelings of unworthiness. Needless to say, the male addict doesn't want to have sex with his disciplinarian mother. Guilt about alcohol-induced impotency may also cause an alcoholic to withdraw.

In early sobriety, if the recovering addict is ashamed and guilt-ridden about admitting his or her addiction and past conduct, some of the past sexual patterns may continue. The addict's spouse may be unable to relax and enjoy sex with the newly sober spouse or may withhold sex after sobriety as a method — sometimes unconscious — to punish the addict for the past or to remain in control.

Dating

In recovery, it's natural to desire an equal intimate relationship. The work of recovery raises your self-esteem so you feel worthy of love and teaches you relationship skills. The healthier you become, the healthier are the people you date and the more able you are to evaluate potential partners. The power of codependency is strong, and it's very difficult to resist repeating old patterns. The best antidote is working on your recovery and attending Twelve Step meetings. Books about dating abound, but here are a few pointers as they relate to codependency.

Types of relationships

There are several types of relationships. Each meets different needs with different levels of involvement. They range from casual to marriage and long-term commitment, being the least frequent, as shown in Figure 12-1.

The most common relationships are casual encounters with strangers you see at a gathering or activity, such as shopping or a sports event, or people who merely serve a function, like a cashier or food server. Codependents with poor boundaries may disclose intimate details of their lives or feel responsible to help them, neglecting their own needs or friends. It's fine to be charitable, but important to maintain a choice and boundaries about when and whom you help. If you interact more frequently with the person, he or she becomes an acquaintance. Someone you meet at a workshop or your hairdresser may become an acquaintance, similar to a classmate, team player, or co-worker. If you decide to socialize and plan to get together, he or she may become an activity partner. The person still isn't a friend because your relationship revolves around an activity, like someone with whom you play golf. As you see and interact with him or her, you gather information about whether or not he or she is honest, reliable, and respectful of your needs and opinions. If the answer is yes, and you enjoy his or her company, you may want to take it to the next level and become friends, which means now you want to talk and spend time together for their own sake. You like doing things together upon which you *both* agree. You get involved with each other's lives and offer support.

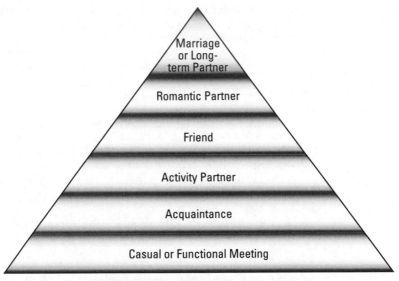

Figure 12-1: Types of relationships.

Friendships can take years to develop. If you expect them to happen in a few months of knowing someone, you may be disappointed as you learn more about the person. If you add sex to the equation, then it's a romantic partner, although some people have sex with a casual stranger, acquaintance, or activity partner. If you do, it's a mistake to expect your lover to want to spend time with you outside of sex, so it may be important to find that out if you can be friends first. Otherwise, you may end up feeling used or let down.

You get to determine the type of relationship you want — an activity companion, a sex partner, a committed relationship, or marriage. It's not always easy to decide. Often codependents are confused because they don't know themselves or have been hurt in the past. If you're not sure if you want commitment, or if you have unconscious fears, your ambivalence will likely attract someone who is not right for you or who is unable to connect or commit emotionally. You still can decide whether to continue a relationship.

For starters

Physical attraction tells you nothing about the person's integrity or capacity to respect you and maintain a healthy relationship. Making good choices is based upon knowing and valuing yourself, your needs, wants, and standards, and knowing the other person.

Dating is an opportunity to gather information about someone and to communicate your feelings, values, wants, and needs. You can determine whether you're compatible and whether your date has the necessary qualities for a successful relationship (see Chapter 16). If you're unaware of your values or don't honor them, sexual attraction can take over and tempt you to go along with your date's values, rather than compare them to their own. After a while, you may be unhappy that your values don't match your partner's.

Self-acceptance means that you don't judge or deny your needs or values in order to make a relationship work. Some people like to spend a lot of time together, whereas others need more space. Some are active, and others are homebodies. Some need a lot of affection, and others don't. To some, security is paramount. Some want adventure and others emotional intimacy. Realize you can be who you are and have what you want without apology or self-sacrifice.

Closeness vs. separateness

Codependents use a self-defeating, all-or-nothing approach to dating. Either you feel intense physical attraction, coupled with an underlying fear of abandonment, or you're bored and indifferent. When you're interested in someone, you soon disclose your history and deep feelings and secrets in order to feel close. Boundaries merge quickly and you become dependent, drop hobbies and plans with friends. Soon you stop being honest and please and manipulate in order to protect the wonderful feelings of being with the other person. The fear of speaking openly and honestly leads to obsession, and when things start to bother you, instead of addressing them, you blame yourself or your date. One of you withdraws or loses interest in order to create a safer boundary — or perhaps flips back and forth or argues about the relationship, but you can neither stay close nor move on. Alternatively, you may move on quickly or spend time alone to get back the Self you lost when you were emotionally close.

Sex

Sex and dating can be a minefield for codependents with poor boundaries and self-esteem. Both men and women use seduction to hide their fears of inadequacy and that they don't know how to be authentic and intimate. The one seduced may interpret the attention to mean more than sexual attraction and manipulation. Women often have difficulty saying "No" to sex that they don't want to have because they feel responsible for their partners' sexual needs and/or so men will continue dating them. Doing so may lower their opinion of themselves and their self-esteem. Sex becomes a substitute for intimacy to reduce their depression and loneliness. Real intimacy takes time together, self-esteem, skill, and trust (see Chapter 16). Before having sex with someone you're dating, think about:

- ✔ What are your desires and expectations concerning having a sexual relationship? Do you want an exclusive relationship?

- ✔ If you haven't discussed this with your partner, why not?

- ✔ How will having sex affect you emotionally?

- ✔ What are the health risks?

- ✔ How do you feel about sexually transmitted diseases (STDs)? If you don't know, get the facts about STDs. Most people don't know when they're infected. Only a test can be relied upon.

Think of dating as a lab to learn more about yourself. Sense how you feel when you are touched — not just pleasurable sensations, but your thoughts and emotions as well. Distinguish feelings of excitement and fear, which may seem similar. You alone have the right to decide whether anyone may touch you. Notice if you start to rationalize negative sensations, thoughts, or feelings. Your body's signaling, "Stop!" Practice listening and verbalizing those words.

Never have sex:

- ✔ If you're afraid

- ✔ If you feel guilty or obligated

- ✔ To win someone's love

- ✔ To change or manipulate someone

Sexual attraction and attachment cause you to overlook red flags. When in the relationship, the very traits you liked can be problems. See Chapter 16 for what to look for and avoid when starting a relationship.

Chapter 13

Going for the Gold – Healing Your Past

In This Chapter

▶ Befriending your wounded child
▶ Healing shame
▶ Grieving your childhood
▶ Finding out about trauma

*R*ecognizing your codependent patterns and sources is a major step in your recovery, but real change involves healing underlying shame and grieving losses from your childhood. This chapter initiates you to that process. You're introduced to the stages of grief, concluding with acceptance. It's a bit like going back and filling in missing pieces from your past. The decision to confront your parent or parents is addressed.

Growing up in a dysfunctional family can be traumatic. Many of you may still be experiencing symptoms as a result. Trauma is explained as well as new treatment options for healing it.

The Wounded Child

In dysfunctional families, it's not safe to be spontaneous, vulnerable, and authentic. You're shamed and even punished for expressing your feelings and for being imperfect, needy, and immature. Some people are neglected or emotionally or physically abandoned and conclude they can't trust or rely on anyone, put aside their child Self, and play an adult role before they're ready.

How you've encountered these experiences are your wounds. Most everyone manages to grow up, but the scars remain and account for problems in relationships and coping with reality. Deeper healing requires reopening those wounds, cleaning them, and applying the medicine of compassion.

The nature of your child Self

Maybe you've heard the expression "inner child." Perhaps you think the idea that you have a child inside of you is absurd or would feel foolish talking about it. That would be expected if you feel silly goofing around. Nevertheless, once you were a child and had all the traits shared by little children. A lot of codependents learned to be mature, responsible, and in control at an early age. If your parents valued those traits, the child in you had to lie low. On the other hand, perhaps you easily allow your child to come out, but there are still feelings from your childhood that were never safe to express.

Your inner child can be compared to your *true, authentic Self.* Psychologist Carl Jung believed that the child was a symbol of the Self and the "bringer of healing" who leads the way for wholeness, individuation, and personality change. The spirit of your inner child went into hiding and is waiting to be recognized and freed.

Your child's characteristics

If you've been around very young children, you know that they're spontaneous and open with their feelings — before they learn to be afraid and guarded. They laugh out loud, cry when they're hurt, and holler and defy you when they're angry. They soon recover and move their attention to something else. Regardless of feeling hurt or disappointed, they forgive, don't worry, and uncondition-ally love their parents. They're always in the moment, are curious, exploring everything, and their ability to become absorbed in their imagination and creativity is limitless. They're happiest playing, singing, and dancing. Above all, they're lovable just as they are. Although you've been conditioned not to behave like a child, all the following child characteristics are still within you:

- ✔ **Imperfect:** Makes mistakes, stumbles, forgets, and spills things
- ✔ **Needy:** Requires love, attention, and affection
- ✔ **Playful and creative:** Uses limitless imagination
- ✔ **Spontaneous:** Responds to changing ideas, feelings, and needs
- ✔ **Dependent:** Needs adults for help, instruction, and encouragement
- ✔ **Immature:** Acts like a child, not a grown up
- ✔ **Vulnerable:** Expresses all needs and feelings
- ✔ **Authentic**: Appears without defenses or pretense
- ✔ **Innocent:** Is unashamed of being bad, defective, or not enough

> ✔ **Enthusiastic and energetic:** Exudes excitement and zeal
>
> ✔ **Loving and lovable:** Gives and deserves love

Your enthusiasm, creativity, and zest for life come alive when your authentic Self — your child — is embraced, expressed, and nurtured. It's your feeling Self that's present when you experience emotions or are spontaneous, creative, playful, or intuitive.

List all the ways that your child expresses itself in your feelings and at play, such as wearing bright colors, gardening, dancing, playing music, a sport, or with a pet, cooking, bubble baths, or any other activity that you fully enjoy.

Your child's needs

Sometimes your child lets you know through depression, anger, addiction, illness, or pain that its needs are being neglected. Core needs of a child are:

- ✔ Unconditional love
- ✔ Safety
- ✔ Being listened to
- ✔ Touch
- ✔ Guidance
- ✔ Respect
- ✔ Nurturing
- ✔ Play
- ✔ Encouragement

If you're overriding or ignoring your needs and desires, working too hard, not setting safe boundaries, or pushing and criticizing yourself, your child will be very unhappy and may throw a tantrum or become anxious, cranky, forlorn, tired, depressed, or sick. Beware of trying to "nurture" it in self-destructive ways through addictive behavior — like drugs instead of relaxation, rescuing others instead of healing yourself, giving it food instead of self-expression, or sex instead of tenderness.

Befriending your child Self

How your parents treated you is how you care for yourself. If you weren't nurtured, you won't be able to nurture yourself. It may be a challenge for you to befriend your child, discover what it needs, and nurture it in healthy ways. It gets easier and fun with time and practice. Your child holds great wisdom for you to uncover.

Getting in touch with your child

Your child can be readily accessed through the emotional and intuitive right side of your brain by way of movement, creative expression, meditation, and writing with your nondominant hand.

1. Sit or lie down. Take several minutes to relax your whole body, starting with your toes up to your scalp. Now imagine that you're visiting the home where you grew up. (If you lived in several, choose one before puberty.) Notice how you feel about being outside your home and entering. Go inside, and pay attention to the smells, sounds, voices, footsteps, décor, and what you feel in your body. Do this slowly in every room, until you find your child. Look into your child's face and discover what he or she's feeling. Speak to him or her gently, with kindness and compassion, and learn what the child part of you felt in the past and wants and needs now. Reassure your child that you're interested and listening, and that you'll do all you can to fulfill his or her needs and desires.

2. On newsprint or inexpensive paper, paint or draw (in color is better) your inner child with your non-dominant hand. Tell your perfectionist and Critic to leave you alone. Whatever you draw is exactly right.

3. Now interview the child you've created. Ask questions with your right hand, and answer with your nondominant hand. Find out what your child is feeling, what matters most, and what exactly it needs and wants you to know.

4. Your child speaks to you through your body and movement. Play instrumental music with a nondistinct beat or rhythm, and allow your body to move however it wants. Stop and notice what you're feeling. Move in a way that expresses or emphasizes that feeling. You may want to curl into a ball, climb the walls, or pound the floor. See if sounds or words want expression. Allow them, howl them, sing them, and write them.

Make a habit of dialoguing with your child on a daily basis to find out what it wants, feels, and needs. Ask your child its opinion about plans, decisions, which friends feel safe, and which don't. Getting to know your child includes happy and play times, too. Ask your child about its early favorites — favorite playmate, discovery, food, place, pastime, teacher, TV show, book, fairy tale, song, and so on.

First impressions

Some infants experience trauma from delivery complications or are premature and spend the first weeks separated from their mothers in an incubator. Others are born unwanted, or to a mother who was an addict or under immense stress.

Write a letter to your child and ask about its first experiences in the womb and coming into this world. Ask your child what your parents felt about your birth. Answer with your nondominant hand. You may not consciously know, but suspend your disbelief and trust that whatever you write contains some truth.

You may not remember much about your childhood, but after you start writing more will come to you. Gather information about your early years from family members, and list events and memories for each year, including, births, deaths, moves, best friends, school teachers, and illnesses. Write a dialogue with your child to learn its feelings about the events, trips, discoveries, memories, and people.

Parenting your child

A good parent respects, listens to, empathizes, comforts, encourages, and guides a child. A parent also sets limits. Practice these parenting skills with your child, and over time you'll develop an open loving relationship.

Nurturing your child

Universal symbols of nurturance and unconditional love are Mother Earth, the Madonna and child, and female deities in other religions. Nurturing your inner child begins by giving him or her love. Most codependents find it easy to love others but not themselves (see Chapter 10). Some end up drained and resentful because they're helping others and neglecting themselves. When you start caring for yourself, you have better boundaries about taking care of others.

After years of judging, pushing, scolding, indulging, abandoning, and neglecting your child, begin building bridges of trust by nurturing, listening, and talking to your child in these ways:

- ✔ **Listening:** Create quiet, alone time to hear what's on your child's mind.

- ✔ **Mirroring:** Repeat what your child says and name feelings, such as "I hear that you're sad."

- ✔ **Understanding:** "It was unfair that you were treated that way. That must have hurt a lot."

✔ **Acceptance:** "It's okay. You're not bad for feeling (angry, hopeless, confused)." All feelings are okay.

✔ **Empathy:** "I know how you feel."

✔ **Consolation and comfort:** "You won't always feel this way. It will get better."

✔ **Encouragement:** "You can do it, and we can do it together."

✔ **Unconditional love:** Say "I love you" in the mirror, even for your seemingly damaged parts.

1. In your journal, writing with your nondominant hand, find out how your child feels about how you've parented it. Encourage your child to be specific about ways you've disappointed him or her. Details provide you with valuable information about your child's needs. Discover how your child wants to be loved.

2. Start by apologizing to your child and proving yourself trustworthy through your actions. Keep your commitments and promises, or your child will feel abandoned and go back into hiding.

3. Write your child a love letter. Be specific about what you love, and then read it to yourself out loud in the mirror.

4. Get in the practice of asking yourself how you feel, what you want and need in the moment.

Protecting your child

Your child is all feelings. Without boundaries, it feels out of control. Your child may be angry and want to break things or hurt you or someone else. He or she may want to rant or confide inappropriately with a co-worker or love someone who is abusive or abandoning. Other times, your child is rebellious, stubborn, or afraid to do things necessary for your well-being. When your child doesn't want to exercise, go to sleep, work, or see a doctor, it's not always in your best interest to let him or her have their way.

Good parenting involves nurturing that dissolves anger and protection and guidance that set limits and finds healthy outlets for it. Try sticking to limits you set, like getting your work done, enough rest, healthy food, and exercise. Your nurturing parent can listen and empathize with the moods and recalcitrance of your inner child. Then the protective parent can offer guidance and set limits, explaining that some things, although unpleasant, benefit you in the long run (see Chapter 9 on your responsibilities). You can mediate a compromise between your child and adult perspectives. Your child may be afraid and just need reassurance and encouragement, but sometimes that fear can be an intuitive warning, especially if your child consistently doesn't want to do something. There's probably a deeper, valid reason, which you should explore through dialoguing.

The protective parent is also the part of you that's a child advocate and stands up for you in the world. Find out what your inner child wants you to do to protect it. Standing up to others takes practice if you were abused and no one protected you, or you weren't allowed to say "No," or "Stop." (See Chapter 11 on setting boundaries.) Psychotherapy can help you find your voice and heal trauma, as discussed later in this chapter. Start by following these suggestions:

- ✔ Make a fist, stomp your feet, and repeat, "I have a right to . . . ." Say it loud, and keep saying it, filling in the blank with different words, such as "be respected, feel safe, get a raise, be listened to," and so on.

- ✔ Practice saying, "I don't like that," "Stop it!" "How dare you . . ." "Don't do that!"

- ✔ After finding out what your inner child needs you to say, do the following role play exercise. Imagine the person you want to talk to is sitting in an empty chair. Stand up and practice asserting what you want to say. Keep it to one sentence without explanations. (Your actual message may be longer. Practice saying what you want succinctly, without explanations.)

- ✔ Take a martial arts class for self-defense training.

Healing shame

Shame is an emotion that comes and goes, like anger or fear. But codependents have internalized shame so that it becomes who they think they are. They think they're bad, unlovable, guilty, self-ish, weak, or responsible for abuse that they experienced. This is untrue. (See Chapters 3 and 7.) Children are innocent, and so were you, no matter what you were told. Even if you weren't accused or blamed, you probably accuse or blame yourself.

When children are powerless to set boundaries or leave their parents, they idealize them and attribute positive traits in order to survive and create a feeling of safety. With parents who range from cold and rigid to unpredictable and out of control, it's more comforting to believe, "If I'm good, Mommy (or Daddy) will love me," than "Mommy (or Daddy) is self-centered, doesn't care about me, or is unreliable." The truth would be frightening and lead to despair. It provides children a sense of control to believe that if they're very good or behave, they can avoid criticism and abuse.

Codependents also blame themselves for not stopping abuse directed toward them or a sibling or for receiving bribes or pleasure from an abusive parent. Some feel ashamed that they didn't stand up to a parent sooner because they finally did as a teenager or adult. They don't realize that their reactions were established when they were very young and didn't have the emotional and mental maturity to respond differently. It's also natural to love and need love and affection from your parents despite abuse. Children will do anything to get it because they need love to grow. They don't understand (sometimes long into adulthood) that they didn't cause and couldn't have changed or stopped their parents' actions. Maybe you have the illusion that you caused or can change someone's behavior today.

Ways to heal shame include:

- ✔ Read Chapters 3 and 10, and describe how and when you feel ashamed.

- ✔ Read Chapter 7 and identify the sources of your shame.

- ✔ Work with the Tyrannical Trio as suggested in Chapter 10.

- ✔ Listen and talk to your inner child. Repeatedly remind your child that he or she is innocent and question the assumptions about what he or she considers shameful.

- ✔ Let your inner child know you love him or her no matter what.

- ✔ Read literature on codependency and abuse. (See Chapter 18.)

- ✔ Join a support group or Twelve Step program and share what happened to you. (See Chapter 18.)

- ✔ Enter therapy for trauma, discussed later in this chapter.

Grieving Your Losses – Feel to Heal

You may know about pain in your past or you may be in denial (see Chapter 5). Everyone, including those raised in healthy families, had disappointments in their childhood. Codependents had more than others. It's also possible that despite growing up in a dysfunctional family, you were happy much of the time. Family life may have included affection, laughter, and fun. Nevertheless, there were also losses. Here are some ideas that get in the way of grieving:

- ✔ **Rationalizing:** "My parents did the best that they could," or "They didn't know better." Even if these statements were true, they deny the effect they had on you.

- ✔ **Justifying:** "My dad had a rough childhood," or "I was a difficult kid."

✔ **Minimizing:** "It wasn't so bad. I know kids who had it worse."

✔ **Avoidance:** Using an addiction (including food, work, and relationships) to avoid feelings. Thinking it's in the past and doesn't bother me. "Grief won't change anything," or "My parents are dead now anyway."

✔ **Intellectualizing:** "I know all about it," but without feelings.

✔ **Premature forgiveness:** Forgiveness before working through grief can abort the process and block the healthy release of emotions that keep you stuck.

When you first discover what caused their codependency — perhaps by reading this book — your knowledge is still intellectual. Even if you know all about your abusive childhood, you must link childhood events or your parents' or siblings' behavior to the effect it had on you and your feelings about it then and now. You must feel to heal.

When you lose someone or something dear, it's natural to have feelings about it. When you experienced losses growing up in a dysfunctional family, emotions go unexpressed (see Chapter 7), and their energy gets stored in your body. Not discharging emotion can lead to depression and chronic emotional and physical symptoms. Healing involves identifying your wounds, feeling the feelings, and sharing those feelings with others. Maybe you've cried or raged about the past, but it's important that you're witnessed by someone you trust. Otherwise, it may be a repetition of your childhood, when you had no one to comfort you in your pain.

Gradually, your past and those emotions lose their power over you. There's never a "good" time to do the work, but postponing it only perpetuates your unhappiness and codependency, which deprive you of your future. Grieving is a process that happens over time — sometimes, several years. It's wise to get professional help.

The childhood you missed

You may not realize what you've lost. If you grew up deaf, you wouldn't know the sound of a symphony. So, too, if you never had nurturing, you wouldn't know the soothing comfort of a mother's voice. One client had never had any closeness with her father, never sat on his knee, never saw him smile at her, or heard a kind word — things most children take for granted. Your losses are particular to you, but here's a suggested list to jog your memory:

✔ Experiencing the death or separation from a loved one or pet

✔ Knowing all the things your friends could do that you couldn't

- ✔ Finding the lack of a happy, carefree childhood
- ✔ Giving up the illusion of having had a happy childhood
- ✔ Giving up the hope you can get today what you didn't before
- ✔ Having parents absent from PTA meetings, athletic events, or your graduation, performance, or award ceremony
- ✔ Not having friends over because you were too embarrassed
- ✔ Preferring someone else as a parent because something was lacking in your relationship with your parent
- ✔ Going through things alone or having no one to talk to
- ✔ Being physically or emotionally abandoned
- ✔ Feeling your parents' divorce and its consequences
- ✔ Not receiving encouragement, guidance, or financial support
- ✔ Being excluded from an inheritance
- ✔ Feeling unsafe or not trusting family members
- ✔ Seeing the damage and lost time your past has caused and the energy and money you must spend to heal now
- ✔ Missing an extended family
- ✔ Experiencing ruined holidays, birthdays, and vacations, or having had none
- ✔ Experiencing the inability to enjoy healthy intimacy and relationships
- ✔ Feeling damage to your self-esteem and ability to love
- ✔ Missing specific feelings, such as spontaneity, joy, and fun
- ✔ Losing innocence, including virginity from incest or rape
- ✔ Missing successes or goals you may have achieved

Write a paragraph about any of these losses or others you remember with as much detail as you can recall. Write the feelings you had at the time and how you feel about it today. Read what you wrote to someone you trust.

Faces of grief

People generally believe that grief entails feeling sad and crying. That's a big component, but grief has many faces and stages. It includes talking about your past and an array of emotions. You may feel self-obsessed, and for a while you may need to be. You may experience some of these feelings:

✔ Mood swings

✔ Fatigue and exhaustion

✔ Memory gaps

✔ Obsessive thoughts

✔ Confusion

✔ Feeling lost, aimless, and lack of meaning

✔ Feeling spacey and disorganized; difficulty thinking

✔ Anger, including rage, self-pity, and bitterness

✔ Shame and guilt

✔ Feeling stuck and unable to move on

✔ Hopelessness

✔ Crying, sorrow, and sadness

✔ Deadness, emptiness, or sense of unreality

 Notice when you have any of the above feelings. Write about them, and see if they connect to a loss, present or past. If it's a present loss, does it remind you of one in the past?

Stages of grief

Grief doesn't always follow a fixed pattern. Professionals have divided it into stages, which may be experienced out of order and can be recycled over and over from the beginning. Elisabeth Kubler-Ross wrote about the following five stages of grief.

1. **Denial:** Believing you feel fine or your childhood was happy, or minimizing or excusing parents' behavior (see Chapter 5).

2. **Anger:** Anger can last a long time; it's important not to get stuck there and to allow your sadness (see Chapter 3).

3. **Bargaining:** Thinking "If only . . . " about the past or making deals with God about the future.

4. **Depression:** Caused by sorrow and sadness, which may include feelings of emptiness and hopelessness.

5. **Acceptance:** Doesn't mean that you forget or are okay with what happened but that you see your past objectively, without denial or strong emotions about what happened to you.

Many codependents, especially women, feel sad when they're angry. Others don't allow themselves to cry or feel sad and only feel anger. Both sadness and anger are necessary stages of grieving. Some professionals add guilt as a stage. Codependents already have more guilt than they should. (See Chapter 3 on guilt and Chapter 10 on self-forgiveness.) Consider whether your guilt is:

✔ To avoid grief

✔ Because you're taking responsibility for someone else's actions

✔ For choices made when you were too young to be responsible

✔ For pain you caused others due to justifiable anger or your natural desire for independence

Suggestions for healing

Ideally, it's recommended that you work one-on-one with someone you trust who is a trained professional and can guide and help you understand and manage painful feelings. Grief and trauma overlap because trauma involves loss, often of trust, security, or innocence. These feelings pass in time *but not on their own.* The therapeutic techniques at the end of this chapter are effective for healing. Sharing at Twelve Step meetings is also useful.

✔ What stage are you with respect to each loss? Track stages as you experience them, but don't judge how far along you've come because the stages recycle.

✔ Allow yourself to feel whatever feelings you've identified, without justifying your parents' actions or blaming yourself.

✔ Share your feelings where it's safe and find productive ways to vent your anger.

✔ Write a letter to your parent(s) stating:

   • What was done to you

   • How you felt then

   • How you feel about it now

   • How it has affected you

✔ Read the letter to someone you trust.

✔ Imagine your parent in a chair, and read the letter aloud.

✔ Deeply relax and imagine your parent and share the letter.

✔ Think about what you want from the person today.

Acceptance

Acceptance is key to moving on, whereas grief and resentment prevent growth. Your fate included your parents, and they're part of you, like it or not. Unconditional love or anger toward them is replaced with an objective assessment of reality and forgiveness. You understand why they behaved as they did but not as a defense to your feelings. Acceptance also includes forgiving yourself and accepting who you are today without regret, shame, or apology.

Some people ask if forgiveness is necessary to heal. Forgiveness shouldn't bypass grief, but be a natural consequence. It's a process, and if given too soon can abort healing — if withheld too long, can prevent you from moving on. Unresolved anger and resentment can turn into guilt, low self-esteem, and shame, and can spill over into current relationships. Keep in mind what forgiveness is and isn't. It:

✔ Means you let go of your hurt and resentment

✔ Means you let go of any desire for retribution or compensation

✔ Doesn't mean condoning the abuser's actions

✔ Doesn't mean forgetting

✔ Doesn't necessarily mean being friends or having a relationship

✔ Doesn't mean trusting or being vulnerable to the abuser

When grieving is completed, you discover new hope and energy to live your life — more than if you don't grieve. You accept your childhood and that these were your parents. A burden has been lifted, and you feel lighter. You can focus on your future because you're not controlled by your past. You gain self-esteem, self-compassion, and a sense of well-being. You're able to risk trusting and loving in more realistic and healthy ways.

Confrontations

A complete discussion of confrontation is beyond the scope of this book. You don't have to confront the abuser in person to heal. The person may be dead, too old, or infirm. Whether or not you decide to have a personal confrontation, follow the suggestions in this book — to come out of denial, strengthen your support system, self-esteem, boundaries, and assertiveness, and to heal grief, anger, and shame. All are essential preparation for confrontation.

Confrontation should be for you — without unrealistic expectations that the abuser will magically change. Prepare to be attacked. You're probably challenging denial that has been maintained for years, and if you're focused on getting something from the abuser, you may be disappointed. If you're seeking revenge, you have unfinished anger work to do, and a confrontation may leave you feeling guilty and prevent or prolong reconciliation if you want it one day.

Before confronting a parent or abuser, ask yourself:

- ✔ What are your motives?

- ✔ What do you hope to accomplish?

- ✔ What are your expectations?

- ✔ Can you live with your worst imagined outcome?

- ✔ Do you have a strong support system?

- ✔ Are you secure in what happened to you in the face of denial?

- ✔ Are you secure in knowing it wasn't your fault?

- ✔ What do you still need and want from your family?

- ✔ Can you live without it or without contact with them?

- ✔ Are you prepared to handle blame and angry reprisals?

- ✔ What if you get no reaction?

If you decide to go ahead with a confrontation, prepare with a friend or therapist, and write down and rehearse what you're going to say aloud. State what boundaries you need and anything else you want in any future relationship. Plan to meet at a place where you can easily leave. Ask to be heard without interruption and succinctly state the points you've rehearsed. Don't judge yourself if you decide to forego confrontation for any reason, such as you couldn't handle your family's reaction, are still dependent on them, or it would expose you to more abuse without any benefit.

Healing Trauma

Trauma can be emotional, physical, or environmental, and can range from experiencing an earthquake to humiliation by a bully. The focus here is on emotional trauma, which is a stressful event or ongoing situation that overwhelms your ability to cope with what's happening. Some of your childhood losses, such as any kind of abuse or divorce, may have been traumatic.

Kinds of trauma

With codependency, traumatization usually starts when you were very young, so you hadn't yet developed coping skills that a healthy adult would have. Events had a greater impact on you then than they would today. Examples of traumatic occurrences are:

- ✔ Betrayal
- ✔ Abuse; remember that it may be subtle or covert and can be as damaging as violence if enduring. Physical and sexual abuse are both physical and emotional traumas (see Chapters 3 and 7).
- ✔ Addiction or living with an addict
- ✔ Death of a loved one or physical or emotional abandonment
- ✔ Pain
- ✔ Threat of physical pain, harm, or abandonment
- ✔ Helplessness
- ✔ Poverty
- ✔ Real or threatened loss of anything of value
- ✔ Witnessing a trauma to someone else, including survivor guilt

Symptoms of trauma

Trauma is a subjective experience and differs from person to person. Each child in a family will react differently to the same experience and to trauma. Symptoms may come and go and may not show up until years after the event. You needn't have all of the following symptoms to have experienced trauma:

- ✔ Over-reacting to triggers that are reminders of the trauma
- ✔ Avoiding thinking, experiencing, or talking about triggers for the trauma
- ✔ Avoiding activities you once enjoyed
- ✔ Feeling hopeless about the future
- ✔ Experiencing memory lapses or inability to recall parts of trauma
- ✔ Having difficulty concentrating
- ✔ Having difficulty maintaining close relationships
- ✔ Feeling irritable or angry

✔ Feeling overwhelming guilt or shame

✔ Behaving in a self-destructive manner

✔ Being easily frightened and startled

✔ Being hypervigilant — excessively fearful

✔ Hearing or seeing things that aren't there

✔ Having restricted feelings — sometimes numb or emotionally flat, or detached from emotions, other people, or events

✔ Feeling depersonalized; a loss of Self or cut off from your body and environment — like you're going through the motions

✔ Having flashbacks of scenes or reliving the past event

✔ Having dreams or nightmares about the past

✔ Experiencing insomnia

✔ Experiencing panic attacks

Post-traumatic stress syndrome (PTSD) is not uncommon among codependents who experienced trauma or grew up with a practicing addict. (For more information about PTSD, see *Post Traumatic Stress Disorder For Dummies* by Dr. Mark Goulson, published by Wiley) Diagnosis requires a specific number of symptoms that last for at least 30 days and may start long after the triggering event. Core symptoms include:

✔ Intrusive thoughts in the form of dreams, waking flashbacks, or recurring negative thoughts

✔ Avoidance of reminders of the trauma, including forgetting or avoiding sleep and shutting down feelings or numbness

✔ Hyperarousal putting your nervous system on alert, creating irritability, exhaustion, and difficulty relaxing and sleeping

Trauma is debilitating and robs you of your life. Often a person has experienced several traumas, resulting in more severe symptoms, such as mood swings, depression, high blood pressure, and chronic pain. Focus on treating both the trauma and codependency.

Treatment

A number of treatments have been shown to be successful to treat trauma. Talking about what happened to you in a group setting is useful, but it won't be as effective as working one-on-one with a trained therapist in an environment where you feel safe to express your feelings and receive feedback. Effective therapies are:

✔ **Cognitive-behavioral therapy (CBT):** CBT is recommended for PTSD and associated thoughts, feelings, and beliefs.

✔ **Eye movement desensitization and reprocessing (EMDR):** EMDR uses eye movements to alter beliefs and feelings. The eye movements affect the brain's patterns.

✔ **Emotional freedom technique (EFT):** EFT is based on tapping acupressure points that reduce emotional reactivity.

✔ **Rational Emotive Behavior Therapy (REBT):** REBT challenges beliefs and thoughts without reviewing the past.

✔ **Visualization:** This lessens the impact of an event by re-experiencing it in a safe situation with the aid of an advocate or protector to gain a new perspective and coping strategies.

✔ **Psychodynamic psychotherapy:** This helps you to identify triggers, change your thoughts and beliefs, handle emotions, conflicts, and symptoms created by the trauma, set boundaries, and increase your self-esteem and self-compassion.

✔ **Desensitization:** This a technique used in various forms of therapy to reduce your reactivity to triggers.

✔ **Support groups, including Twelve Step programs:** Telling what happened and listening to others discharges your emotions, informs you about trauma, breaks down shame, and helps you to handle emotions and rebuild confidence and trust. Groups are an excellent adjunct to individual therapy. They don't usually afford you the privacy and individual attention needed to focus on the personal aspects of the trauma you experienced.

Chapter 14

Healing Pleasures

*F*ocusing on your problems can sap your joy and pleasure. Healing entails coming out of denial and feeling your pain, but it also includes developing healthy habits to increase positive feelings and their healing chemicals that combat hopelessness, anxiety, and depression. This chapter focuses on bringing pleasure, enjoyment, and nourishment into your life through physical, sensual, spiritual, creative, and social activities. Sometimes focusing on a problem becomes a problem in itself, while engaging in activities that inspire, relax, and fulfill you revives your enthusiasm and creativity and gives you a new attitude, focus, and perspective. The inner child you met in Chapter 13 is not only emotional and vulnerable, but also playful, spontaneous, creative, and energetic. So lighten up and let your child enjoy some healthy fun. Real changes happen when you do.

Coming to Your Senses

Freud saw man as a pleasure-seeking animal who passionately strives for happiness. You're wired for pleasure. Your brain contains centers that respond directly to pleasurable sensations that guide and maintain health. The healthiest people are pleasure-loving, pleasure-seeking, pleasure-creating individuals who have a joie de vivre. They pursue healthy pleasures and live optimistically, with zest and commitment that improves their health and prolongs their life.

The unity of mind and body was recognized as early as Aristotle. Your thoughts and feelings affect your body, and your body's movement and sensations affect your mind. For example, depression saps your physical energy and can lead to illness and pain, and illness and pain can make you irritable and depressed. To experience the body/mind connection, try these experiments:

✔ Close your eyes; now imagine opening your refrigerator and taking out a bright yellow lemon. See yourself slicing the lemon on a cutting board. Smell the tangy aroma as you slice it. Imagine the sour taste. Imagine you're picking up a lemon wedge and sucking on it until the juices mix with your saliva. Notice if your mouth starts to water. This is an example of how your mind and imagination actually cause chemical changes in your body — just as seeing a scary movie can make your heart race.

✔ Now smile and laugh for one minute. The physical sensations caused by these facial movements trigger the release of mood altering chemicals that can lighten you up. If you don't notice a difference, try exercising for 20 to 30 minutes, which will do the same thing.

Today we have empirical evidence of this interdependence. Psychoneuro-endocrinological and psychoneuro-immunological research, supported by positron emission tomography (PET) scans and other techniques, has revealed intelligence throughout the body. The autonomic nervous system is made up of the sympathetic branch that prepares you for action — to fight or flee — and the parasympathetic branch that relaxes you. When you can neither fight nor flee when facing danger, you freeze in a state of constant anxiety. In contrast, the parasympathetic nervous system is associated with pleasurable sensations and nourishment, healing, and regeneration. See the contrasting effects of both branches of the autonomic nervous system in Table 14-1.

Table 14-1 Effects of the Autonomic Nervous System

Sympathetic Nervous System	Autonomic Nervous System
Increases pulse	Slows and strengthens heartbeat
Pale, cold skin	Rosy cheeks, warm skin
Constricts circulation	Dilates blood vessels
Increases blood pressure	Lowers blood pressure
Tightens muscles	Relaxes muscles
Shallow breathing	Slow, deep breathing
Constricts digestion	Stimulates digestion and elimination
Increases metabolic rate	Slows metabolic rate
Suppresses immunity	Stimulates immune response

Loving your body

How you treat your body reveals a lot about your self-esteem — what you think and feel about yourself. The media encourages the creation of imaginary ideal standards of how the body should look and perform. Would you say that a bloodhound's ears are too long, a hummingbird is too small, or a Dalmatian has too many spots? Each is different and perfect. If you hate or hide parts of your body, work it like a machine, or don't care what you feed it, you're not being loving to yourself. Although many people act as if their body is a slave to serve them, you and your body are one, and it's up to you to care for it as nature intended.

It's said that your body is a temple — a temple of God. What does this mean? The divine lives within you and everyone else. The spirit of God flows through every one of your cells. This is the power of life that resides within you, and the life within you and all other creations is an expression of God. Your relationship with your body is a template for all your relationships. Giving and receiving love freely and uninhibitedly start with acceptance of your body.

Are you kinder to your pet than to your own animal self? Your animal body needs to be touched gently and lovingly. This stimulates the release of feel-good chemicals, like serotonin, that maximize health. Touch inhibits the sympathetic nervous system's production of stress hormones and activates the parasympathetic nervous system, promoting immune function, relaxation of the body/mind, pain reduction, longevity, and cellular growth and repair. A comforting touch can even stabilize heart function and blood pressure. You can honor your body by:

✔ Thanking your body and praising it every day.

✔ Pretending your body is newborn, and from now on, bathing it consciously and gently, like a baby.

✔ Preparing healthy food lovingly and eating slowly to savor each bite. Enjoy relaxing music or candlelight while you eat.

Relaxation is essential to healing the mind and the body. Living in your head, obsessing, worrying, and analyzing exhaust and paralyze you. By nurturing your body and putting into practice the suggestions described in this chapter, you can switch into relaxation mode. It doesn't relax you if you take a bubble bath and worry the entire time. The following exercises can help you nurture yourself and become more present.

✔ Sit or lie down comfortably. Close your eyes and put one hand on your belly and one on your chest. Breathe normally. Feel your breath. It's very important not to alter or think about your breath. Just feel it.

✔ Repeat the previous exercise, and this time pay attention to sensations in your toes, shoulders, buttocks, fingers, and thighs. Move around the body and really feel sensation both internally and at your skin. Sense the texture of your clothing, the support of gravity, and your body's weight. If you're outside, smell the air, hear and feel the breeze, and feel the sun's warmth.

✔ Sit or lie down comfortably. Begin at your toes and contract them for 5 seconds, then completely relax for a few moments. Contract your feet for 5 seconds; then release. Contract, hold, and release all the muscle groups of your body, including your face and scalp. When finished, scan your body for any tension, and release it. Think about completely letting go.

✔ Put powder or cornstarch on your belly and stroke it very, very slowly.

Smelling the roses

The whole point of the proverb, "Stop and smell the roses," is to stop and make time for simple sensual pleasures. Slowing down is key, and in the modern world, everything moves faster, people work harder, and simple pleasures, like smelling flowers, walking in the grass, watching a sunrise, or gazing at a starry night sky are rare. To truly relax, you must lose your mind, and come to your senses. Leave thinking, talking, and working behind, and move into the realm of sensation to open your heart and intuition. It takes time. Any one of the senses is a portal to the brain centers that release endorphins, chemicals that heal and provide pleasure and euphoria when you experience music, beauty, nature, or art. Research shows that post-operative patients who can see trees from their hospital rooms require less medication and are released sooner.

Music heals

Certain frequencies of music slow down and entrain the body/mind to maximize healing. A waltz releases endorphins and reduces stress hormones. The sound of rain, waves, babbling water, or chimes, wind in the trees, or a caring voice can have the same calming effect — comparable to 2.5 mg. of Valium. Hayden's "Cello Concerto in C" and Bach's "Air on the G String" are used to supplement treatment for cancer, stroke, arthritis, and kidney dialysis, as well as in intensive care units to reduce pain and anxiety and speed post-operative recovery. Music reduces the need for anesthesia and pain medication, and has helped patients with Parkinson's, Alzheimer's disease, and autism.

Your body naturally responds to rhythm, singing, and chanting, which reverberate through your tissues and bones, bypassing the brain's frontal cortex and stimulating spontaneous movement, memory, and emotion.

Pleasant aromas are also healing. A whiff of spiced apple can reduce your stress response and stimulate relaxation. Aromatherapy is effective for treating insomnia, anxiety, panic attacks, back pain, migraine, and food cravings.

Sensing nature and living organisms awakens you to the transcendent dimension of life, creation, the universe, and God. When you look deeply at a flower's magnificence and perfection, feel the softness of cat fur, sense the ocean's power, or the splendor of a meadow, sunset, or sunrise, you connect to something larger than yourself that feeds your soul and calms your mind.

✔ Spend an entire day unplanned but follow your body's impulses and senses — ignore your "should's."

✔ Lie in the grass and watch clouds.

✔ Make a CD of relaxing music. (Some of my favorites are Chopin's "Nocturnes," Massenet's "Meditation" from *Thais*, Mozart's "Clarinet Quintet in A," Francisco Tárrega's "Alhambra," Saint-Saens' "The Swan," and Michel Colombier's "Emmanuel.")

✔ Watch a fire.

✔ Listen to a fountain, a brook, or the ocean.

✔ Watch animals or babies play.

✔ Arrange flowers.

✔ Visit an art museum.

✔ Gaze at an aquarium. This has been proven as effective as hypnosis in reducing pain, anxiety, and blood pressure.

✔ Bake something aromatic.

✔ Use scented oils, soap, incense, or perfume.

Moving your body

Your body is made to move. The first fetal sensations are rocking, floating, and moving in the womb. Gentle holding and rocking stimulate relaxation. Health depends upon movement. Endorphins are released from subtle internal movements in martial arts, dance, and exercise. You derive pleasure from the motion of your muscles, limbs, breath, tissues, fluids, and cells. You've undoubtedly heard about the health benefits of exercise. Exercise, even walking on a regular basis:

- Increases oxygen intake and circulation

- Increases heart health

- Reduces "bad" cholesterol and increases "good" cholesterol

- Helps protect against and manage type 2 diabetes, arthritis, depression, and some cancers

- Reduces anxiety and depression and elevates mood

- Increases energy, strength, and endurance

- Reduces and controls weight

- Improves confidence and self-esteem

Ask your child what form of exercise is best for you. You can find movement and exercise classes at a local YMCA, YWCA, or community college. If you belong to a health club, ask a trainer to design an individualized exercise plan for you. For motivation, exercise with a friend. Focus on your pleasure, and choose an activity that you're passionate about, like surfing or dancing. If you enjoy swimming, do it at a pace you enjoy and not as a race. Same goes for walking. You may want to increase your distance over time but don't turn it into a competition with yourself. Look around and enjoy the sky, the trees, and other sights and sounds around you. If you exercise in a natural setting, you gain the added benefit of being outdoors in nature. The greater your pleasure, the more transformative are your results.

Miraculous movement

There are many stories of passion overcoming the limitations of the mind and body. A former professional dancer, who could walk only with a quad cane due to a stroke, amazingly danced with grace when her favorite music was played. Most notable is the story of cellist Pablo Casals, who suffered from rheumatoid arthritis and emphysema. Each morning, head and back bent over, he shuffled to the piano bench. He unclenched his hands, his back began to straighten, and his breathing relaxed. Casals began to play Bach's "Wohltemperierte Klavier" with skill and alacrity, humming as he played. Then he played a Brahms concerto with agile fingers that flew across the keyboard. His whole body became fluid and moved to the music. Afterwards, he rose and stood several inches taller, had a hearty breakfast, and took a walk.

Making Time to Play

Children easily feel joy when they play. If you've forgotten, just visit a playground or park. Watch the enthusiasm and aliveness of children at play. Everyone has latent memories of playing as a child — a time when you were at one with the world, with love, and pleasure.

Play is purposeless, yet meaningful. It occupies you in spontaneous amusement that isn't self-conscious. During play you're united in the timeless present with the object of your experience. Your Self is enjoying the world while enjoying itself. This relaxed, joyful oneness is both healing and pleasurable.

✔ Write a story about a joyful or fun time you remember from your childhood.

✔ Draw a picture of your playful child with your nondominant hand.

Recreation and vacations

Recreation does just that. It refreshes the mind and body through stimulating or amusing activity. It recreates and unifies the body, mind, and spirit, inspiring and revitalizing you. Recreation enhances your health and quality of life. It's effective rehabilitation for healing trauma victims, grief, and many illnesses. It's hard to worry when you're gardening, camping, golfing, or flying a kite — but don't plan activities with someone who adds to your stress.

Leisure is freedom from time-consuming duties, responsibilities, or activities, without purpose. Leisure may include play and recreational pastimes, such as fishing or playing cards, going to movies, reading, lying on the beach, or doing nothing. Seemingly meaningless activities nourish and relax you. How often do you just let a day unfold, talk to your neighbor, sit outdoors doing nothing, play old music you saved, or write a letter? The point is to maximize your care-free time.

✔ Ask your child what it wants to do for a play date and answer with your nondominant hand.

✔ Make a collage of the things that your inner child enjoys. Use magazine clippings or download pictures from the Internet.

✔ Take one day or afternoon each week to do them.

✔ Go to a toy, crafts, hobby, or art supply store. Pick out something fun. Then play.

✔ Plan a costume party or a party with games and fun activities.

✔ Read bedtime stories to yourself.

✔ Plan a vacation. If you can't take one, pretend you're on vacation in your own town. Plan the day and make it an adventure. Allow your child to help.

Laughter is a great antidote to pain, stress, and negative emotions. It triggers the release of endorphins, relaxes muscles, and reduces stress-related hormones that indirectly raise blood pressure. It's promoted by the American Cancer Society. Norman Cousins completely reversed painful ankylosing spondylites and avoided heart by-pass surgery by supplementing his medical treatment with visualization, laughter, and the love of family and friends. He watched the Marx Brothers' films and "Candid Camera" reruns, and attributed his healing to laughter and the endorphins that elevated his mood. Research has confirmed that watching an hour of comedy lowers stress hormones and boosts immunity. Laugh with a friend. It really is contagious.

✔ List all the things that make you laugh and practice them.

✔ Read joke books.

✔ Watch comedic movies and TV episodes.

✔ Make up jokes and limericks with a friend.

✔ Plan a laugh-in with a friend and laugh for no reason. Soon you'll be in stitches.

Hobbies and creative expression

A hobby is an activity you enjoy that isn't your vocation. You enjoy it for its own sake. It may be collecting stamps, researching, raising butterflies, using a microscope, or doing something creative. Creativity uplifts the soul. It can be expressed numerous ways, such as in art, crafts, music, dance, photography, writing, dramatics, and other hobbies. It provides relaxation, pleasure, inspiration, and is a powerful channel for healing, especially if you're having fun and approach it as play. On the other hand, perfectionism and focus on effort, technique, or an expected outcome restrict your creativity and the flow of expression and information in your body, taking you further from the awareness and joy of the moment. Whether you enjoy the arts, knitting, cooking, or sports, you're happiest when you lose yourself and are in "flow" with the activity.

In the zone

Mihály Csíkszentmihályi was the researcher and founder of the concept of being "in flow." According to Csíkszentmihályi, flow is when you're totally immersed in performing and learning. It harnesses your motivation and emotions to enhance your performance of whatever you're doing, whether a sport or creative learning activity. It stimulates positive, energizing emotions and joy. The activity is so engrossing and rewarding that you lose a sense of yourself and time, even bodily needs. The activity must have some challenge. If it's too difficult, you become frustrated — too easy, and you'll be bored. Flow improves your performance, motivation, and skill.

Consider taking adult continuing education or community college classes to develop new skills. Whatever you do, it's key that your Critic doesn't step in and squelch your fun. It's really okay to make mistakes or be messy. The idea is to allow your feelings and intuition to guide you. Young children do this before they learn to judge their creations. It's important to enjoy the process and not focus on the product.

✔ Ask your child how it feels about your creativity in your life today. Answer with your nondominant hand.

✔ Ask your child to recall hobbies and creative activities you enjoyed as a child. Was there something your child longed to do that you didn't — take acting lessons, learn to fly, or play an instrument?

✔ Writing with your nondominant hand, find out what your child wishes to express or do. Then do it. If you always wanted to fly, take flying lessons. It's never too late to learn something new. It keeps you young, passionate, and enthusiastic.

✔ Get some butcher paper or newsprint, marking pens, and poster paints. Paste the paper on a wall, and paint a mural of your life — how it was, how it is, and how you want it to look. You don't have to paint figures. You can use colors and shapes to express your feelings. Use the pens to add captions and call-outs with your thoughts and feelings. If it helps you to relax, put on some music while you paint.

✔ Make a collage of objects, pieces of fabric, wire, clippings, and/or pressed plant material. (They can be pressed in a heavy book such as a telephone book, and dried in a few weeks.)

Creating a Spiritual Practice

Even when you're doing typical relaxing pastimes such as reading a newspaper, playing a game, or watching television, you're not truly relaxed. They can cause stress, even competition, and don't stimulate the parasympathetic nervous system in the way that letting go of mental activity does.

A spiritual practice is a regular activity done for the purpose of enhancing your *spirituality*. It can deeply relax you and be a valuable source of healing. What spirituality means varies among different cultures and religions. Whether it includes praying, practicing martial arts, calligraphy, or mediating, you're developing the ability to focus your attention and do one thing at a time. If you don't already have a spiritual practice, consider creating one to reap its many benefits.

Benefits of a spiritual practice

Maintaining a consistent spiritual practice is an important component of your recovery. It can help you heal codependent symptoms, such as a weak sense of Self, being focused on others, compulsive behavior, obsessive thoughts, anxiety, unhappiness, and depression. It's common for people to worry about the past or some imagined future event and then react as if it has occurred. When you're thinking about the past or future, you're missing out on enjoying the present. Bringing your mind into the present enhances your ability to make constructive changes to avoid repeating past mistakes and allowing anticipated problems to materialize.

Meditation is a simple, spiritual practice that focuses your attention. You can do it on your own anytime. Although training can be helpful, it's not necessary. You may think you have no time to meditate, but actually meditation makes you more efficient and productive, creating more time in your life. Its benefits are many, such as:

- ✔ Improves physical, emotional, and mental health
- ✔ Enhances concentration and clarity of thought
- ✔ Increases emotional balance
- ✔ Enhances sense of spiritual fulfillment
- ✔ Increases creativity and intuition
- ✔ Enables you to be present — in the "now"
- ✔ Increases calmness

✔ Strengthens the Self and will

✔ Provides guidance

✔ Provides motivation, courage, and power

✔ Enhances joy and feelings of well-being

✔ Reduces reactivity

✔ Provides benefits of the parasympathetic nervous system and increases alpha brain waves

✔ Reorganizes and strengthens the personality structure

Types of meditation

There are many forms of meditation, enough to fill a book, and some require advanced training. Different religions, cultures, and schools of study emphasize different techniques. The following are a few simple suggestions to get you started. Several overlap in practice and are by no means comprehensive. Experiment with a different type for a week or two at a time, and then continue with one that suits you best. Everyone is different. In choosing a practice, It's important that it feels comfortable to you. Look for small signs of improvement in your mood, clarity, concentration, and interactions with others. After months or years of practice, you become increasingly *mindful,* or aware, of your body sensations, feelings, thoughts, and perceptions in your day-to-day life. This, in turn, enhances all the benefits of your meditation practice. If you like meditation, acquire more information through reading and meeting with a meditation group or teacher in the genre you select. (See *Meditation For Dummies,* by Stephan Bodian published by Wiley) Meditating with others is more powerful and helps you maintain awareness.

Watching your breath

Simply notice your breath *without changing it.* Sense the air passing in and out of your nostrils or the rise and fall of your chest or belly. There are many breathing exercises to enhance relaxation, such as extending your exhale or breathing in and out of one nostril at a time. In this meditation you're not doing anything special, just observing. Thoughts may arise, but you bring your attention back to your breath. Your respiration naturally slows. Slowing your breath relaxes your mind and nervous system.

Observing sensations

Notice sensations as they come and go in different areas of your body. If thoughts or feelings arise, try to notice them at the level of sensation before they turn into thoughts and emotions. Even if you have some discomfort, notice it. One practice is to then move on to another area, while another suggests that you get curious about the discomfort and experience the texture, temperature, volume, pressure, and so on at the level of pure sensation. This may neutralize your discomfort. Experiment with both techniques and discover the difference.

Observing thoughts

You may not be aware of how busy your mind is until you start to meditate. Many people resist or quit meditation because their Critic bashes them for thinking. Well, guess what! Everyone's mind is full of thoughts. It takes a meditative discipline to alter that. The point is not to banish thoughts — impossible — but to observe them. This isn't easy. When you first begin mediation, perhaps you notice your thoughts, but within a few minutes, you've forgotten what you're doing and are thinking about something in the past or future. You're no longer in the *now,* but are off in worry, fantasy, a feeling, reaction, or plan. It takes practice to observe your thoughts dispassionately, which is very different from just thinking. One technique is to allow thoughts and feelings without stopping them. Let them run their course. The key is to remember to observe them.

 Noticing that you're thinking tends to minimize thoughts. You may ask yourself — each time you remember — "Who is thinking?" See what happens. Visualization may also be helpful. Compare your thoughts to ripples in a pool of still water or clouds passing in a blue sky. Watch them float by without getting attached to the content. Another tool is counting. Count your thoughts or count your exhales, starting over each time you have a thought. It's best not to count past 4, because beginners have difficulty maintaining awareness beyond that, or even getting to 4 without thinking about something — including the counting — so be easy on yourself.

 A common problem is forgetting that you're meditating and becoming lost in thought. Another is to think about your meditation, which is also a story you don't want to get into. It generally leads to an evaluation of good or bad. Beware not to compete with yourself, which defeats the purpose. Return to noticing your thoughts again. If you're judging yourself, label each judgment as judging 1, judging 2, and so on. Another trap is to get caught up in pleasurable or creative thoughts. Continue to bring yourself back to the present. This noticing tends to dilute the power of your thoughts. Pretty soon, your mind gets tired of being interrupted and quiets down, like a puppy you're training over and over.

Looking at an object

Focus your attention on something outside of yourself, such as the sound of chimes, an object such as a rock, twig, candle flame, or a mandala, which is a picture of a religious symbol or a diagram. You can make a mandala by drawing a circle, triangle, or square on paper. Look at it for a few minutes. If you're looking at an object, explore *nonverbally* every detail available to your perception but do not stare. Imagine you're touching it and try to sense it with your eyes. Now, close your eyes and look at the afterimage until it fades, then repeat the process.

Moving meditation

If you get restless sitting, there are many forms of movement meditation, such as hatha yoga, t'ai chi, karate, qi gong, aikido, Sufi dervish dances, Alexander movement, contact improvisation, authentic movement, and Continuum. To experiment, practice a walking meditation. This can be done indoors or outside. Take a few breaths to center your awareness and step slowly, paying attention to each section of your foot and toes as they make contact with the ground. Notice the muscles and bones flexing in your ankle and calf, along your leg and into your hip, the movement in your belly and pelvis, and the counterpoint sway of your arms and shoulders. If thoughts or feelings arise, just notice them and bring your attention back to your body in motion. There's plenty to occupy your attention with each step. Walk slowly to take in as much information as you can. Focus on one body part for a while — your feet, for example — noticing every aspect of each step and which area of your foot strikes the ground first. Don't judge what you observe.

Mantra

Mantras are sacred words, sounds, or phrases repeated over and over. They're prayers or chants that are part of all religions and indigenous traditions. A mantra is said either out loud or silently and may be timed to your breath. In some traditions, a mantra is given to you by a guru or teacher and may be based on your astrological sign. There're mantras for different purposes — to achieve different states of consciousness, to resonate with various aspects of divine energy, and to manifest different qualities, such as compassion. Examples include "Elohim" and "Adonai" in Judaism, "Jesus Christ" or "Amen" in Christianity, "Allahu Akbar" in Islam, and "OM" (or "AUM") in Buddhism and Hinduism. You may also use words, such as peace, or love, or phrases, such as "I am God," or "I am that I am." To start, use one that is familiar and meaningful. (See Chapter 9.)

The Relaxation Response

The Relaxation Response is a secular technique developed by Dr. Herbert Benson, a pioneer in body-mind research. It has been shown to stimulate the parasympathetic nervous system and reduce stress, anxiety, depression, and anger. Benson developed it after studying experienced practitioners of Transcendental Meditation at Harvard University.

1. Sit in a relaxed position and close your eyes.

2. Starting at your toes and progressing to your face, relax each muscle, and keep them relaxed.

3. Breathe normally through your nose and repeat "one" silently with each inhale and again with each exhale. Do not control your breath.

4. Do this daily for 10 to 20 minutes and take a few minutes before getting up.

Contemplation

Contemplation on an idea, problem, image, or spiritual passage is sometimes considered an unstructured form of meditation. Contemplate one of the mantras in Chapter 9. Reflect on it, and let your mind consider different aspects, reactions, and feelings about it, without straying away to other topics. Allow your thoughts and feelings to occupy you. In contrast, Christian contemplative prayer is emptying the mind to achieve oneness with God.

General guidelines

Unless you're doing a movement meditation, it's best to sit comfortably. You needn't sit cross-legged, although there're physiological benefits to sitting is certain prescribed positions. If sitting is too uncomfortable, lie down or try a movement practice. It's best to meditate at the same time each day for a definite length of time. You can set a timer. Start with 5 or 10 minutes. It's important not to try too hard. Trying to relax makes you tenser. Think about meditation as an opportunity to let go (you can come back to your worries), rather than another challenge. Whatever form you practice, when self-judgment arises, observe it like any other thought and return to the object of your attention. If you get sleepy, meditate with your eyes partially open, looking ahead and down at a 45-degree angle. Finally, meditation is not a means to escape your problems but to help you face them with greater courage and equanimity.

Reaching Out to Friends

Codependency has a way of narrowing your lifestyle and connections with people outside of your family or primary relationship — especially if you're living with addiction or abuse. You get so wrapped up and preoccupied with these relationships that you probably haven't had the time or mental and emotional energy to develop friendships with others or be involved in the community in which you live. In addition, more and more people live alone or are single parents.

Part of healing entails reaching out and establishing new ties and friends. This helps you realize that there is life outside of your codependent relationships that provides stimulation, different points of view, and support. Conversation, sharing, being in touch with others who have active, involved lives provides involvement, encouragement, and a sense of belonging, especially when you don't have, aren't close with, or don't live near extended family to offer support. It's said that sharing your joys doubles them, and sharing your woes halves them. Perhaps, this is why people with strong social ties live longer, have fewer colds, lower blood pressure, and lower heart rates. In fact, a good social network provides the same health benefits as exercise! When you're out of school, it can be difficult to establish new relationships. Here are some suggestions.

- ✔ Attend a support group (see Chapter 18) and talk to people after the meeting. Join others if they invite you out for coffee.

- ✔ Volunteer at a senior center, nearby hospital, animal shelter, or other nonprofit organization. Consider mentoring a child with Big Brothers or Big Sisters.

- ✔ Join a committee at your children's school or at a religious organization to which you belong.

- ✔ Take a class and learn something new. Talk to others during the break. Make plans to meet for dinner or coffee before or after class.

- ✔ Volunteer as a docent at a local museum.

- ✔ Through local schools or libraries, become a tutor and help children or adults read.

- ✔ Participate in political fundraisers and campaign activities.

- ✔ Find meet-ups online with others who share a common interest.

- ✔ Connect with old friends via Internet social networking such as Facebook or Twitter.

✔ There are clubs for just about every interest, and the Internet has made it easier than ever to locate them. Find a club for people who share your hobbies or recreational interests, such as a sailing club, the Sierra Club, the Audubon Society, a bridge, baseball, coin, or book club.

✔ Although face-to-face contact is always better, participate in online chats and forums, including the subject of codependency. If you're housebound or live in a remote area, this is a great way to connect with others who share your problems and interests.

Chapter 15

Coping with Relapse

This chapter is about the challenges faced in recovery. They include maintaining vigilance about *codependency creep*. It can sneak into your relationships and reactions and show up at work or in other settings. Another problem is shifting from codependency to a different addiction. You also may think you've recovered and are in a healthy relationship, only to find that you've brought your codependency along. Some suggestions are offered about handling relapse.

Replays Are Normal

In most Twelve Step programs, members celebrate birthdays for the period of time they've been sober or abstinent, unless they *slip*. This doesn't really apply to codependency. In Al-Anon and Codependency Anonymous, when birthdays are celebrated, it's for length of membership, not abstinence. In other words, you're acknowledged just for showing up and trying. Hence, I hesitate to use the term *relapse* because it denotes judgment and going backwards. Codependents slip all the time. Replays of past behavior are a normal part of recovery, which is actually a learning process that progresses in spirals (see Chapter 6).

Codependency is a life-long journey

The Twelve Step programs emphasize progress, not perfection. Remember that addiction is never cured but is a disease requiring life-long attention. Most people object when they first hear this concept. They're ashamed and don't like being labeled codependent, an addict, or alcoholic. They feel damaged and want to quickly recover and be "perfect." The problem is that those feelings and attitudes are part of the addiction itself and can lead to a false sense of security that you've overcome codependency. For addicts, this denial can lead to risky behavior that turns into a full-blown relapse. When it comes to codependency, it's the same story. Codependency can creep into your relationships unless you maintain awareness or at least check yourself regularly.

Codependency is so basic — the underbelly of all addictions — that recovery calls for a fundamental shift in your personality, coping mechanisms, and behavior. Recovery entails changes in your attitude and behavior in all interactions, even with yourself. It's impossible to be abstinent from people, much less your relationship with yourself. You may start out enthusiastically wanting to make major changes but discover that despite your best efforts and intentions, you're repeating old, codependent behavior. This is not a relapse or slip but part of an on-going learning and relearning process. Recall from Chapter 6 that recovery progresses in spirals — just like the shape of your DNA. Imagine trying to untwist your DNA! It's an apt analogy because codependency is learned very early in childhood and passed on generationally. Your codependent behaviors are deeply engrained, and it takes patience, strength, and perseverance to unlearn and replace bad habits and attitudes with new ones. They're part of who you are, and they feel comfortable, like worn jeans. You don't want to part with them — despite the fact that your jeans are threadbare.

Why progress is cyclical

Recovery entails learning new alternative behaviors and attitudes. If someone tells you not to think about a monkey, every time you try to not think of one, you think about not thinking of a monkey. But if someone tells you to think about an elephant, you'll do that, too. The point is that recovery isn't just about stopping old habits. It necessitates replacing them with new ones. These changes are long-term goals. Detaching from a loved one's problems and the habit of giving well-meaning advice isn't easy. Controlling your temper and impulse to react in habitual ways takes awareness and restraint. Assertiveness requires that you acknowledge your wants, needs, and feelings, and gain the courage to express them. Learning to accept and love yourself is a lifelong journey.

Additionally, refraining from old patterns creates anxiety, anger, and a sense of loss of control. New attitudes and behaviors feel uncomfortable and arouse other emotions, including fear and guilt. Dealing with these emotions frequently causes people to return to old codependent behavior.

Recovery from codependency takes years of practice. Learning a new language demands correction and repetition. When you become aware that you're reverting to old habits, you're actually becoming more conscious of yourself, which is part of growth. You start to experience an incongruity between how you act and how you want to act, and that discrepancy is becoming more uncomfortable. You're gaining a deeper understanding and able to witness the negative consequences of the old behavior.

Changing codependent habits is also difficult because your old ways served a self-protective purpose. You may want to change but letting go of them leaves a void that may be scary and painful. Just saying "No" to someone ushers in tremendous anxiety. The fear of abandonment or retribution may cause you to revert to old behavior. Learning how to deal with these feelings and new coping skills is crucial. For instance, you may learn to say, "I'll think about it," when asked to do something you don't want to. Then you may write or pray about it and examine your motives, desires, and the consequences of your response. You can talk to a friend, therapist, or sponsor. Over time, you become more spontaneous and authentic. This is where having a support system and spiritual practice are invaluable in navigating the uneasy waters of change.

Signs of codependency creep

Codependent behavior ebbs and flows in recovery. Sometimes it's a constant reminder that you're in a learning process or relearning something you thought you had down pat. It can surprise you and return when you're overtired, lonely, or haven't taken care of yourself, which is, of course, a codependent symptom. Learning to value and nurture yourself and meet your needs are the cornerstones of recovery. Here are some warning signs to look out for:

- ✔ You're putting in extra hours at work to the detriment of your sleep, health, and relationships.
- ✔ You're building a list of faults about someone.
- ✔ You're continually tired or getting colds.
- ✔ You're harboring resentments.
- ✔ You're writing speeches in your head to someone.
- ✔ You're dishonest or keeping secrets.
- ✔ You stop going to meetings.
- ✔ You're focusing on the needs of someone else and dropping your own needs and activities.
- ✔ You're waiting for someone else to do something with you rather than do it yourself.
- ✔ You're hiding relationship problems from family, friends, your therapist, or sponsor.

✔ You set unrealistic goals and expectations for yourself.

✔ You're obsessing about someone else.

✔ You're impatient and irritable.

✔ You're feeling self-pity.

✔ You're watching, criticizing, or nagging someone.

✔ You have a negative attitude about things.

✔ You're isolating or withdrawing from people.

✔ You're being overly self-critical or comparing yourself to others.

✔ You stop making time for your spiritual practice.

✔ You're not making time for play and recreation.

Triggers

There may be certain people or events that trigger your codependent patterns. (See Chapter 9.) Sometimes, it means you have more healing to do. It can also mean you should avoid the person or situation if it's unhealthy for you. In time, triggers diminish, and you learn to trust yourself. Typical triggers are people or events that remind you of a past trauma. For example, if you were sexually abused, starting a new relationship may resurrect feelings of distrust, fear, and shame. If your ex cheated on you, you may interpret an innocent conversation between your lover and someone of the opposite sex as flirtation and feel distrust, rejected, and humiliated. You're dating someone new who has wine with dinner and you're afraid he or she is an alcoholic. There is no limit to the number of possible triggers, and they vary depending upon each individual's past experience. You may not be able to tell if you're reacting to the present or the past — or both. Sometimes, the new person really is flirting or abusing alcohol. What you can do is the following:

✔ Work on healing your past (see Chapter 13).

✔ Journal about the trigger, your memories, and your past and present feelings.

✔ Talk to a therapist.

✔ Have a frank conversation with the new person about it and share your feelings and needs.

Many people make significant strides in their recovery, but when they're around dysfunctional family members they revert back to their codependent patterns (see Chapter 12). Some people say they actually feel like they regress to a younger version of themselves.

The roles and communication patterns with your family were established when your personality, defenses, and coping style were formed, and unless your relatives have changed, it's very difficult to maintain your new behavior with them for very long. Follow the suggestions in Chapter 12 and those outlined later in this chapter regarding coping.

Talking to your ex can also make you revert to codependent patterns that were part of your former relationship. If a prior relationship was traumatic, then in addition to being triggered by your ex and the relationship dynamics, you may also re-experience emotions triggered by the trauma. Psychiatrist Carl Whittaker, founder of experiential family therapy, believed that when you deeply love someone, he or she may always trigger unconscious feelings from your childhood. This process is called *transference,* and can apply to your close relatives and ex partners, as happened to Ella.

Ella's ex-husband Max was very self-centered and typically monopolized the conversation, while she played a passive, codependent role as listener, believing she had nothing worthwhile to contribute. She was now happily married to someone unselfish and interested in her, and in this marriage she had an equal voice. She still talked to Max regarding co-parenting, but inevitably he got into long-winded monologues. She didn't know how to stop him or end the conversation. Each time she got off the phone, she was furious at him and at herself for allowing it. After months of intermittent success in setting boundaries verbally, she found a solution in restricting communication to e-mail and texting.

Crossovers and Sequels

It's not unusual for people in recovery to make progress and then discover that their codependent behavior returns in new or different situations. For some, relationships aren't that difficult, but work or functioning in a group is a challenge. For others, it's the reverse.

Some addicts are successful in stopping one addiction, and then discover that they have another one. When codependents start letting go, occasionally they cross over to a new addiction. There are individuals who have multiple addictions, and codependency underlies them all. It's been said that codependency is the hardest to recover from because it goes to the core of who you are.

It's typical for people to repeat codependent patterns in new relationships — sequels. It's also common for codependents in recovery to unwittingly substitute one codependent relationship for another.

Groups, jobs, and organizations

Many people don't think about changing their codependent patterns at work and don't believe that they have any power in that environment. They think their problems come with the job and don't understand that unconscious dynamics are operating. Whether you blame your job or organization or blame yourself, you can apply the principles and suggestions throughout this book to your interactions at work or in an organization.

Just as in a relationship, in a group there are always actions and reactions, conflicts of needs, different points of view, and communication problems. You can respond in a healthy or dysfunctional manner. When you join a group or organization, there are rules and a certain culture and hierarchy, and you have to establish your place. Often an unconscious alchemy happens that mysteriously recreates your family dynamics. Before you know it, you're playing the role that you did in your family. If you were the Adapter or Mascot, you begin acting that way in a group setting (see Chapter 7). If you were the Scapegoat in your family, you may start to feel like one at work. If you were the responsible Hero as a child, at work or in an organization, you end up working long hours and become a leader or go-to person — maybe experiencing burnout. You may react to a boss or chairperson of a committee as if he or she were one of your parents and react to co-workers as if they were siblings. If you don't know the role you played in your family, just think about your styles of reacting. Are you a pleaser, withdrawer, martyr, and so on? (See Chapter 9.)

Clara volunteered to help a fund-raising committee at her church. The committee leader was very bossy and rigid about doing things her way, even though the rules required that decisions be made by majority vote. When Clara made suggestions, the leader dismissed them the way Clara's mother had done whenever Clara expressed her opinion. As a child, Clara had learned to discount her own ideas and give up on them and was starting to do that again. At committee meetings, other members passively accepted the leader's authoritarian style and resented and complained about her behind her back. From going to Codependents Anonymous, Clara became aware that her childhood pattern of passive accommodation was being triggered. Instead of continuing to repeat it, she talked with other committee members, and they all agreed to speak to the leader about following the church guidelines for majority vote. When confronted, the leader changed her style, and the entire committee was grateful and energized with new ideas and productivity.

Daniel had been a freelance marketer, but had to take a job with a marketing firm to make ends meet. Daniel was used to working independently and continued to act that way, ignoring some of the company rules that he thought were petty. Growing up, Daniel had rebelled against his father's strict rules. After several months on the new job, Daniel was being watched and reprimanded, and his hostility for his boss noticeably increased. In therapy, he realized that he was recreating his family drama and to save his job decided to change his role. He admitted to his manager that he was having difficulty adjusting to his new position, but that he wanted to make a contribution and be a team player. He asked his manager for more feedback on what was expected of him. To Daniel's amazement, his manager was appreciative and in time began seeking Daniel's input, instead of perceiving him as a problem. Daniel went from the rebel to confident.

Some jobs and organizations are dysfunctional. Usually, it's a reflection of codependency, addiction, or mental illness of top management, which sets the entire organization's rules and culture. That doesn't mean you can't make changes in how you're treated or what you're willing to do. Even after you do, you may decide that another environment would be more supportive and motivating. Sometimes, you must improve your self-esteem before you're able to leave.

Here are some questions to explore in group and job settings:

- ✔ Are you more comfortable interacting in groups or one-on-one?
- ✔ What are your feelings in a group setting? How old do you feel?
- ✔ How old do you feel interacting with a supervisors or leaders?
- ✔ Assess the rules in the group or on the job.
- ✔ How do you react to the rules and the group structure?
- ✔ Look at the characteristics of functional and dysfunctional families in Chapter 7 and compare them with those of your job or group.
- ✔ How do you react to members or employees?
- ✔ What role do you play in a group setting?
- ✔ How are your feelings and role the same or different from those with your family?
- ✔ What are the boundaries among members or employees?
- ✔ What are the boundaries between leaders and members or between supervisors and employees?
- ✔ How do you react to leaders and supervisors?
- ✔ What can you do to change the way you're behaving, reacting, and feeling?

Rachel worked as a loan officer for a large bank. Everyone in her department was intimidated by the senior vice president, who was rude and insulting to the employees. Even though she'd learned to be assertive in her personal relationships, she was convinced that she had no choice but to accept the abuse. It was a real eye-opener when she overheard a conversation between the VP and his temporary secretary. He abrasively scolded the secretary for the way she'd handled a document. The temp calmly responded, "Please don't speak to me in that tone of voice." Even more shocking was that he politely apologized and softened his tone. He knew how to be nice if he couldn't get away with behaving badly. It wasn't easy for Rachel to copy the temporary secretary. She felt more powerless at work than at home, but this experience showed her that it was possible and became a goal in her recovery.

Sam was hired as dean of a private college to oversee, revamp, and improve the academic performance of the students. On the job, he discovered that there was a lot of political infighting among the directors, and different factions had different agendas. He was given conflicting assignments that absorbed his time. He received approval to execute one plan, only to have it aborted by someone else. His staff became disillusioned and lacked motivation because they felt their work was for nothing. He'd been doing well in recovery but became depressed due to the job. Sam wasn't used to this. His family had been hierarchical, and he liked to work in situations where the rules were defined and predictable. It was also his pattern to blame himself and feel like a failure. He kept trying to make a difference, but it was impossible because of the dysfunctional board of directors. Finally, he realized it wasn't just him and found another position.

Shifting addictions

When you start detaching and accept that you're powerless over others in your close relationships, it leaves a void previously filled with mental and physical activity trying to control and manipulate others. It can also be a shattering to realize that the addict you love has a life-threatening addiction, subject only to a daily reprieve, over which you're powerless. The emptiness that was masked by codependent addictive behavior is revealed, and feelings of anxiety, anger, loss, emptiness, boredom, and depression may arise. These feelings and the stress of change described earlier may cause you to turn to a new addiction or relapse with one you quit years before, like smoking or an eating disorder. Whether you're spending more time eating, shopping, or working, some pivotal questions to ask yourself are:

✔ Are you preoccupied thinking about the habit?

✔ Are you acting compulsively?

✔ Is it taking time from your relationships and self-nurturing?

✔ Are you spending money that you don't think you should on it?

✔ Are you secretive about your behavior?

✔ Are you ashamed of your behavior?

With a new addiction comes more denial and avoidance of the feelings that are part of change and recovery from codependency. Maybe you think your new preoccupation doesn't matter because it helps you cope — so that you're not being codependent. Wrong. Codependency underlies all addictions, and substituting addictions is merely a cover-up that detours your recovery. It avoids the necessity of learning to manage your thoughts and feelings in new healthy ways. The best strategy is to get counseling or support in a Twelve Step program to help you stop the compulsive behavior. Practice the suggestions in Chapter 14 and get increased support for dealing with your codependency (see Chapter 18).

New relationships

Many codependents in recovery decide to leave a problematic relationship after gaining more independence and self-esteem, and their lives improve. Others are living with an addict who finds recovery. They think their codependency is cured.

If you leave a troubled relationship, you may become involved with someone emotionally healthy and available, but your self-esteem hasn't caught up, and after a while you start sabotaging the relationship because you don't feel worthy or are afraid that it can't last (see Chapter 16). In other cases, you may avoid dating another abuser or addict, which is a definite plus, but enter a relationship with another codependent. In either case, if core codependency issues and causes haven't been addressed, codependent patterns reoccur that affect your self-esteem, communication, and intimacy.

Cynthia ended her relationship with a controlling, abusive man. She was happy, focusing on her career, and thought her codependency was a thing of the past, only to be dismayed to see her behavior return in a new relationship with a sober, easy-going, and kind man, who was fun to be with. Cynthia was convinced he was her soul mate, but his schedule never allowed them enough time together. She started obsessing about him and dropped plans with friends and other activities she enjoyed to be available when he called. After bending herself into a pretzel to be with him, she became as unhappy as she'd been with her ex, whom she began to miss because at least he needed her. When the relationship ended, she had to work on her issues of abandonment, intimacy, and low self-esteem to really feel worthy of kindness and love.

Arnie had been married to an alcoholic, whom he'd taken care of after frequent bouts of drunkenness. He'd been responsible for supporting the family and the majority of the parenting. When he met Denise following his divorce, he was impressed that she was health conscious and was starting a business fixing up and reselling homes. Arnie had stopped attending Al-Anon meetings after his divorce, thinking them unnecessary because he was no longer involved with an alcoholic. Before long, he was in love, helping and giving Denise business advice and loaning her money. He didn't find out until later that she had a history of failed ventures and debts. He started feeling resentful and judgmental, and his old enabling and controlling behavior returned full-blown by the time he crawled back to Al-Anon.

Coping with Relapse

Whether you call it a slip, a replay, or a relapse, the most important thing is to get back on track. How you think about your behavior and how you treat yourself are key in making that turnaround. The path back requires both humility and self-nurturing.

You're human!

Some people think the idea that you should be perfect and not make mistakes comes from a sense of pride. Actually, it comes from shame. Either way, it's your codependency that blows your "mistakes" out of proportion, making you feel terrible and worse than others for making them and at other times judgmental and impatient with people for their mistakes. Maybe you grew up with guilt and criticism. When you exaggerate your errors, you're in reaction mode. (See Chapter 9.) The Critic that berates you for your slip or relapse is not the voice of health that you believe it is. *It's your codependency talking!*

It may be hard to admit that you're human and make mistakes, and, in addition, that you're powerless over your own recovery. Although a great deal of focus and effort is required to heal from addiction and codependency, you may be disappointed if you rely only on self-will. In fact, your will can get in the way. Sometimes, you won't be able to discern whether or not you're being controlling, whether or not you're in denial, or whether or not your actions reflect good or poor self-esteem. Just when you think you're doing great, you discover that all along you were in a major relapse. The path of recovery has twists and turns and isn't black or white. It's a murky, messy process. Recognizing this is a huge step in recovery because help is necessary — whether it comes from God, your unconscious, a Twelve Step program, or counseling — often all four.

Take responsibility

With humility, it's easier to realistically assess yourself. Taking responsibility is a step toward change. It comes from a place of self-acceptance. (See Chapter 10.) Rather than stay stuck in self-judgment and guilt, you admit, "Okay, I did (or said) that. Now, what am I going to do about it?" It's also important to ask, "Whom did I hurt?" Don't forget to put yourself at the top of the list because your self-judgment hurts your self-esteem. Staying guilty continues to do so, whereas taking responsibility and self-forgiveness improve your self-esteem and behavior.

The Serenity Prayer (see Chapter 9) emphasizes "changing what I can." You can't change the past and you can't change the future if you're stuck looking backwards and judging yourself for what you did. You surely will have another opportunity to behave differently and you've gained greater consciousness to do so. Moreover, dwelling on defects and mistakes only reinforce them, whereas positive actions today determine build a better future. If you did something that embarrassed you or about which you feel ashamed, you're gaining experience about the consequences of your actions. Consider it a wake-up call to take your recovery seriously. Try to understand how and why you got off-track. Here are a few questions to ask:

✔ How do you feel about making mistakes?

✔ How were your mistakes treated as a child?

✔ Does expecting perfection improve your life overall?

✔ In what way does perfectionism and self-blame hurt you?

✔ What or who may have triggered you?

✔ What emotions did you have?

✔ What were your motives?

✔ What needs were not being met by you and by others?

✔ How did your actions meet those needs, or not?

✔ How did your emotions and thoughts lead to your actions?

✔ What healthier beliefs, thoughts, feelings, and actions would have led to a better result?

✔ How did your actions affect yourself and others?

✔ Whom did you hurt?

✔ How can you make amends? (See Chapter 10.)

✔ Do the circumstances that led to your actions remind you of something from your past?

Self-care

You're more likely to relapse if you're not practicing adequate self-care and attending to your needs (see Chapter 8), including rest, recreation, exercise, inspiration, and emotional support (see Chapter 14). Not surprisingly, self-care is not only preventive, it's also the remedy. Emotional support begins with you. Self-nurturing actually furthers your growth. A relapse is an opportunity to practice self-acceptance, empathy, and self-love (see Chapter 10), as well as self-examination in the foregoing section. Try these suggestions:

✔ Dialogue with your Critic (see Chapter 10).

✔ Look back on when you first began recovery, and reflect on your progress.

✔ List your achievements in recovery.

✔ Focus on your assets and strengths.

✔ Write yourself a compassionate letter of understanding and forgiveness.

✔ Ask for help from God or your higher power.

Part IV
Standing on Your Own: Leaving Codependency Behind

The 5th Wave   By Rich Tennant

"I don't know, Mona — sometimes I get the feeling you're afraid to get close."

In this part...

Part IV prepares you for a full, healthy life. Here, you learn about healthy relationships and self-empowerment outside of relationships. This section helps you uncover your dreams and passions and discover your skills and talents. You've neglected yourself; now you can turn your attention back to you to help you begin creating your confidence and your future. This part also gives you a comprehensive look at where to get help, from meetings to psychotherapy to a list of emergency phone numbers.

Chapter 16

Relationships that Work

· ·

· ·

*H*ealthy relationships are the minority in America. In fact, the majority is dysfunctional — probably 80 percent, give or take a little. So, "normal" isn't necessarily healthy. Unfortunately, the media encourages dysfunctional relationships. Love stories are about falling in love, and marriage is the happy ending. In reality, that's just the beginning. This chapter describes the criteria and necessary skills that make relationships work. Intimacy is the lifeblood of relationships, and I explore this topic in this chapter. Finally, I suggest some tips for dealing with loneliness. Knowing how to cope when you're lonely can sustain you before and after a relationship and make you a better partner.

Relationship Success

A healthy long-term relationship doesn't preoccupy your thoughts. It becomes background instead of foreground. It supports you in living your life, like the battery that enables a watch to tick. If you have to keep checking the battery, you're not enjoying the watch — which is your life. The battery doesn't need repairing, just recharging, and similarly, like maintaining a skill level or caring for your pet, even healthy relationships require time and nurturing.

You don't control who you fall in love with, but you can choose with whom you spend your time and commit to. Most people are in love when they get married. But it doesn't last for the multitudes that get divorced each year because love neither solves marital problems nor predicts a relationship's success. In addition to love, you must deal with the process of relating — how you treat each other, communicate, and make decisions together. The process of relationships and the behavior that makes them last require more than the feeling aspect of love. Mixing up these components causes problems. When you accuse your partner of not loving you because he or she wants time alone or disagrees, you are confusing your feelings with process.

Love and hate go together. It's not abnormal to feel intense hostility toward your mate. When you live with someone, over time there are constant disappointments, small and large. In opening yourself to love and intimacy, you open yourself to being hurt and disappointed. If there's enough redeeming good in the relationship, you can talk about it, let go, and move past the hurt.

The three of us

It may seem obvious, but for a relationship to be successful, there must be two separate individuals who come together to form a couple, which isn't a blending or merger. There're three distinct entities:

1. I

2. You

3. We

Codependents emphasize the "we" or the "you" of relationships, and lose sight of "I." They go from physical attraction to thinking *we* are a couple, sometimes ignoring whether the other person agrees. Typically, they want to spend all their time together and drop their friends and interests. Usually, they expect their partner to have the same interests and are hurt if their partner wants to do something independently. Codependents think the ideal relationship is when "we" are "one." Ignoring differences and separateness, both of which are essential for successful relationships, results in lack of respect and attempts to control, change, or fix your partner. People in healthy relationships seek closeness, not oneness. They make their relationship a priority, but enjoy the rest of their lives and don't neglect themselves. There are disagreements and compromise, separateness and closeness. The more you develop your individual "I," the more that differences and separateness can be tolerated. (See Chapter 3.)

The basics

Healthy partners don't want intensity, and they don't want the drama, fights, or fear of abandonment that creates it. They desire contentment. They aren't addicted to the highs and lows and adrenalin rushes of break-ups, make-ups, fear, and crazy sex. They steer clear of addiction, infidelity, someone with too many problems, or who is dishonest or abusive. Bottom line is that you want to feel safe not only from physical harm, but also to be yourself. You may think such a person is a great catch. Maybe — maybe not. Before getting serious, look for someone who:

- ✔ Is safe

- ✔ Takes care of him- or herself and doesn't need to be rescued

- ✔ Treats you and others with respect

- ✔ Is reliable and trustworthy

- ✔ Wants to spend time together

- ✔ Values you and the relationship

- ✔ Has connections to other friends and his or her family

Codependents sometimes confuse excitement with the anxiety of not feeling safe because it's familiar and reminiscent of not feeling safe in their family as a child. Personal qualities that go into creating a feeling of safety and trust make up the basics. Table 16-1 compares traits to look for that make or break relationships.

Table 16-1	Relationship Recipe
Safe	**Unsafe**
Reliable	Unpredictable, doesn't keep word
Honest	Evasive, dishonest
Respectful	Rude, discounting, dismissive, bossy
Listens	Preoccupied, interrupts, ignores
Accepting	Judging, rejecting
Open	Secretive
Eye contact	No eye contact
Clear boundaries	Inappropriate, invasive, rigid
Supportive	Competitive, indifferent
Authentic	Phony, bragging, words don't match actions
Caring	Self-centered
Practices self-care	Neglects self

(continued)

Table 16-1 (continued)

Safe	Unsafe
Compromises	Rigid, inflexible
Allowing	Controlling
Giving	Selfish, needy, withholding
Understanding	Cold, insensitive

Love, and then what?

When love is shared in the early stages of a relationship, it changes you. You're catapulted out of your ordinary personality to become more expansive. Tension and striving subside, and you feel wonderful — generous, kind, playful, happy, secure, alive, strong, blessed, accepting of yourself and others, and connected to the world. Some people experience this as blissful moments, while others can sustain it for hours, an entire day, or longer. All is well — for a while. Just being with or even thinking about your beloved arouses these feelings. Everyone wants *that experience!* Love allows you to let go of defenses, lose control, and "fall" into the current of your own energy and of life itself. You share your past and private feelings and feel accepted and loved. You believe your prayers and dreams for the future may finally be fulfilled, that your pain and loneliness are over, and that these good feelings will last forever. There's a lot of hope and expectations about this new love. Some people get married at this stage and commit their lives to each other.

Reality starts to chip away at the great love experience when conflicts, awareness of differences, disappointments, and the sheer stress of living arise. You have hurt feelings you didn't before you met and miss the good feelings you had. You want *that love experience* back and don't want your partner to leave, because you need a relationship in order to feel calm and to enliven you. You start to manipulate and control the relationship, hiding your true feelings to keep it going. Yet, precisely those defensive tactics designed to maintain the relationship block the magic you first discovered together. You start to wonder, "Should I be with this person?" and "Are we compatible?" You're no longer content being the present and begin worrying about the future. Maybe you won't accomplish your educational or career goals or will have the responsibility of supporting a family. Your ordinary personality and its defenses hanker to return because they've helped you survive. What would happen to you without them? Who would you be? Certainly not like anyone in your dysfunctional family. If there's enough good in the relationship, you don't want to let go. Codependents hold on even when there isn't. They're either afraid of being alone again or feel too guilty ending the relationship. You placate your partner or withdraw for a while to avoid conflict, or try to change him or her with demands, criticism, or guilt. You rationalize your doubts and hope things will improve. If you can connect to the love and forget about your differences and worries, or if you're given an ultimatum, you may get married.

Most of the fears that challenge love revolve around how whole and secure your Self is and how worthy you feel of being loved. You wonder, "Will I get hurt?" "Will I be secure?" or "Will I get trapped?" Usually, this is unconscious, but generally boils down to, "Will I get enough love or be abandoned?" or "Will I lose my autonomy or be smothered?" The thought that you're becoming dependent upon your beloved is terrifying, as are the fears that your flaws and insufficiency may disappoint him or her. If you don't feel worthy of love, you push your partner away. If you're afraid of being alone, you cling to the relationship. Power struggles ensue about relatives, chores, career decisions, or where to live, but if you look deeper, one partner is wondering whether he (usually men) has to give up too much independence or whether she (usually women) matters enough to him. Your relationship can get stuck — sometimes a lifetime — at this power struggle stage of mutual dissatisfaction, thinking your partner is the problem. See the discussion about levels of intimacy later in this chapter.

Beyond the basics

To get past power struggles, you must have enough self-esteem to maintain your identity. With a stronger Self, you're not afraid it may disintegrate if you're rejected or alone, nor afraid of losing it by getting closer and opening up. When your Critic quiets down (see Chapter 10), you feel worthy of love and don't reject it when it shows up; otherwise you're stuck being a pursuer or distancer — pursuing someone unavailable who can't or doesn't love you, or bored or finding fault with someone who does. Lasting relationships require more than the basics. They involve:

Developing your Self and self-esteem

Creating safety

Being realistic

Communicating assertively

Accepting each other's differences

Making decisions and problem-solving together

Spending quality time together and apart

> Giving and cooperating
>
> Having compatible needs and values
>
> Sharing a common vision
>
> Maintaining friendships

Couples strive, but aren't able to, maintain and express these qualities perfectly, nor all the time, and sometimes not even well. You get hurt, angry, and disappointed, and in spite of yourself, you both want and don't want to wound your partner. You do your best, and sometimes your best is your worst. Then you forgive yourself and each other.

Developing your Self and self-esteem

The greater your sense of Self and self-esteem, the more successful will be your relationships. Couples with independent identities each continue to focus on and pursue individual goals and growth. When you finding sustenance in your relationship and with yourself, you're more able to give, which enhances your intimacy as a couple. With high self-esteem, you don't expect or need as much validation and support. If your self-esteem is low, you place unrealistic demands on your partner to make you happy and feel good about yourself. These are your responsibilities. Hence, working on yourself can really improve your relationships. Self-esteem also allows you to be open without being ashamed to reveal yourself. You won't be as sensitive to criticism and differences, nor as threatened by closeness or separateness. You're not so afraid of being rejected because you can stand on your own. Knowing you're free to leave, you don't have to please or change people; you can enjoy them and negotiate for what you want.

Creating safety

Safety is basic and is reflected in the other ingredients of a healthy relationship, such as healthy communication and problem-solving, which includes respect, listening, and not abusing your partner. These qualities enable you to feel safe and be open with one another, rather than keep to yourself, withdraw, and become resentful. When you feel safe, you're free to be yourself. If you're unreliable and don't deliver on commitments and promises, you can't be counted on. This erodes trust and goodwill that are the bedrock of safety. If you or your partner goes through a tough time, you want to know that the relationship is a safe haven and that you're there for each other.

Being realistic

Happy couples are realistic about their expectations of each other and the relationship. They don't expect the initial phase of romance and infatuation to last forever because they're not relying on the relationship to make them happy. They also accept that it won't fill all their needs. They know that perfection doesn't exist and that relationships have problems and challenges. They're willing to talk and work them through. They also each accept responsibility to make themselves happy.

Communicating assertively

Healthy communication in a healthy relationship involves sharing your present, inner experience, listening to the other person, and then sharing your present, inner experience about what you heard. (See Chapters 3, 8, and 11.) Notice that this includes listening, which is essential for a relationship to last. Healthy communication is assertive and involves setting boundaries and asking for what you need and want. Asking is not the same as having expectations, which may be heard as a subtle demand. If you practice self-care and self-responsibility, then you're more prepared to share your feelings and make requests without reacting to, manipulating, or punishing the other person when you don't get the answer you want. This also gives you greater freedom to say "No."

Healthy communication also means that there is room for anger and disagreements, but you have ground rules. You avoid abusive communication and don't attack or denigrate each other or blame, nag, interrupt, or criticize. You both agree to take timeouts if anger starts to escalate, but you either let go of or talk through things and don't' stockpile resentments.

Accepting each other's differences

Differences are guaranteed in relationships. Happy couples know this. They respect one another and accept each other's differences. The greater your sense of Self, the greater your ability to tolerate differences without getting angry, pretending they don't exist, or trying to change the other person. Usually, after about six months with someone, qualities and behaviors you don't like begin to bother you. Acceptance doesn't mean that you agree, nor that you accept or condone hurtful behavior or abuse, but acceptance is necessary if you don't want to be miserable living with a trait or habit you can't tolerate. (See Chapter 9.) Don't expect the person to change for you! If he or she does, it's probably a short time before habitual behavior returns. You still get to determine your own bottom line and ask yourself whether you can accept the *whole* person.

Making decisions and problem-solving together

Because differences are inevitable, you must develop problem-solving skills. (See Chapter 11.) Some couples avoid conflict by allowing one person to become the decider, parceling out areas of responsibility, or by ignoring problems. These strategies may lead

to repressed resentment that creates walls and breeds hopelessness, which erupts without resolution, again leading to distancing
and hopelessness. Such couples are afraid of being disappointed
again, keep to themselves, and operate at a functional level without real intimacy.

Couples who communicate and problem-solve effectively can
respect and discuss each other's differences without blame or
giving up their own position. Because they value each other's happiness and realize it's crucial to their own and the welfare of the
relationship, they seek compromise. Instead of problems dividing
them, problem-solving brings the couple to a deeper level of understanding and closeness.

Spending quality time together and apart

If you want an intimate nourishing relationship, spend time
together where you're both enjoying yourself. It may be as simple
as talking or as complex as developing a community project. If
you share hobbies or interests or a joint pursuit, it's easier to find
commonality, but common interests aren't a necessity in a good
relationship, as long as you're both willing to make time to be
together. Commonality without the other components of successful relationships is insufficient.

Equally important is being able to enjoy interests, work, and
friends separately from your partner. You renew your own aliveness and bring new energy and experiences to the relationship.
You're not using the relationship as your sole source of nourishment, which drains it. Quality time apart also makes you miss your
partner, keeping romance alive.

Giving and cooperating

In relationships that work, couples know that their happiness
depends on making their partner happy. They do their best to
cooperate when their partner makes a request. Because they're
able to take care of and nurture themselves, there isn't a power
struggle or competition over whose needs get met. They feel
enough and are able to give without expectation. Cooperation
doesn't diminish or deplete them. In fact, they receive in the act
of giving. They're also unafraid to give because they can say, "No"
when it matters.

Having compatible needs and values

Usually, needs for closeness and novelty are similar among satisfied couples. If you want more closeness than your partner, you
may always feel unhappy or rejected. On the other hand, if you
want greater separateness, you may feel smothered. In either
case, the cause isn't personal to you, but a reflection of differing

priorities between you and your partner. Realizing this can help you accept your differences. Partners that make new experiences a high priority are happiest because they're always learning and bringing fresh ideas and experiences to the relationship. If one partner likes to have new experiences, the relationship can work if the other is willing to go along.

Your values needn't be the same but compatible enough that they can survive long term. You don't have to have the same political or religious beliefs to be happy together, unless your values in those areas are deal-breakers, but it's vital that you mutually respect each other's values. There are numerous other values, such as fidelity and security. In relationships that work, honesty and fidelity are high priorities, because trust is essential. Broken trust takes time and effort to repair.

How much you value security also impacts your relationship. If your values for security are mismatched, it can lead to problems in making changes and financial decisions. If one partner wants to live for today, sell everything, and travel the world, and the other wants to pay off the mortgage and save for their future, the risk-taker feels constrained, and the spouse feels insecure. Both think the other is wrong-minded, and neither is happy.

Both you and your partner prioritize a list of values. (See Chapter 8.) Identify which of your needs and values are given the same priority. Discuss your differences and how have you compromised.

Sharing a common vision

Having a common vision of the future helps you build that future together, whether it's a family, a business, or a retirement home. It solidifies you as a unit that includes each other. It also directs your attention and commitment to something greater than yourselves, which you both are working toward. Think of the excitement that can be generated when you're working on a team — whether it's an athletic team or working with others on a political campaign, or a community, work, or creative project. People often meet and fall in love doing that because it produces a synergy.

Maintaining friendships

Maintaining friendships outside your relationship is essential for codependents whose close relationships tend to be closed. It can feel like lockdown. (See Chapter 7.) It's unrealistic to expect one person to share all your interests and meet all your needs for companionship, support, and closeness. Encourage each other's outside friendships and integrate your friends into the relationship. Ideally, you develop friendships with other couples to do things with.

Review your present and past relationships and compare them to the traits mentioned in this section; then answer the following questions:

- ✔ Have the qualities you're looking for in a partner changed over time?

- ✔ Have your relationships improved over time? How?

- ✔ If you're in recovery, how has what you've learned changed your relationships?

- ✔ What percent of your time and mental energy is focused on you verses your partner?

- ✔ What skills or attitudes do you need to improve to have healthier relationships?

Self-Development and Relationships

Much of the work of recovery and building self-esteem is repairing and furthering your individuation — becoming a whole Self. The individuation process (see Chapter 7) of developing a psychologically healthy, autonomous Self is impaired in codependent children, which affected your ability to have satisfying intimate relationships. Another way of looking at individuation is the degree to which you've healed childhood wounds and increased your capacity to think about and perceive the world and other people clearly in the present, not filtered through beliefs, rules, and reactions to triggers originating in your past. When achieved, individuation also means that you view and accept your parents for who they are, without idealization, grief, or resentment.

There are three premises about individuation and relationships:

1. You can function more easily and are happier in your relationships to the degree you've developed your Self and self-esteem. This means that you're more individuated.

2. The greater your individuation, the greater your intimacy. Intimacy in healthy relationships is based upon closeness, not sameness or oneness.

3. You select a mate at about the same level of individuation. You can still continue to grow and individuate further.

Everyone has the dual needs of autonomy and intimacy. Most relationship problems revolve around negotiating how you can satisfy your needs for physical and emotional closeness and your individual needs, which include needs for separateness, career goals, personal hobbies, individual friends, creativity, spirituality, and so forth. In her book, *Intimate Partners,* Maggie Scarf outlines five types of relationships based upon the partners' level of individuation. The levels were originally categorized by Stuart Johnson, M.S.W., and are renamed here (see Figure 16-1). Notice that five is the lowest level, and level one is the most harmonious and individuated tier. The majority of marriages range between levels two and four — four being the most content, and two being more conflictual and dysfunctional. Your relationship may vary depending upon your stress, which may cause you to revert to a lower level of functioning due to greater fear and generally less nurturing.

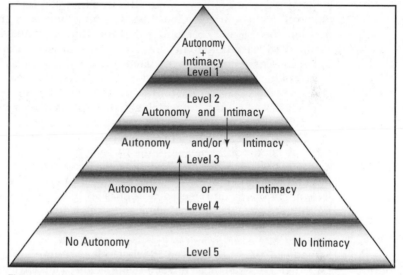

Figure 16-1: Levels of self-development in relationships.

No Self — level five

At this level, you suffer when it comes to relationships. Your boundaries are so weak that alone you feel lost and afraid you can't survive in a world you experience as indifferent. (See Chapter 3 on boundaries.) You may feel depressed, empty, lonely, or disintegrating. You long to be with someone to validate your existence and to feel more substantial, but getting close poses problems, too. Your lack of boundaries makes close relationships frightening because you lose yourself in them. You may feel smothered or devoured, or just not be able to hold on to your own opinions, feelings, and identity. This is not an intellectual thought process about you and the relationship, but it's quite visceral and automatic. You must push your partner away for self-preservation. You feel badly in, as well as out of, a relationship. In either case, your survival feels

threatened. At this level the problem of separateness and closeness is insoluble. There's a lot of drama and pain, and relationships are very unstable.

Pursuer and distancer — level four

At level four, you're able to experience autonomy and also closeness, but they're mutually exclusive. You only experience one at
a time, while the other operates unconsciously. On your own, you
can manage better than level five, but in order to be in a relationship, your partner must play out the need that you repressed and
"split off" from your consciousness. Often in conjoint therapy, one
partner (the pursuer) complains that the other (the distancer) is
too busy to make time to be close. The pursuer isn't aware of his
or her needs for autonomy or space, and the distancer is unconscious of his or her need for intimacy. However, the distancer
creates more separateness for the pursuer, which he or she consciously doesn't want, but which satisfies the pursuer's unconscious need for separateness. The pursuer creates more closeness
for the distancer, which he or she consciously avoids, but unconsciously needs. Still, they continue to be unhappy and blame one
another. The distancer may feel nagged, pressured, claustrophobic, and want to create even more distance, whereas the pursuer
feels abandoned and rejected, and pursues more vigorously.
Neither is aware that part of him- or herself is being projected onto
and acted by his or her partner.

Sometimes, the truth is revealed when one partner plays the role of
the other. For example, a husband complains that his wife doesn't
want sex. At a friend's suggestion, she starts asking for more sex.
To her surprise, whenever she asks, her husband makes an excuse.
They had had an unconscious agreement to forego sexual intimacy.
She was the foil for her husband, who was able to preserve his feelings of pride and virility, not aware of his intimacy fears.

Splitting and knitting — level three

If there's abuse or addiction, it's difficult to progress beyond level
two, which requires self-reflection and awareness of your feelings.
At level three, when you're emotionally triggered you may still
think it's your partner who's the entire problem, but later you're
able to talk it over and acknowledge the feelings inside you that
you've projected onto your partner. You *split off* the unconscious
need for autonomy or intimacy but then integrate or knit it back
into awareness. In other words, when you reflect upon your experience, you're able to feel your own conflicting needs and feelings.
The need for closeness or separateness is not your partner's, but
you can acknowledge that it lives within you. This allows for an

intimate conversation and sharing of feelings without blame. You can talk about fears of losing your individuality and autonomy as well as your need for closeness and intimacy. Conversing together dilutes potential arguments, enabling you to compromise with your mate. Because the conflict is within you, you may come up with solutions not before imagined. If you're in couples' therapy, in time, you have more experiences at level three. Eventually, you're able to shift on your own or with the help of a recovery program.

In the previous example about sex, the wife would not only ask for sex, but also feel her desire and be able to discuss her conflicting needs for intimacy and time alone on her separate interests, such as reading a novel or talking to a friend. The husband could acknowledge anxiety about closeness and satisfying her and his desire to be alone, which he's afraid to admit to himself or his wife.

Containing opposites — level two

At level two, instead of experiencing intimacy and autonomy as mutually exclusive as in level four, you realize that they're opposites on a continuum. You're aware of and take responsibility for your conflicting feelings most of the time and struggle to balance your dual needs for closeness and separateness. Neither one frightens you, and you can address and talk about both sides of the coin when making decisions. You don't impose expectations, blame, or make demands on your partner, since you're able to emotionally survive on your own. Nor do you please your partner without weighing the cost to yourself. The compromise is not so much with your partner as within yourself; however, you still experience compromising as giving up one need to satisfy the other.

You're able to contain ambivalence and opposites within yourself, which fluctuate in the relationship. There's a much greater sense of fluidity and choice. Sometimes, you're strong, confident, and courageous; other times, you feel afraid, incompetent, and weak. You're both playful and serious, intellectual and emotional, giving and receiving. Your relationships aren't role determined, nor do certain feelings or traits reside only in one person as happens in level two. Both partners express all their feelings. At times, they slip back to level three, but return to level two.

Harmony — level one

Rare is the person who reaches this level, where autonomy and intimacy are now not in conflict but are equally satisfying. There's no tension between the two. Emotions don't escalate when decisions are made about doing things together because there's neither projection, nor inner conflict. You're able to express a need for separateness with love and affection instead of blame or guilt. You don't feel rejected when left because you're more whole and autonomous. You don't take your partner's need for autonomy personally. You accept that he or she is a separate person with different needs. In fact, you can feel close when physically apart. Supporting each others' autonomy makes you feel more loved and appreciated as individuals. Likewise, being sexually and emotionally intimate doesn't feel like a loss of autonomy, but a celebration of your own sexuality and your mutual love. The integrity of your Self is maintained and fully integrated, rather than parts being projected onto your partner. Giving and receiving blend, but you can ask for your preferences and wouldn't do something you were comfortable doing. Rather than feeling a loss of yourself with closeness, you feel more completely yourself with your partner.

Intimacy

Everyone wants intimacy, but few know what it is or how to have it. The word *intimate* generally refers to a long or very close, personal relationship. It is also refers to your innermost, essential, or core Self. Sometimes it's used to describe very personal information or sex. The focus here is on emotional intimacy.

Pseudo-intimacy

Codependents aren't good at intimacy. Because of poor boundaries and feeling empty or incomplete, they consciously suppress differences (or don't know themselves enough to be aware of them) in order to merge and feel whole. However, intimacy is being close, not merging. Attaching to someone quickly creates a sense of intimacy and closeness. Codependents confuse this attachment and sharing with love and real intimacy. Often, one person is the caretaker and the other has the problem. The Top Dog — Underdog dynamic (described in Chapter 3) gets set up, and they feel intimate by listening and sharing pain and problems. Each person feels important or cared for, but that's not the same as intimacy. In fact, shame may motivate such disclosures too soon in order to push another person away, as if to ask, "Do you still want to go out with me?"

On his first date with **Betsy, Brandon** shared all of his anguish about his graduate studies and parents' disapproval of his chosen profession. He got so worked up, he started to cry. When he wanted to kiss Betsy goodnight, she refused. Brandon was hurt and confused, thinking they were close because he'd shared his sorrow. To his shock, she responded honestly saying that she didn't know him well enough, that that would take time, and that she hadn't opened up to him yet.

Codependents have sex soon after meeting to feel close, but sex may not make you feel closer. In fact, it can be used to avoid intimacy. Instead of feeling safe and close afterwards, you can feel emptier than before. If you're friends, then the feelings of safety, warmth, and closeness should continue. But friends aren't always intimate either. Intimacy is something special that requires more than trust and closeness. You may feel safe and trust your same-sex friends, but still not be emotionally intimate and feel comfortable talking about your feelings concerning the friendship.

Couples who've been together for awhile fall into routine patterns of communication and bury their resentments in order to preserve the relationship. They're now attached to one another and don't want to rock the boat. They don't know they have to work at intimacy and believe that they're protecting their love by keeping secrets and not being honest and authentic. Instead, while the relationship is withering, they try to hold on to the exhilarating romantic and loving feelings they once had by creating romance with flirtation, candlelight, gestures, and expressions of love, but romance isn't intimacy and pales in comparison.

When it's real

Intimacy creates feelings of contentment, integration, aliveness, peace, and well-being. It's nourishing and can transform both you and the relationship. Physical closeness, sex, and romance are important in maintaining a relationship, but emotional intimacy renews and enlivens it and supports you. Couples married decades may love each other, have sex, lie in bed together, and yearn to be close, but don't know how.

True intimacy is about being authentic and feels riskier than sharing a problem or something about your past. By revealing yourself in the present, you honor your separateness and drop your defenses, which allow you to be vulnerable and seen by your partner. It requires the courage and confidence of a soul warrior, especially when you're revealing something negative that you fear may jeopardize the relationship. It does the opposite. It builds feelings of trust, brings you closer, and deepens the relationship. This requires the safety of knowing the other person, which minimizes fear. Fear, caretaking, control, and reacting get in the way of intimacy. Intimacy also requires that you're present and can articulate your true feelings — not a reaction. All the things that prevent a healthy relationship will generally prevent intimacy, as well, and the qualities of successful relationships increase the likelihood of intimacy. Dialogues vary in their degrees of intimacy, but the most intimate conversations have the following characteristics:

✔ They're expressions of your *feelings*, not facts, thoughts, or judgments.

✔ They're vulnerable and honest without regard to the consequences.

✔ They're your feelings in the present.

✔ There's an acknowledgement of each others' differences, minimizing reactivity and projection.

✔ They describe *feelings* about yourself or the person you're with. (See Chapter 11.)

When you're having trouble being present, the antidote is to *admit it*. By acknowledging you're not all here, you're stating *what is*, which brings you into the present moment. A way to start speaking authentically may be to say, "I'm confused," or "I don't know what I'm feeling." Intimacy naturally fades. Usually, you or your partner become afraid and interrupt the closeness. People fear that intimacy unchecked may take over their productive and autonomous sides, and they'll dissolve into the other person or become blithering space cadets.

Intimacy can also be nonverbal when two people let down their defenses and have an open and loving attitude toward one another. At those times, talking is a defense that prevents intimacy. Intimacy can be a precious soul encounter, accompanied by a transpersonal, mystical experience. There's a sense of oneness with boundaries merging or disappearing. Practicing mediation and mindfulness increases your ability to sense this and sustain intimacy. The following exercises may increase your awareness about your comfort with intimacy.

✔ Write a dialogue between the parts of you that seek intimacy and autonomy. Allow them to negotiate what each one fears and desires. See if they can reach a compromise.

✔ Recall and list your most intimate moments with someone.

- What did you feel during and after?

- How did each experience affect the relationship?

- Who ended the closeness and how did the closeness end?

- If you ended it, examine what frightened you. Was it related to a past experience?

- What defenses did you use?

- If the other person ended it, how did you feel? Did that remind you of a past experience?

Coping with Loneliness

Prepare to be alone. Loneliness is part of the human condition — especially today, when serial monogamy is the norm. You're alone before, between, after, and at times during a relationship. Even an ideal relationship ends with death of one spouse. Getting comfortable with yourself, learning how to meet your needs, reaching out, and standing on your own two feet allow you to enjoy life alone and make you a better partner when love comes along.

Solitude and being alone describe a physical condition. You may not feel lonely and may feel comfortable, even enjoyment. On the other hand, loneliness can be felt in a marriage or in a crowd when you feel disconnected from others or empty inside. It's a feeling of isolation when you need social interaction. Some people are depressed, sad, or bored and don't know that they're lonely. Others know and still find it difficult to reach out.

Beware of isolating. Rigid boundaries due to fear, shame, hurt, and grief cause many codependents to isolate to avoid a dysfunctional relationship. They're stuck between the fear of a painful relationship and the pain of being alone. Although friends and activities can help your loneliness, you may need counseling to feel safe enough to risk getting close to someone again.

Spending more time alone and developing your interests and a supportive circle of friends help you become comfortable with being single. It's empowering to know you can do things on your own, and although you may believe you won't enjoy them, experiment and find out. Go to a movie, live theatrical performance, art opening, or concert. This enables you to feel secure in yourself, as well as minimizes the need to rush into a relationship with someone inappropriate or unavailable because you're lonely. If you've had a break-up, rather than date right away, it's best to spend some time with yourself to grieve any loss you feel. (See Chapter 13.) Meanwhile, in addition to the suggested activities in Chapter 14, here are some ways to deal with loneliness:

- ✔ Plan social activities on weekends in advance.
- ✔ Call a friend or relative and admit you're lonely.
- ✔ Visit or help a neighbor.
- ✔ Plan a vacation with a friend or tour group.
- ✔ Plan your birthday and holiday celebrations in advance.

Sometimes loneliness takes you by surprise. You think you're fine and the next day you're blue, or you have a good time at a party and you return home lonely. You may not feel like talking to someone, even though it would help. As with all feelings, what makes loneliness worse is resistance to feeling it. If you constrict your heart around a feeling, it just stays stuck there. Part of you is afraid that you may be swallowed up by the pain, and to avoid it you have to distract yourself or engage in some addictive behavior, like overeating, calling an unavailable ex, working, or using a drug. Here are some exercises you can do to work with loneliness:

- ✔ Rather than resisting feeling lonely, allow yourself to experience the fullness of yourself and emotions. Notice what else you feel — perhaps sadness or compassion. You may be surprised that as the feelings move through you, they aren't as painful as you imagined or don't last more than a few minutes. Once you release them, your mind-body is no longer using energy to suppress them, and you feel lighter, peaceful, invigorated, or tired. You definitely shift. You may feel content in your solitude instead of empty and lonely because you've now connected to yourself and are more full than empty. You may decide to call a friend, go for a walk, or welcome a rest from exhaustion you've avoided.

- ✔ You may also experience sadness or grief. They can be connected to feelings of loneliness and emptiness from long ago that are resurfacing. Writing about your feelings and associated memories is one way to heal pain from the past. (See Chapter 13.) Sometimes, feelings of loneliness and isolation can occur if you were at home alone every day after school.

- ✔ Get curious about what event may have triggered your feelings. Think about the past 24 hours. Did you have a disappointment or conversation that didn't go well? Journal about your thoughts, beliefs, and feelings. What different conclusions about the event can you draw from the facts? What different feelings may have resulted?

- ✔ If you're missing an ex, think about what attracted you to the person and any warning signs you may have overlooked. Consider your part in why the relationship didn't work out and what you learned. Ask yourself what you would do differently in the future.

Lonely in America

Twenty percent of Americans feel lonely, and more than 10 percent say they have no close friends to confide in or hang out with. Loneliness is growing. The number of people who have no one to discuss important matters with has tripled, and the number of people they confide in has dropped by a third in the last 20 years.

Chapter 17

Empowering You

*E*mpowering yourself to take initiative in your life both builds and reflects your self-esteem. This chapter is about putting into action the work you've been doing in recovery. Now you're ready to uncover your dreams and passions and discover your skills and talents. If you've been waiting for someone else to bring you happiness and security, you've neglected yourself. This chapter turns that attention back on you to help you begin to create your confidence and your future. It starts with empowering yourself.

Self-Empowerment

Self-empowerment doesn't exist in the dictionary. That's because it's a new word used by advocates of personal growth, the Women's Movement, and the gay and civil rights movements. To *empower* something is to give it authority. Recovery is about making yourself your own authority — what you like, what you want, what you decide, rather than deferring or reacting to someone else. Even rebelling is a reaction that disempowers you. To give yourself authority means *you become the author of your life*. That may feel like a daunting responsibility. (See Chapters 9 and 10.)

Internal locus of control

Most codependents have an external locus of control (see Chapter 3), meaning that they think external factors are the cause of what happens to them and how they feel. Codependents expect and hope that change will come from the outside or some other person. Their focus and power are outside of themselves. They look to others to make themselves feel better and approve of them, especially when it comes to relationships. They also tend to make excuses or blame others or circumstances for their problems and when things don't go as planned. As you stop doing that and begin to take responsibility for your life and your feelings, actions, and inactions (see Chapter 9), you're gradually taking your power back, and the locus of control becomes internal, on yourself. Every time you don't please, react, or control someone, or voice your feelings, opinions, and limits, you're building your self-esteem and an internal locus of control. You stop being a victim. You stop spending your energy trying to change or control someone else. If you're unhappy and get that familiar victim feeling, you take the responsibility to make changes to become happy, even when you can't "fix" the problem. This is a process that involves building self-esteem (see Chapter 10), becoming self-nurturing (see Chapter 14), setting boundaries (see Chapter 11), and healing your past (see Chapter 13).

The final step is manifesting that newfound self-esteem and self-confidence. Expressing not just your voice in your relationships but also your talents, skills, and creativity in the world. When you learn something new, when you solve a problem on your own, when you're doing what you love, and when you're accomplishing your goals, you feel independent and confident, and look forward to each new day. You know you can stand on your own two feet, and it's a great feeling.

People with an internal locus of control are more successful in all aspects of their lives. They believe that outcomes are contingent on their actions and effort rather than luck, unfair circumstances, and things beyond their control. There are quizzes online you can take to determine your locus of control. The good news is that you can change your locus of control. After you realize that you can make a difference in own life and sense of well-being, you begin to take your power back.

Affirmations

What you believe and think determine your actions and success. Sometimes, believing you can achieve a goal is the most difficult step in accomplishing it. If you've been in the habit of making excuses and thinking "I can't," persuade yourself that you *can* by changing the way you talk to yourself. You may not think that affirmations have any value, but every time you negate yourself and your abilities, you're affirming the negative. Making positive affirmations consistently followed up with action begins to convince your unconscious mind that you *can*. When you do, you're able to set and accomplish goals and tasks more easily, without procrastination.

Another unconscious attitude that prevents people from accomplishing what they want is the belief that they don't deserve it. Shame and experiences of being abandoned, abused, or deprived can lead you to conclude that you're not worthy of happiness, success, love, good health, financial security, or supportive friends. It's important to understand your past programming (see Chapter 7), not for the purpose of blaming your family, but for identifying and then discarding false, negative messages that still influence you.

Affirmations work best when they're:

- ✔ Statements that don't contradict your reality

- ✔ Statements that you don't consider false

- ✔ Present tense — not "I will" or reference to a future date

- ✔ Clear and concise

- ✔ Rhythmic or rhyming

- ✔ Positive; avoid statements that contain negative words, such as "don't," or "not," and verbs such as "stop," "avoid," or "give up"

- ✔ Inspirational or move you emotionally and use emotional adjectives and verbs

- ✔ Both written and spoken

- ✔ Repeated consistently for at least a month

- ✔ Reading or listening to uplifting positive ideas

When creating an affirmation, see what negative beliefs arise and modify the statement until you can agree with it at least somewhat. You can use words such as "I'm in the process of . . ." "Every day I'm ready to . . ." "I'm open to . . ." "I welcome new ideas," "I'm building my self-esteem daily," and "My confidence in myself grows and grows."

Don't give power to others who tell you that you can't, shouldn't, or won't be able to do what you desire. Avoid telling your dreams and goals to people who laugh at or doubt you. Instead, talk to those who support you.

Overcomers

Sylvester Stallone claims he was turned down more than 1,500 times for acting jobs because of his facial disfigurement. Despite being broke, when his "Rocky" script finally got the attention of United Artists, he insisted on the starring role and turned down $350,000 **not** to act in it. United Artists eventually agreed to pay him only $35,000, plus a percentage of profits.

Stephen King's first novel, *Carrie* was turned down 30 times before it was accepted for publication.

NFL player Mark Herzlich had been told he'd never play football again after doctors operated on his leg for cancer.

Walt Disney had to dissolve his first animation company and was so broke that he ate dog food.

J.K. Rowling was on welfare, but with hard work and determination wrote *Harry Potter*.

Steven Spielberg was rejected from University of Southern California film school three times and dropped out of another program.

Oprah Winfrey overcame an abusive childhood and was fired from her job as a television reporter because she was "unfit for TV."

Michael Jordan was cut from his high school basketball team.

Norman Cousins fired his doctor and proved him wrong by healing himself of Ankylosing Spondylitis.

Making decisions

A lot of codependents know what other people should do but have a tough time making decisions for themselves, even small ones, like what to order off a menu and what to do with their free time. They may avoid decision-making altogether and practice their addiction, daydream, or worry about someone, or ask others their opinions. Trouble with deciding can stem from:

- ✔ Not being allowed to make choices in childhood
- ✔ Growing up with strict rules or a controlling or authoritarian parent
- ✔ Not being taught how to problem-solve
- ✔ Not having an internal locus of control
- ✔ Not being aware of your feelings
- ✔ Wanting to please someone else

✔ Fear of making a mistake

✔ Fear of disappointment

If you grew up in a family with strict rules, or if one parent was controlling (see Chapter 7), you didn't have an opportunity to make important decisions, nor have the support of parents to help you to learn how to discover your feelings about something and weigh alternatives and consequences. Children can quickly learn how to think for themselves. Good parenting allows them to make age-appropriate decisions and includes listening and reflecting back to a child their feelings and needs and brainstorming consequences of different choices. The same dysfunctional parenting style deprived you of getting to identify and trust your feelings in order to develop an internal locus of control to guide you in knowing yourself and what you want and need. When you don't know what you feel and you're not skilled in thinking through the consequences of your actions and probable outcomes, small decisions can feel monumental. Instead, you act without forethought and/or avoid them and develop a passive attitude toward your life. You may get in the habit of looking to others for guidance, and their opinions can become more important than yours. If you're a pleaser, you won't want to displease them.

Beware not only of friends who tell you what you should do, but authority figures as well. Even when you're paying a professional for advice, explore various options and make sure the action you take is aligned with your values. It may be tempting to ask a psychotherapist to make your decisions. Instead, seek help in thinking through the consequences of your options, which empowers you to make your own decisions and solve your problems.

In many dysfunctional families, children are punished for making innocent mistakes. In some cases, punishment is severe, arbitrary, and unpredictable. (See Chapter 7.) Those fears survive even when you're no longer living with your parents. That parent still lives inside you as your Critic (see Chapter 10), and won't allow you to forgive yourself for mistakes. Perfectionism and the desire to be infallible can haunt every decision, so that you have to research every purchase, rehearse intimate conversations, and avoid new experiences. Another factor is fear of disappointment. In troubled families, parents rarely take the time to comfort children when they're disappointed. Coping with disappointment is a part of maturity, learned when parents understand and empathize with their children's feelings.

Here are some tips in making decisions:

✔ Write down all possible options.

✔ Write the consequences of each, including your feelings.

- ✔ To help you, visualize the results and experience how you feel in your body.

- ✔ Talk over your options with someone you trust who won't judge you or tell you what to do, but who listens and lets you decide for yourself.

- ✔ A graph can help you visually compare aspects of different choices. List your options down the left side of the chart and write the elements to consider along the top, such as cost, convenience, time expended, value, and reward. You can add a column for consequences, and rank them from 1-10. Factors will vary depending on the type of decision. Comparing which car to buy would include things like maintenance, comfort, price, depreciation, and mileage. (This technique doesn't work as well with decisions that are more feeling based.)

Decisions aren't right or wrong, there are only consequences. Many times you won't know until you take a risk and make a choice. Give yourself permission to experiment, change your mind, and make mistakes. This is how you grow and get to know yourself and the world.

Following Your Bliss

The expression, "Follow your bliss" was made famous by the renowned mythologist Joseph Campbell. He urged, "Follow your bliss, and the universe will open doors for you where there were only walls." Whenever he spoke, he encouraged people to do what they love and to find their passion. Following your bliss means living a purposeful, joy-filled life. You may be one of the lucky ones who has always had a life goal and pursued it. Most people, however, muddle through life not knowing, knowing and giving up, postponing, or not trying, or doing what their friends or family think or expect. If you don't have dreams, passions, or know what makes you happy, there's a good chance you won't be. How can you discover your bliss?

Dreams, passions, and work

This book emphasizes listening to your inner voice, feelings, and intuitions. For most codependents, that voice was squelched or ignored for so many years that they stopped listening.

That voice and their hunches became dimmer and dimmer. Recovery is about repairing that inner dialogue. Paradoxically, to discover your goals for the future, you must pay attention in the present and listen to what's calling you in the moment. Listen to your body and mind. What feels right and what do you want? Where do you want to go? With whom do you want to spend your time? What do you want to learn more about? (See Chapter 8.) These are clues to your passion.

Fulfilling your dreams and expressing your passions bring joy to life. Whether it's a hobby or a career, when you're doing what you love, you're feeling your bliss. If you can turn that into a livelihood, then it doesn't feel like "work." You look forward to each day, and your enthusiasm brings you more success.

Consider taking workshops and classes to help you identify your passions and interests, write about your ideas in your journal, and talk to your school guidance counselor or a career planning counselor. Look in the want ads of a newspaper or online, and highlight any that sound interesting or exciting — regardless of pay, skill, or educational requirements. Finding the right field is the first step in doing work that brings you fulfillment. When you do, you're focused and motivated to develop your skills or get the education required.

Answer the following questions to identify your passions. Some examples are suggested. They're not exclusive, but just to get you thinking.

- What future life did you daydream about in childhood?
- What did you want to be when you grew up?
- Who were your idols?
- Whose life would you want?
- Whom do you admire today? In which field?
- What were your favorite classes in school?
- What gets you excited?
- What do you like to talk about? Read about?
- What hobby gives you the most pleasure?
- What do you do where you lose track of time?
- What activities do you most enjoy — building, designing, computing, repairing, negotiating, teaching, analyzing, organizing, brainstorming, researching, or making music?
- What kind of store interests you — a hardware store, bookstore, arts and crafts, electronics, or antique store, nursery, or music shop?
- Where would you most like to spend time — on a campus, a stage, the ocean, or in a national park, laboratory, library, office, or hospital?

✔ Do you prefer working alone or on a team — selling, having clients, or being around children, animals, seniors, doctors, performers, athletes, or scientists?

Ruling out what you don't want to do can be a first step in discovering what you do want. I spent many years as an entertainment lawyer before I owned up to the fact that it wasn't fulfilling me and I didn't want to do it anymore. Codependents are especially influenced by outside forces. What are yours?

✔ What were your father's dreams for himself?

✔ What were your mother's dreams for herself?

✔ What were your father's dreams and advice to you?

✔ What were your mother's dreams and advice to you?

✔ Did a grandparent, sibling, or other relative share his or her dreams or offer advice?

✔ What positive or negative work role models did you have?

✔ Growing up, who influenced you the most?

✔ Did you not follow a passion because of someone else's fears, doubts, or criticism?

✔ Has your culture or religion influenced your work?

✔ How did you decide upon the work and goals you pursue today?

✔ What were your motives for your choices?

✔ What have been the consequences?

Often parents with good intentions guide their children into a life-style or career that will provide financial security or fulfill their unlived dreams. If you discover that you were negatively influenced by your parents or someone else, or if they didn't help you discover what's right for you, realize that your choices were based on the circumstances and who you were at the time. Use the new information to clarify what you really want and make changes.

✔ Do you manifest who you really are?

✔ What prevents you from imagining all you can become?

✔ Have you sacrificed your passions? Why?

✔ Has it made you happy?

✔ Have you been seeking someone's approval?

✔ Is it worth it?

✔ What fears hold you back now?

Sometimes you know what you like, but you're not inspired or motivated to make changes, or you have many talents and interests and can't decide which to pursue. Often the timing isn't right. You may be mentally or emotionally preoccupied with the stress of the present or the pain of the past. When you can't seem to move forward, turn your thoughts and prayers to the belief that guidance and understanding will come, and that when the time is right, your courage and desire will be ignited. Have a heart-to-heart conversation with yourself or God in mediation and write in your journal. Ask that your goals, passions, and ambition be clearly defined. You may need to spend more quiet time listening.

It's not too late

I felt very old at 40 when I realized law wasn't for me. I wasn't sure what I wanted to do. After several years of soul searching, I knew I wanted to be a psychotherapist. I went back to school to earn a master's degree in psychology, do an internship, and work hard to become licensed as a marriage and family therapist. I thought, "If I don't, I'll be that much older without the license, so I may as well." Once I acted on my intuition, a bright, inspiring world and new friendships opened to me.

Looking back, 40 seems young. Grandma Moses' first exhibition was when she was 78 — in a drugstore. There're octogenarians biking more than 500 miles, playing soccer, dancing, and even skydiving — not to mention the 100-year-old marathoner, Fauja Singh, and the 100-year-old bestselling Japanese poet, Toyo Shibata, who began her career at 92. One Senior Olympics champion is 93 years old and winner of six gold medals, including in pole vaulting! The only thing stopping you is your negative beliefs about yourself and your possibilities. Beliefs are not reality. It's the effort toward your goal that counts and changes you. If you have a disability, it only means that you have to pace yourself and find help and methods that enable you to achieve your goals.

Setting Goals

Growing means moving ahead, trying and learning new things, and taking risks; otherwise you stay the same and don't grow. Perhaps you've put off things you wanted to do — waiting for "One day" — for motivation, a partner, or something else to change. Nothing happens until you make it happen. Your life and your future are determined by actions taken today. Today and this minute, and this hour are all you have to work with. A journey begins with the first step — sometimes that first step is the hardest and takes many more years than the following steps. You build momentum as you go. You know you're moving, and you enjoy the journey. The opposite — stagnation and procrastination — only leave you with regret.

Trying new things and setting new goals stretches you. It's normal to be afraid and have doubts. Watch out for the naysayer and Critic that put up roadblocks and tempt you to give up. Transform your Critic into a helpful coach (see Chapter 10). Empower yourself with encouragement and praise whenever negativity arises. When you're afraid, comfort and reassure your inner child. (See Chapter 13.) When you make a mistake or don't follow through, acknowledge it, and learn from it. (See Chapter 15.)

Identifying your skills and talents

Talents and gifts come naturally, and with practice, you can improve them. Everyone has a talent for something. Do you have intuition or perceive things in some area that others don't? Do you do things easily that others are slow at or take the lead in certain situations? Maybe you know what you're good at, or like a lot of people, you may take your talents and abilities for granted. Activities and classes at which you excel probably utilize your talents. You can learn new skills and improve upon them with training and practice. If you enjoy what you're doing, you're more motivated to learn faster.

Perhaps you enjoy babysitting and have a knack for understanding children. Not everyone does. Are you often voted team captain? Do you keep budgets, mediate friends' disputes, repair things easily, take the best pictures, entertain people, or run the fastest? Some people can sing on any note, learn a language, grow plants, win arguments, persuade others, draw what they see, make up stories, match paint, design clothes, or create recipes. I never suspected I had a high aptitude for spacial relationships until it was pointed out to me, but I knew how to pack a tight suitcase and could always tell whether pictures were evenly hung or furniture would fit in a space.

Think about jobs and positions you've held, including volunteering at church, club, and school functions. List the skills that were required and those you learned. For instance, if you had a secretarial job, you used many skills, such as, typing, computer skills, organizing, editing, drafting letters, filing, handling phone calls, calendaring meetings for your boss. If you wrote a grant, you had to research, strategize, write, analyze, organize, edit, create persuasive arguments, budget, coordinate with staff, and possibly negotiate the proposal.

Career and personal goals

The first step in creating goals is developing your vision. When you have an idea about what you want, then sensually embellish it with details to make it feel real. Imagine yourself in your new role or activity. THINK BIG. Your vision should include as many of your five senses as possible, especially how things look and feel.

1. Do the relaxation exercise in Chapter 8, and when your mind and body are relaxed, free your imagination and see yourself embodying each step toward your goal and achieving it. Imagine it with every sense. If your goal is to lose weight, see yourself in your present clothes that are too roomy and big for you. See yourself getting on a scale and the weight measuring lower and lower each day. See your thin self in the mirror and wearing clothes you want to wear, doing the things you're able to do, feeling thinner, and looking down at your toes. Feel your body as lighter, more active, and nimble. Imagine yourself turning down food you'd otherwise eat, and enjoying the aroma and taste of healthy food. Hear people complimenting you. Feel your self-esteem, pride, confidence, and happiness swell.

   If your goal is educational, see yourself studying, taking tests, getting As, receiving compliments from your teachers, family, and friends, and holding your diploma. Feel how proud you're of your accomplishment.

2. The next step is to write about your goals in your journal. Don't let any obstacles, such as age or money, limit your goal.

3. List your short-term and long-term goals in each of the areas in Table 17-1.

Table 17-1		**My Goals**		
Category	*Short-Term Goal*	*Completion Date*	*Long-Term Goal*	*Completion Date*
Social				
Finances				
Fitness				
Personal				
Career				
Nutrition				
Educational				

4. Pick one or two to focus on and write affirmations that support your ability to accomplish that goal.

5. Imagine accomplishing your goal for at least five minutes when you wake up and again before you go to sleep. Feel all of the feelings from the visualization exercise. Do this for at least 30 days.

6. Tell someone who won't criticize you about your goal.

Gathering information

In developing an action plan to accomplish a goal, you must gather information about what you need to achieve it. If it's a career goal, find out the skill and educational requirements, potential income, special licensing permits and requirements, and the approximate time, cost, and experience required to accomplish the prerequisites. You can gather information from the following sources:

- Interview people who work in your chosen field.
- Research online and books and periodicals at the library.
- Attend seminars and workshops.
- Take classes to inform you and develop skills.
- Talk to college and university department heads in your area of interest.
- Find a mentor.
- Talk to a career counselor.
- Visit career planning resources at your school or college (even if you've already graduated).

Make a list of everything you require to accomplish your goal, including qualifications, money, time, support, skills, transportation, tools, contacts, and your determination. Also list distractions and hurdles that may sidetrack or stall you. Foreseeing problems can help you circumvent them. Strategize what you can do to avoid getting deterred from your plan. For example, "Don't tell Dad, because he doesn't support my idea," or "Cancel movie and magazine subscriptions to have more time to study."

Baby steps

The three biggest emotional obstacles to achieving your goals are:

1. Overwhelm

2. Doubt

3. Fear

To be successful in meeting your goals, break them down into stages, and each stage into achievable action steps. I once learned rock climbing to help me overcome my fear of heights. If I looked up or down, I became frightened, but when I focused on the next foothold, I made progress one step at a time, until I reached the summit. The point is, not to look too far ahead, but do what's right in front of you. However small the step you must take, do that. Keep it manageable. You're making progress, rather than procrastinating or giving up because you're overwhelmed and paralyzed with fear that your goal is too hard or impossible to attain. All things great are achieved one step at a time.

Break down one of your goals in Table 17-1 into smaller stages based on the information you've gathered. For example, if you want to be an opera singer, you may need training, practice singing, and studying Italian. A later stage may be performing, starting at community theatres, orchestras, and cafes. If you can't afford a private coach, don't allow that obstacle to stop you from getting started. Other ideas will come to you, and doors that you're unaware of will open.

The first stage of training your voice can then be broken down into smaller actionable steps, such as researching coaches and classes offered in your community at colleges and elsewhere. You may discover a private or community singing league or a choir at local churches, synagogues, or other organizations. Some may be free or only request a donation. The next steps would be contacting them and gaining more information. Through new connections, you may be referred to an affordable private coach. Financing comes further down the road. You start with what you can do and don't worry about steps you don't know how to accomplish. Do the same breakdown and research for learning Italian. Don't forget self-help methods, such as books, CDs, and DVDs. After you start taking steps toward your goals, possibilities you hadn't imagined show up, along with the means to continue on your path. See this illustrated in Table 17-2.

Creating a plan and writing it down maximize your motivation to take action. Outline the goal into stages. Think about the necessary actions and the order required to complete each stage. Estimate the time required to accomplish each. You're creating an action plan. You can mark the status of each action weekly.

**Table 17-2   My Action Plan for Becoming
                       an Opera Singer**

Stage	Step Description	Tasks	Completion Date	Status
One – Begin training			June 1	
	Step 1: Research classes at local colleges and universities	a. Look online and in phone books	Jan 15	X
		b. Ask other singers		X
	Step 2: Contact administrative offices regarding schedule, fees, and other sign-up requirements	a. Make a list of contact information for all schools	Feb 10	Contacted 3 of 6 colleges – waiting for brochures
		b. Call, e-mail or download to obtain brochures		Obtained 2
	Step 3: Visit each one and listen to the class or performance		March 15	
	Step 4: Talk to the instructor and other members there		April 10	
	Step 5: Decide on the best choice		April 15	
	Step 6: Apply for a student loan, if necessary	a. Research loans available	April 20	
		b. Obtain and complete forms		
	Step 7: Apply to join class		May 1	
Two – Practice singing			Feb 1	

Stage	Step Description	Tasks	Completion Date	Status
	Step 1: Home practice – one hour daily		Feb 1 - ongoing	
	Step 2: Research local singing groups		September 1	
		a. Research religious choirs	May 1	
		b. Research professional groups	June 1	
		c. Research local singing leagues	June 1	
		d. Research community organizations and clubs	June 15	
	(Repeat Stage One, Steps 2-5 and 7 but applied to singing)			
Three - Learn Italian – Level One	Step 1: Research classes	a. Research local and online college classes	December 31, 20__	
		b. Research local and online private schools		
	Step 2:	Research self-help methods		
	(Repeat Stage One, Steps 2-7, but apply to learning Italian)			

After completing your action plan, you can further break down each step with daily, written to-do lists. Writing things down helps you get them done. It's a good idea to make a list the night before, so you can spring into action the next morning. For Step 1.a of Stage 1 in Table 17-2, your to-do list may include:

1. Go to a library to look online and through all local phone books.

2. Make a list of local private colleges, community colleges, and universities.

The following day your to-do list may look like this:

1. Research extension classes at universities XYZ.

2. Research continuing education classes at XYZ schools.

3. Make a list of classes offered related to singing and opera.

As you start to take action, new ideas for future steps may come to you. Jot them down in a journal devoted just to this goal. Record your mistakes, so you're more likely to avoid them in the future, and be sure to log your successes. Celebrate them by rewarding yourself.

Chapter 18

Where to Get Help

In This Chapter

▶ Finding out about Twelve Step meetings

▶ Deciding on psychotherapy

▶ Sourcing other educational materials

▶ Obtaining emergency numbers

This chapter provides more specific information about Twelve Step meetings, support groups for trauma and domestic violence, and how to choose the right kind of psychotherapy and therapist for you. Some of the misconceptions about psychotherapy are explained.

Twelve Step Meetings and Support Groups

As discussed in Chapter 6, support is crucial in your recovery. It's difficult to alter your habits and thinking even with support. Without it, it's next to impossible to objectively see your behavior, beliefs, and attitudes and know how to change. Support provides:

Information

Encouragement

Validation

Empowerment

Friendship

Insight

Twelve Step meetings

You don't have to believe you're codependent in order to attend a meeting. You don't have to raise your hand and say that you're codependent or say anything for that matter. If you're curious about meetings, it's recommended that you go for six months and see if you don't feel better.

Finding a meeting

There are dozens of Twelve Step programs that are based on the Twelve Steps of AA. Each program has its own meetings, and each meeting has its own flavor and focus. Many of the programs have online meetings and chats; however, it's always best to attend a meeting and talk to people face to face. Chapter 6 provides an overview of Twelve Step meetings and what to expect. When you're new, it's recommended to attend a few meetings a week. If you're living with an addict, going to more meetings provides additional, necessary support.

You can find the time and place of the meetings by checking the program's website or by calling its national or local office. The number is listed on its web page and in your local phonebook. The local office can also give you the phone number of someone who attends a meeting near you to answer any questions or meet you at the meeting. If you don't have transportation, someone may pick you up and take you to a meeting. They're glad to do this, because being of service is part of their program.

Co-Dependents Anonymous (CoDA) is specifically focused on your codependency. Several of the other programs listed are for friends and relatives of someone who has an addiction. Al-Anon Family Groups is the oldest and addresses many issues of codependency. The following programs provide helpful information, support, and tools for recovery.

> **ACA (Adult Children of Alcoholics):** Meetings for those who grew up in an alcoholic or dysfunctional home
>
> **Al-Anon Family Groups:** Include Al-Anon for adult relatives of alcoholics, Alateen for teenage relatives, and Ala-tot for children of alcoholics; meetings also specifically for parents and children of alcoholics.
>
> **Co-Anon:** For friends and family of cocaine addicts
>
> **CoDA (Co-Dependents Anonymous):** For people working to end patterns of dysfunctional relationships and develop functional and healthy relationships
>
> **COSA (Codependents of Sex Addicts):** For relatives of sex addicts

COSLAA (CoSex and Love Addicts Anonymous): For friends and relatives of sex or love addicts

Gam-Anon/Gam-A-Teen: For friends and family members of **gamblers**

RCA (Recovering Couples Anonymous): For couples with varying addictions seeking healthy intimate relationships

FA (Families Anonymous): For relatives and friends of addicts

Other programs relevant to codependents that you may find helpful include:

SIA (Survivors of Incest Anonymous): For survivors of sexual abuse

LLA (Love Addicts Anonymous): For recovery from love and romance addiction

SLAA (Sex and Love Addicts Anonymous): For recovery from sex or love addiction

EA (Emotions Anonymous): For help with emotional issues

EHA (Emotional Health Anonymous): For recovery from mental and emotional illness

There are other Twelve Step programs for addiction to drugs, work, food, gambling, debting, sex, smoking, and clutter. You can find information about these on the Internet and in your local phone book.

Double winners

If you're a recovering addict, it's a good idea to first achieve abstinence or sobriety in a Twelve Step program that focuses on your primary addiction before starting a second one. When you feel ready to work on your codependency and relationship issues, you become a "double winner" by attending a second program, such as CoDA, ACA, or Al-Anon.

Sponsorship

Sponsorship is one of the benefits of Twelve Step programs. After you attend meetings for a while and you've heard or met members who have several years in that program, consider asking someone you respect to be your *sponsor*. A sponsor is a guide you can call between meetings to discuss personal problems. Your sponsor also makes suggestions about how to progress in your recovery, including how to follow the 12 steps. In addition to attending meetings, following the steps helps you to change and grow. Sometimes people who are in two programs have two sponsors and work the 12 steps of both because each program has its own focus.

Other support groups

For **trauma survivors,** you can find information at the following websites:

> **Trauma Survivors Network:** Find information and a peer support group near you (www.traumasurvivorsnetwork.org/home;index)
>
> **Sidran Institute:** For help with trauma and dissociation (www.sidran.org)
>
> **PTSD Forum:** An online forum for those suffering from post-traumatic stress disorder (www.ptsdforum.org)

For **victims of domestic violence,** shelters and support groups are organized by state, in contrast to Twelve Step programs, which are international, so you need to search for groups within your state. There are usually informational and group meetings at local shelters. Websites that can provide you more information and help you locate a group or shelter in your area are listed here. Some also provide legal information, such as how to obtain a restraining order.

> **National Coalition Against Domestic Violence:** For information and conferences (www.ncadv.org/)
>
> **The Hotline:** For information and a 24-hour hotline for emergency help (www.thehotline.org/)
>
> **Womenslaw.org:** For legal information, links to shelters and help in your state, and a list of chats and message board (www.womenslaw.org/index.php); similar information is available at this site, which also has a stress-reduction toolkit (www.helpguide.org/mental/domestic_violence_abuse_help_treatment_prevention.htm)

Psychotherapy

Psychotherapy is the best option if you don't want to attend a Twelve Step program. It's also a valuable adjunct to joining a Twelve Step program in order to do deeper recovery work individually or with your partner in couples counseling (see Chapter 6). People make the most progress when they combine therapy and a Twelve Step program.

Your insurance company may or may not pay for therapy. This is something you should find out before you seek a therapist. Many therapists are *providers* with specific insurance companies, meaning they will submit their bill and get paid directly from the insurance company, and you're responsible only for a small co-pay. Depending upon your insurer and where you live, you may or may not find a provider sufficiently experienced in the issues you want to address and with whom you feel comfortable. There are many excellent therapists who are "out-of-network" and aren't providers with your insurance company. Your insurance plan may reimburse you for a portion of the out-of-network therapist's fee. In that case, you may have to submit your bill to the insurer for payment. Some health plans limit the number of sessions you have. Insurance companies have a right to know your diagnosis, and some ask for treatment plans and progress reports. The federal HIPAA Privacy Rule makes this information inaccessible to your employer.

Find an experienced therapist, with whom you feel comfortable and safe. A therapist needn't be very friendly or outgoing, and many maintain a reserve for therapeutic reasons, but they shouldn't be cold or indifferent. A therapeutic relationship is unique and not the same as with a friend or a teacher. You are the center of attention, in contrast with a teacher, who does most of the talking, or a friend who shares personal stories and problems. Here are some misconceptions about therapy:

- ✔ **A therapist should give you advice.** An experienced therapist won't give you specific advice on handling a situation. He or she may urge you to attend a Twelve Step meeting or pursue your goals, but even in those cases, a good therapist will explore your point of view. There's an episode of "Curb Your Enthusiasm" where Larry David's therapist tells him exactly how to win back his wife's affection after she left him. It back fires in a hilarious string of unintended consequences because Larry didn't follow his own instincts.

- ✔ **A therapist can see through you.** It's surprising that some people think a therapist has magic x-ray vision to see into them. Through intuition and experience, a therapist develops hunches about patterns and causes, but doesn't know facts you're unwilling to disclose.

- ✔ **If you just show up, you can change.** Therapy requires attention and work on your part. The therapist is an ally — a partner — to support and guide you as you explore your memories, thoughts, and feelings. The more you think about yourself and your therapy, the more you get out of it.

- ✔ **Therapy ends when the session ends.** In fact, most of the work of therapy happens between sessions in your fantasies, dreams, actions, and fleeting thoughts. Therapy can be a laboratory for you to try new perspectives and behaviors in a protected environment. Think about what you felt and learned in each session and practice it during the week. Then return to your therapist and tell him or her how it went.

✔ **Therapy makes you dependent.** You're going to therapy to overcome your codependency. Even if you're not in a relationship with someone, you may be afraid that you'd become dependent if you were. Staying away from relationships or therapy won't heal that issue. Therapy is designed to make you more independent and interdependent in relationships, unless you and your therapist collude to use your therapy as a regular source of advice.

✔ **Therapists can predict the future.** Many clients want to know if they can get their girlfriend back or whether their marriage will last. Even psychics are wrong half the time. Therapy can empower you to change your future, rather than feel powerless or at the mercy of unseen forces.

✔ **Therapy isn't working if you don't better afterwards.** As you change and recover, your emotions go up and down. Therapy stirs the pot, and painful feelings come up in the process. Sometimes you feel depressed or anxious, particularly as you let go of old habits.

✔ **A therapist will judge you.** If you're feeling judged by your therapist, confront him or her right away. Therapists are human, and there may have been a misunderstanding. If this is a repeated pattern, or if you feel put-down or shamed, consider changing therapists.

It's surprising to most clients that their therapist cares about them. They don't feel that they're likeable or loveable, or that they make an impact on the therapist, because the relationship isn't mutual and they're not helping the therapist. These are things to talk about in therapy because they go to the core of codependency.

Individual therapy

Individual therapy is focused on you, not your partner. Sometimes people come and want to complain about their partner or the addict and convince the therapist why that person is so frustrating or in the wrong. They really want their pain to be heard and witnessed, but it doesn't help them to grow or change. A support group would be a good place to do that. Often it takes time to help them focus on themselves. If you're ready to do that, you can make the most of individual therapy. It can help you individuate from your family and build a solid, confident Self, by understanding your behavior, beliefs, thinking, and history in a way that's more concentrated and specific to you than you can in a Twelve Step meeting. You can also learn to problem solve, raise your self-esteem, accomplish goals, and resolve issues from your past. Therapy is particularly important if you are or have suffered from trauma or abuse, or have a mental illness or a mood disorder, such as depression or anxiety, which is not relieved by going to meetings.

Couples counseling

Couples counseling includes marital therapy and is ideal if you want to work on issues in your relationship. It probably won't be useful with a partner who is regularly using drugs or is newly sober or abstinent. Their focus has to be on getting clean and sober. Twelve Step meetings don't address communication, abuse, and intimacy issues. Relationships do change if only one person makes changes, but progress is enhanced if you and your partner work together in therapy. It takes two to have a conversation, and a therapist can view the dynamics between you and your partner.

In couples counseling, the couple is the client. There are no secrets between one of you and the therapist. If you're in individual therapy and want to switch to couples therapy, it's advisable to be referred to a new therapist to see you as a couple, so that there's more balance. However, as part of couples counseling, the therapist may see both partners individually to work on personal issues.

Recommended Reading

There is a lot of helpful literature (books, pamphlets, and so on) available on relationships and addictions — too many to list here. Some of the known authors on codependency include Melody Beattie, Pia Mellody, Robin Norwood, Earnie Larsen, Claudia Black, Charles Whitfield, Sharon Wegscheider-Cruse, Anne Wilson Schaef, and Janet Wotitz. You may also want to check out books on trauma, violence, depression, conflict resolution, self esteem, or abuse. Two *For Dummies* books that you may find helpful are:

> *Post-Traumatic-Stress Disorder For Dummies,* by Marc Goulston (Wiley Publishing, Inc., 2008).

> *Addiction and Recovery For Dummies,* by Brian F. Shaw, Paul Ritvo, Jane Irvine, and M. David Lewis (Wiley Publishing, Inc., 2004).

Be sure to check out books and pamphlets at Al-Anon and CoDA websites and meetings. You can also find pamphlets, ebooks, and blogs at www.WhatIsCodependency.com and www.darlene lancer.com, including "Are You Codependent?" *Going Bonkers* (2010); "Recovery in the Twelve Steps," *The California Therapist* (2004); "The Dance of Intimacy," "10 Steps to Self-Esteem," "How to Be Assertive," "Codependent Issues," "Breaking-Up: Should You Leave or Can You Get the Change You Want?" and "Your Primary Spiritual Relationship — Loving Yourself."

Emergency Numbers

The following are some national phone numbers to keep handy. It's a good idea to look up local numbers for services in your area. Some programs have only state hotlines. Resources for domestic violence and hotlines for shelters vary from state to state, but you can find that information in your local phone book and on the Internet. You may be able to locate a nearby shelter through your local police department. If you anticipate violence, keep the number on your refrigerator and get information about a shelter in advance. If you're in immediate danger, call 911.

Al-Anon and Alateen: 757-563-1600; meeting line: 888-425-2666

CoDA: 602- 277-7991 or 888-444-2359

Co-Anon: 520-513-5028 or 800-898-9985

COSA: 763-537-6904

National Domestic Violence Hotline: 800-799-SAFE (7233)

National Child Abuse Hotline: 800-4-ACHILD (422-4453)

National Suicide Prevention Lifeline: 800-273-TALK (8255)

Part V
The Part of Tens

"Let's see if we can identify some of the stress triggers in your life. You mentioned something about a large wolf that periodically shows up and attempts to blow your house down..."

In this part...

This is The Part of Tens, and it contains ten suggestions on how to love yourself and be good to you! It also contains ten daily reminders to help you put into practice everything you've learned from reading this book.

Chapter 19

Ten Ways to Love Yourself

1f I had to sum up this entire book in two words, it would be "Love Yourself." Doing that may sound strange because you're used to loving other people. You may not know how to love *you*. Love involves actions as well as feelings. Think about those you love. You want to know them, support them, encourage them, give to them, and make them happy. Do you do that for yourself? This chapter suggests ten ways in which you can love and give to yourself. Maybe you think all this preoccupation with loving yourself is selfish. It's not. Selfishness comes from a feeling of lack. In contrast, when you're happy and fill yourself with love, like being in love, you have more to give to others. They enjoy being in your presence and feel better without your having to "fix" or change them.

Have a Spiritual Practice

Love yourself by spending time alone. Whether or not you believe in God, a spiritual practice is an excellent means of creating a deeper relationship with your Self. What better way to honor you. A spiritual practice doesn't require religious beliefs. Your intention may simply be to find a centered, calm place to access inner guidance, to develop reverence for life, or to experience harmony with yourself and others. Listening and finding your truth gives you greater confidence, clarity, and peace. It helps you let go of control and not react, despite what's happening around you.

Receive Support

Love yourself by asking for and receiving help. Human beings are social animals and need each other. When you're lonely, confused, anxious, overwhelmed, or in the dumps, reaching out is a way of giving to yourself. Sometimes, turning to God brings comfort and guidance. Other times, your emotions take over, and you're unable to think or calm yourself. That's the time when you need others.

There are times when everyone needs support. When problems persist and don't go away on their own, you require more than friends can offer. Unfortunately, some people believe that asking for and receiving help are signs of weakness. If you're used to helping others, you probably don't feel worthy of or comfortable receiving. Changing that pattern is growth. Whether it's going to a meeting or seeking professional counseling, getting support isn't an indulgence or a character flaw. In fact, it takes self-honesty to know your limits, and humility and courage to ask for help. Doing so allows others to give and feel close to you. Appreciating their love and support is human and healthy.

 Throughout this book, the importance of friends and a support system as a necessary part of recovery has been emphasized. You can't and don't have to do it alone. Make sure your friends are actually supportive and knowledgeable about codependency, and reach out to people who are.

Meet Your Needs

Love yourself by attending to your needs. If you've been tending the needs of others, but neglecting your own, it's time to turn that around and put yourself first. The reverse also happens — you expect others to fill needs that are your responsibility. Be sure to address your basic, physical needs, such as healthy food, rest, exercise, and medical and dental check-ups. Give special attention to needs you may be overlooking (see Chapter 5). When you're lonely, sad, angry, afraid, overwhelmed, confused, tired, or feeling like a victim, ask yourself what you need. If you're depressed, you may have been avoiding and neglecting yourself for a long time. This isn't rocket science. The simple equation is:

> Neglect your needs — feel bad
>
> Satisfy your needs — feel good

Some needs are met by others, such as needs for intimacy and friendship. It's your obligation to speak up and ask for what you need and want. Expecting others to read your mind leads to resentment and conflict.

It takes awareness, practice, and skill to balance your needs with those of others, especially when needs conflict. Do you silently cave in? Do you state what you want and then quickly yield to objection? You may feel that holding your ground is selfish. Remember, saying "Yes" to you sometimes requires that you to say "No" to someone else.

Have Fun

Love yourself by planning pleasure, recreation, and hobbies. These are needs, too. Focusing on a problem often makes it worse. Without balance, pain can turn into self-pity and become a way of life. There are also people who take themselves too seriously. They develop tunnel vision when it comes to work and problems. For them, living is a struggle, a competition, or a test of endurance and achievement.

You may have forgotten how to laugh and enjoy yourself, which is important in maintaining balance in your body's chemistry and in your life. Life isn't meant to be a burden, but to be enjoyed. Celebrate it by making time to relax, play, and be creative — activities that are rejuvenating and bring you into the present. Sometimes, when you take a break and have fun — even for a short time — your worries magically dissolve, and you gain a new perspective on a problem. Pleasure restores your energy and sense of well-being, which not only nourishes your soul, but also enhances the productivity and quality of your work.

Protect Yourself

Love yourself by protecting yourself from physical, mental, and emotional abuse. Loving someone doesn't mean you have to accept insulting or demeaning words or behavior. If you think you're being abused, don't waste your energy or risk your safety trying to change the abuser, explaining your position, or proving your innocence. It doesn't matter. You didn't cause, nor are you responsible for, other peoples' words or behavior, but you do have a responsibility to protect yourself and your children. You have a choice to speak up, set limits, disengage from the conversation, leave the room, get professional help, call the police when there's violence, or end the relationship.

Accept Yourself

Love yourself as the unique individual you are, including your appearance, feelings, thoughts, and addictions. You don't have to earn respect or prove anything. You're deserving of love and respect as a human being with flaws and failures. Notice if you're trying to change for someone else's validation. Instead, remind yourself that being yourself is more important. When you practice self-acceptance, you stop worrying about what others think and can be more authentic and spontaneous.

Are you your own abuser? Watch for whenever you judge or evaluate yourself, or compare yourself to others. Observe whenever you scold or are harsh with yourself and others.

Becoming and accepting yourself takes time. Forcing change with constant self-evaluation and self-judgment keeps you stuck, but self-acceptance allows change to happen with little effort. When you slip or make mistakes, remember that self-criticism compounds them. It's much more productive to forgive yourself, and focus on your behavior in the present.

Gentle Yourself

Love yourself with gentleness and compassion. Modulate your inner voice so that it's calm and kind. When you're afraid or in pain, blaming yourself or thinking there's something wrong with you makes matters worse. When you're tempted to ignore your feelings and distract yourself with more activity, obsessions, or addictive behavior, practice just being with yourself. Be the one who is there for you with gentleness and compassion in your anxiety, sorrow, hopelessness, anger, and terror. The child within you needs you. Comfort yourself with all the tenderness you would a crying child or wounded animal. Listen, forgive, and embrace your full humanness. Develop trust that you can count on yourself.

Encourage Yourself

Love yourself with encouragement and enthusiasm. Transform your inner Critic into a positive coach. Get in the habit of finding things you do well and acknowledge them. Don't wait for others to appreciate and compliment you. Appreciate and compliment yourself. In fact, repeat praise over and over. Instead of taking your good qualities for granted, notice them, and give yourself credit. Look for small things you do right and well. How good it feels hearing encouragement! Stop doubting yourself, and pay attention to every small sign of progress toward your goals. Tell yourself you can make it — you can do whatever you desire. When you love yourself with encouragement, watch your self-confidence and success grow:

Positive encouragement — positive action — positive confidence

Cheer yourself onward. Make a big deal over it. Celebrate yourself everyday!

Express Yourself

Love yourself by expressing yourself. Your Self has been hidden too long. Healing shame requires that you risk being seen. Commit to stop hiding, and honor yourself by communicating your feelings, opinions, thoughts, and needs. You have a right to think and feel what you do without explanation or justification. Your self-respect and the respect you receive from others will grow.

Self-expression also includes your creativity. Express yourself in music, writing, design, art, cooking, crafts, dance, or wherever your creativity leads you. Tell your inner Critic you're creating for fun and not to bother you.

Pursue Your Passions

Love yourself by following your passions. Only you hold the keys to your happiness. Talking yourself out of pursuing your desires leads to discontent and regret. Even if your desires are impractical or unprofitable, don't allow those obstacles to discourage you. Every day, take one small step toward realizing your goals or doing something that excites you. If you're uncertain about your passions, pay attention to what stimulates you. Listen to what calls to you, follow your inspiration, and take risks to experience the fullness of who you are.

If you're depressed or overwhelmed, it can be hard to think about positive goals. For now, make your recovery your number-one objective. In time, you will have more energy and motivation about the future and your desires. Be patient. Goals or a specific direction eventually emerge.

Chapter 20

Ten Daily Reminders

. . . .

In This Chapter

▶ Remembering to focus on yourself

▶ Honoring and trusting yourself

▶ Letting go of hurry, worry, and control

▶ Reaching out to others

. . . .

By now you understand a lot about codependency, and if you've done the exercises throughout this book, you've learned more about yourself. Putting it together may be overwhelming and a lot to remember all at the same time. This chapter distills ten daily reminders — five Do's and five Don'ts. Write them in your journal and check yourself each day. This will help you remember and speed your recovery.

Do Focus on Yourself

Remember that focusing on others is the hallmark of codependency. It's easy to slip back and become preoccupied with thinking about those whom you love — worrying about their problems or wondering what they're thinking or what they said, did, or didn't do. You can lose hours or days of your life in fruitless obsessions. On the other hand, you reap a multitude of benefits from focusing on your own life. The only thoughts and behavior you can control are yours. Every time you turn your attention back to yourself, you're recovering by becoming your own center and master of your life. Mind your own business, and let other people live their lives. You always have a choice about how you respond.

Aside from worry, daydreaming about romance or a happier relationship also prevents you from living your life — which is happening right now. You may be escaping an unhappy present, but you're also not taking responsibility for changing what is within your power, and you're the only one who can. Each time you escape, you miss an opportunity to build a happier today and tomorrow. It's far more constructive to allow your feelings and

utilize coping skills, such as journaling, calling someone supportive, going to a meeting, taking a walk, doing something creative.

Throughout the day, pay attention to what you feel and need, and
to whether your thoughts are helping you. Ask yourself what's
necessary to meet your needs and goals. This sounds like a lot of
work. It is, and you're worth it! Even if you're only 10 percent effective, that's 110 percent more effective than when you're thinking
about someone else, over whom you have no control.

Do Let Go

Remember that the refusal to accept reality causes pain, and you
create more pain when you attempt to control, resist, or escape
reality and your feelings about it. Accepting reality is a step toward
emotional health and maturity. Life is in constant flux and unpredictable. But realizing this and deepening your relationship with
your spiritual Self allow you to find security despite insecurity.
That's not always easy and takes practice. A helpful reminder is
the wisdom of the Serenity Prayer:

> "God grant me the serenity to accept the things I cannot
> change . . ."

Whether it's the loss of a loved one, your own limitations, someone
else's decision or feelings, or an unhappy childhood, "letting go"
is a reminder to encounter reality with equanimity. Sometimes, all
that's necessary is awareness and a change of perspective; other
times, it involves grieving. Mostly, it's requires a deep recognition
and constant reminder that you're not in control of other people,
situations, and events. The past is also beyond your control.
Dwelling on what you "should have" said or done is the Critic's
favorite weapon. Reflecting on the past in order to make amends
and grow is helpful, but ruminating about it is fruitless.

Acceptance doesn't require passivity. It prepares you to take
appropriate action. Yet, sometimes silence and calm allow things
to unfold in a better way than you could have planned. Forcing
your will can make matters worse and add unnecessary stress to
an already frustrating or painful situation.

Do Trust Your Experience

Remember to pay attention to and validate our own experience.
Putting trust in others sooner or later disappoints you. God may have
disappointed you, too. Recovery means developing trust in yourself.
Looking to love, prestige, money, or other people to trust over your
own experience eventually leads to confusion and discouragement.

If you're new to recovery, you may be unable to trust anything, including yourself because you've been disconnected from your inner experience for years. It takes time and practice to listen to and trust yourself. The more you do, the more your self-confidence and willingness to risk grow. Developing trust is an evolving process. Often it follows these stages:

1. Trusting a sponsor, therapist, or Twelve Step program helps to center and calm you

2. Trusting God and/or your experience gained through reading spiritual material, mediation

3. Listening to your feelings, inner guidance, and intuition

4. Trusting the process of risk, experience, and faith in yourself

Do Honor Your Feelings

Remember that honoring your feelings is a way of saying that you and your feelings matter. Society spends billions of dollars to not feel any discomfort or pain and provides constant and plentiful opportunities for distraction. Beware of avoiding feelings through denial, obsession, caretaking, and control. Recovery means experiencing, naming, and allowing your feelings. If you stay with them, they ebb — like a passing cloud or stormy weather. If you run from them, they follow you, until you're forced to feel or become numb. Feelings aren't logical and don't have to make rational sense. That doesn't mean they're less valid or significant. Journal daily. Describe the situation that's bothering you, and ask yourself how you feel about it.

Never ignore, minimize, or rationalize away your feelings — not just your emotions, but all your bodily sensations. Eat when you're hungry, sleep when you're tired, and wear a jacket when you're cold. Don't ignore your feelings and sensations because someone else has a different experience or disagrees. Your feelings are yours, valid, and unique. You have a right to your feelings without explanation. Don't allow anyone to tell you how you "should" or "shouldn't" feel — especially you! You've probably been doing that for years. Start honoring your feelings today.

Do Be Yourself

Remember that you're unique, and your life happens only once. You have one chance to live it. Fully expressing your true Self is what it means to recover. Every creation is meant to grow and develop its complete, singular expression. The rose bud blossoms into an exquisite rose, and the caterpillar transforms into a marvelous butterfly, which is why it's often seen as a symbol of the Al-Anon Twelve Step program. You, too, are meant to realize your full potential. But unlike plants and other animals, effort and self-knowledge are required to develop and become all you're intended to be. When you deny your needs, desires, thoughts, values, and feelings, or people-please and manipulate out of fear, you're not being authentic. Self-realization requires mindfulness of those impulses and translating them into authentic action and honest communication. This takes courage. Realize this, and get support.

Don't React

Remember that other people's words and actions reflect who they are, just as your words and actions reflect you. If you were at a restaurant with a companion and began to rant in a rude or obnoxious manner, it wouldn't discredit your friend, nor would his or her behavior reflect well upon you. The reverse is also true.

When you react to someone else, you lose your power, and problems escalate. Rather than react (see Chapter 10), listen, think, feel, and respond. If you don't know what to reply, say that you'll think things over. Then, write about your triggers and feelings. Consider productive options in the situation that may include doing nothing, a conversation about your needs, setting boundaries, or getting professional information and help.

Don't Hurry

Remember Emmet Fox's simple slogan used by Twelve Step programs, "Easy Does It." You may believe that if you don't push yourself or try harder, nothing would get accomplished, and you'd become a slacker. Probably you already do a lot and more than your share. The verb "to push" means to shove, thrust, force, bear down, muscle, press. Would you want to work for a boss who did that? Does that person live inside of you? Pressuring yourself makes life harder and less enjoyable. You make mistakes and are less productive.

When I'm late for an appointment and stuck in traffic, I remind myself of composer Hoagy Carmichael's words, "Slow motion gets you faster." Getting tense and agitated won't get me to my destination any sooner. I may as well relax, smell the roses, and make life worth living.

Don't Worry

Remember to lighten up. Fretting feeds your fears. You can't know what the future holds, nor can you anticipate your future feelings. When you worry, you project the worse. Your fears grow and grow, setting up a vicious cycle, until you lose touch with reality. The world and your mind become dangerous places. Yet the disasters you imagine may never come to pass. Even if they do, in the interim, you lose precious moments today. Preparation, on the other hand, differs from worry because it's constructive action.

Having a spiritual practice helps you stay in the present. When you catch your thoughts drifting into the past or future, focus your awareness on your immediate perceptions — your breath, sounds, and your environment.

Don't Try to be Perfect

Remember that everyone makes mistakes, but perfectionists don't accept this reality or themselves. They believe that their only choice is to be perfect or fail. Trying to live mistake-free creates constant tension. Humans are imperfect. If you can't admit making mistakes, it's because you fear that *you're a mistake.* But being human isn't a mistake.

What do Scotchgard, penicillin, and chocolate chip cookies have in common? They all originated from a mistake. When it comes to creativity, mistakes can be a blessing that take your work in an unintended direction that you never could have imagined. When perfection tempts you, take a look at the painting of a man with three legs, titled *People Reading Stock Exchange,* by famed illustrator Norman Rockwell, and have you noticed that Michelangelo's women all look like the males who were his models?

Giving up perfectionism isn't easy. When you stop trying to make things perfect, expect to feel uncomfortable. Making something "perfect" may take only a few seconds or may be impossible. See if you can leave things undone, unclear, or a little messy, dirty, or asymmetrical. Notice how it makes you feel. Question your beliefs, practice self-forgiveness, and have heart-to-heart talks with your Critic and Perfectionist.

Don't Isolate

Remember that recovery involves sharing your problems, reaching out, and allowing others in. Isolating is a bad habit. If you tend to isolate when you're depressed or in pain, it's probably because you haven't had positive experiences of being loved and comforted when you were. You may not be aware that you're lonely or need others or comforting, nor be able to imagine that it can make you feel better. People also isolate because of shame or feeling like an outsider. Unfortunately, isolation or maintaining your distance reinforces those negative beliefs, keeps people at a distance, and prevents the restructuring of these unhealthy attitudes. Doing the opposite is often the way to break an unhealthy habit.

Index

Apple & Mac

iPad 2 For Dummies,
3rd Edition
978-1-118-17679-5

iPhone 4S
For Dummies,
5th Edition
978-1-118-03671-6

iPod touch For
Dummies, 3rd Edition
978-1-118-12960-9

Mac OS X Lion
For Dummies
978-1-118-02205-4

Blogging & Social Media

CityVille For Dummies
978-1-118-08337-6

Facebook For Dummies,
4th Edition
978-1-118-09562-1

Mom Blogging
For Dummies
978-1-118-03843-7

Twitter For Dummies,
2nd Edition
978-0-470-76879-2

WordPress For
Dummies, 4th Edition
978-1-118-07342-1

Business

Cash Flow For Dummies
978-1-118-01850-7

Investing For Dummies,
6th Edition
978-0-470-90545-6

Job Searching with Social Media

Job Searching with
Social Media
For Dummies
978-0-470-93072-4

QuickBooks 2012
For Dummies
978-1-118-09120-3

Resumes
For Dummies,
6th Edition
978-0-470-87361-8

Starting an Etsy
Business For Dummies
978-0-470-93067-0

Cooking & Entertaining

Cooking Basics
For Dummies,
4th Edition
978-0-470-91388-8

Wine For Dummies,
4th Edition
978-0-470-04579-4

Diet & Nutrition

Kettlebells
For Dummies
978-0-470-59929-7

Nutrition For Dummies,
5th Edition
970-0-470-93231-5

Restaurant Calorie
Counter For Dummies,
2nd Edition
978-0-470-64405-8

Digital Photography

Digital SLR Cameras
& Photography For
Dummies, 4th Edition
978-1-118-14489-3

Digital SLR Settings
& Shortcuts
For Dummies
978-0-470-91763-3

Photoshop Elements 10
For Dummies
978-1-118-10742-3

Gardening

Gardening Basics
For Dummies
978-0-470-03749-2

Vegetable Gardening
For Dummies,
2nd Edition
978-0-470-49870-5

Green/Sustainable

Raising Chickens
For Dummies
978-0-470-46544-8

Green Cleaning
For Dummies
978-0-470-39106-8

Health

Diabetes For Dummies,
3rd Edition
978-0-470-27086-8

Food Allergies
For Dummies
978-0-470-09584-3

Living Gluten-Free
For Dummies,
2nd Edition
978-0-470-58589-4

Hobbies

Beekeeping
For Dummies,
2nd Edition
978-0-470-43065-1

Chess For Dummies,
3rd Edition
978-1-118-01695-4

Drawing For Dummies,
2nd Edition
978-0-470-61842-4

eBay For Dummies,
7th Edition
978-1-118-09806-6

Knitting For Dummies,
2nd Edition
978-0-470-28747-7

Language & Foreign Language

English Grammar
For Dummies,
2nd Edition
978-0-470-54664-2

French For Dummies,
2nd Edition
978-1-118-00464-7

German For Dummies,
2nd Edition
978-0-470-90101-4

Spanish Essentials
For Dummies
978-0-470-63751-7

Spanish For Dummies,
2nd Edition
978-0-470-87855-2

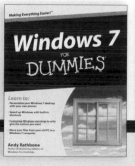

Math & Science

Algebra I For Dummies, 2nd Edition
978-0-470-55964-2

Biology For Dummies, 2nd Edition
978-0-470-59875-7

Chemistry For Dummies, 2nd Edition
978-1-1180-0730-3

Geometry For Dummies, 2nd Edition
978-0-470-08946-0

Pre-Algebra Essentials For Dummies
978-0-470-61838-7

Microsoft Office

Excel 2010 For Dummies
978-0-470-48953-6

Office 2010 All-in-One For Dummies
978-0-470-49748-7

Office 2011 for Mac For Dummies
978-0-470-87869-9

Word 2010 For Dummies
978-0-470-48772-3

Music

Guitar For Dummies, 2nd Edition
978-0-7645-9904-0

Clarinet For Dummies
978-0-470-58477-4

iPod & iTunes For Dummies, 9th Edition
978-1-118-13060-5

Pets

Cats For Dummies, 2nd Edition
978-0-7645-5275-5

Dogs All-in One For Dummies
978-0470-52978-2

Saltwater Aquariums For Dummies
978-0-470-06805-2

Religion & Inspiration

The Bible For Dummies
978-0-7645-5296-0

Catholicism For Dummies, 2nd Edition
978-1-118-07778-8

Spirituality For Dummies, 2nd Edition
978-0-470-19142-2

Self-Help & Relationships

Happiness For Dummies
978-0-470-28171-0

Overcoming Anxiety For Dummies, 2nd Edition
978-0-470-57441-6

Seniors

Crosswords For Seniors For Dummies
978-0-470-49157-7

iPad 2 For Seniors For Dummies, 3rd Edition
978-1-118-17678-8

Laptops & Tablets For Seniors For Dummies, 2nd Edition
978-1-118-09596-6

Smartphones & Tablets

BlackBerry For Dummies, 5th Edition
978-1-118-10035-6

Droid X2 For Dummies
978-1-118-14864-8

HTC ThunderBolt For Dummies
978-1-118-07601-9

MOTOROLA XOOM For Dummies
978-1-118-08835-7

Sports

Basketball For Dummies, 3rd Edition
978-1-118-07374-2

Football For Dummies, 2nd Edition
978-1-118-01261-1

Golf For Dummies, 4th Edition
978-0-470-88279-5

Test Prep

ACT For Dummies, 5th Edition
978-1-118-01259-8

ASVAB For Dummies, 3rd Edition
978-0-470-63760-9

The GRE Test For Dummies, 7th Edition
978-0-470-00919-2

Police Officer Exam For Dummies
978-0-470-88724-0

Series 7 Exam For Dummies
978-0-470-09932-2

Web Development

HTML, CSS, & XHTML For Dummies, 7th Edition
978-0-470-91659-9

Drupal For Dummies, 2nd Edition
978-1-118-08348-2

Windows 7

Windows 7 For Dummies
978-0-470-49743-2

Windows 7 For Dummies, Book + DVD Bundle
978-0-470-52398-8

Windows 7 All-in-One For Dummies
978-0-470-48763-1

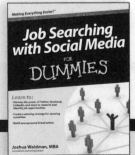

Available wherever books are sold. For more information or to order direct: U.S. customers visit www.dummies.com or call 1-877-762-2974. U.K. customers visit www.wileyeurope.com or call (0) 1243 843291. Canadian customers visit www.wiley.ca or call 1-800-567-4797.

Connect with us online at www.facebook.com/fordummies or @fordummies